THE CROSS AND THE RIVER

THE CROSS AND THE RIVER

Ethiopia, Egypt, and the Nile

Haggai Erlich

LYNNE
RIENNER
PUBLISHERS

BOULDER
LONDON

Paperback edition published in the United States of America in 2015 by
Lynne Rienner Publishers, Inc.
1800 30th Street, Boulder, Colorado 80301
www.rienner.com

and in the United Kingdom by
Lynne Rienner Publishers, Inc.
3 Henrietta Street, Covent Garden, London WC2E 8LU

Hardcover edition published in 2002 by Lynne Rienner Publishers, Inc.

ISBN 978-1-62637-192-7 (pbk. : alk. paper)

Printed and bound in the United States of America

The paper used in this publication meets the requirements
of the American National Standard for Permanence of
Paper for Printed Library Materials Z39.48-1992.

5 4 3 2 1

To my mother, Yehudit,
1910–1966

Contents

Contents

Preface

The idea of writing this book was conceived in the late 1980s. The memory of the great famine in Ethiopia was still fresh. The images of the walking skeletons of young children, victims of their country's failure to store water and develop a modern irrigation system, refused to fade away. The absurdity of the land of the Blue Nile dying of thirst was combined with the fact that Egypt at that time was about to face a similar catastrophe. Egypt, the "gift of the Nile," had fully developed its water system, but its dependence on the river, and on rains in Ethiopia, remained. In the early summer of 1988, after five years of drought in Ethiopia had reduced the waters of Lake Nasser to an alarming level, experts predicted the imminent demise of Egypt's agriculture. The good rains of that summer brought some temporary relief, but no rest to my mind. As a student of both countries' history, I was aware of their historic interdependence, of their mutual strategic, cultural, and religious relations. I was also aware of their failure, through many centuries of meaningful relations, to cope together with the challenge of the great river. The intensive Egyptian-Ethiopian efforts to reach understanding that resumed in the early 1990s have not been facilitated by old legacies of mutual suspicion. A common, long-term, multifaceted history continues to send double messages, blurring an aggravating issue.

In 1995, I began to work on the present volume. It is an attempt to reconstruct cultural-conceptual developments beyond the concrete, ancient Ethiopian-Egyptian relations. My research was assisted by two institutions. The Israel Science Foundation, founded by the Israeli Academy for Science and Humanities, granted me a three-year scholarship. The United States Institute of Peace, based in Washington, D.C., generously financed the fourth year of gathering materials. It is my honor and pleasure to thank the leaders of these two prestigious bodies. They saw the connection between my proposed approach and the contemporary Nile crisis. It is indeed my greatest hope that this study will serve the principal purposes of each of these two entities: promoting a scholarly understanding of intercultural history and that of facilitating international appeasement and peace. A 1999–2000 sabbatical year in San Diego, California, under the auspices of the Lipinski Institute was the ideal time and place to write the book.

I would also like to thank dozens of my students at Tel Aviv University with whom I shared my ideas and from whose responses and papers I benefited. The greatest help was rendered by Relli Shechter, who, while a Ph.D. candidate at Harvard University, resourcefully gathered a lot of material for this study in Egypt and the United States. Draft chapters of the book were read by a number of leading scholars. The early chapters, dealing with the medieval period, were read by Emeri van Donzel, Stuart Munro-Hay, Steven Kaplan, Amalia Levanoni, and Michael Winter. The entire draft was read by Israel Gershoni, Paul Henze, Yoram Meital, and David Wasserstein. They all offered constructive criticism and corrective comments. I hold Israel Gershoni in the highest esteem for his insightful comments on the Egyptian dimension, and I acknowledge with the same spirit Paul Henze's authoritative comments on the Ethiopian side. During the last twenty years it has been my privilege to work together and constantly share ideas with each of these two experts and original minds. Of special value, as well, was the highly informative response to the whole manuscript by the distinguished Ethiopianist Thomas Kane. A true, noble soldier in the service of scholarship, Thomas Kane, the embodiment of knowledge and modesty, wrote a list of detailed remarks for me during his very last days. He died of cancer in October 2000. My gratitude goes to all of the above.

I also have the pleasure of thanking Dana Hargil for editing my English and the Open University of Israel for financing that stage. I am further grateful to the Open University for twenty years of cooperation in promoting the humanistic study of both Ethiopia and Egypt in Israel. The Irene Halmos Chair for Arabic Literature of Tel Aviv University and its Entin Faculty of Humanities financed the dust jacket of this book. I am grateful to Sasson Somekh, the incumbent of the Chair, and Dean Dan Laor for their help. Special thanks are due to Lynne Rienner and her staff for all our previous productions, as well as for the pleasure of working again with her publishing house. Finally, my deepest thanks go to my wife, Yochi, the ultimate friend.

The responsibility for the final product is of course entirely mine.

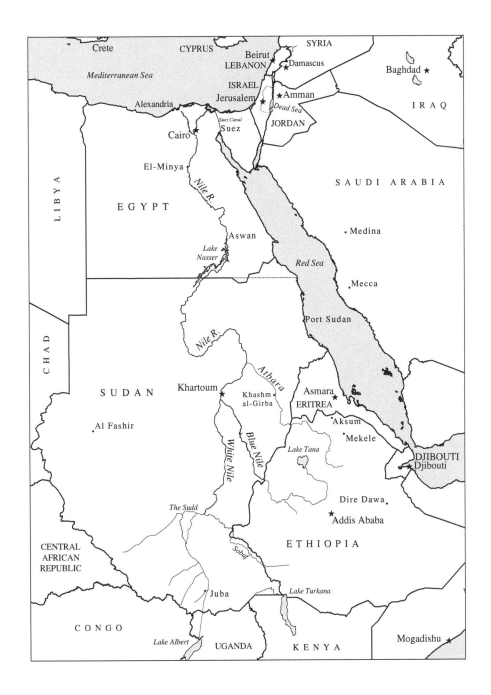

The Nile Basin Today

1

Introduction:
The Crisis of the Nile

This book is about a history of collective identities and their role in intercultural and political international relations, but it is closely relevant to a contemporary issue of immense practical importance. It has to do with the very existence of Egypt. As these lines are being written, the "gift of the Nile" enters the twenty-first century facing an ever-deepening controversy over its waters. In the coming decades, gradually and perhaps inescapably, the Nile River will become an issue of life and death.[1]

At the heart of the matter is the fact that 86 percent of the water irrigating Egypt comes from Ethiopia and that Ethiopia itself intends to use a part of it. The waters of Ethiopia flow down the Nile tributaries of the Atbara River (the Takkaze in Ethiopia) and the Sobat (the Ethiopian Baro-Akobo) but mainly through the Blue Nile, or the Abbai—"the big (river)" and "the father of rivers" for the Ethiopians. The Blue Nile begins in Lake Tana (1,700 meters above sea level) and makes an 1,000-kilometer loop through Ethiopian territory, carving a 600-meter-deep gorge through the highlands. During its passage through Ethiopia the Abbai harnesses waters from over ninety tributaries before it meets the White Nile in Khartoum. The contribution of the White Nile is much smaller. Originating in the Great Lakes of Equatorial Africa, the White Nile is then lost in the vast marshes of the Sudd (meaning "obstruction") region, before it emerges in the northern part of southern Sudan. Having been thus subject to intensive evaporation in the Sudd, the White Nile's steady but slower stream yields a mere 14 percent of the total amount of the combined river reaching Egypt. The Blue Nile is much more energetic. Not only does it cascade through the huge, steep, rocky walls of the highland plateau, but its flow changes in an annual drama, peaking from June to October, the rainy season in Ethiopia. It is there and then that the lifeblood of Egypt is created.

1

The Ethiopian waters constitute by far the greater share of the Nile, and their sudden arrival creates the August floods that for many millennia have irrigated, or sometimes flooded, the fields of Egypt. Egypt itself has practically no rain. It contributes no water to the Nile, but it needs every drop. Egypt was not only born of the Nile, it also lives by it, and its dependence increases in accordance with the pace of its modernization and population growth. The 1987–1988 period demonstrated how increasingly vulnerable Egypt has become. After several years of drought in Ethiopia, the water level in Lake Nasser, behind the new Egyptian Aswan High Dam inaugurated in January 1971, was reduced to an alarming level. The volume of the reservoir had fallen from the normal level of 165–175 meters above sea level (173.04 in 1978) to 153 meters by early July 1988. Had the rains in Ethiopia continued to fail for another two months, the water would have dropped to 147 meters, halting the massive production of hydroelectric power from the Aswan Dam. The amount of water then left in Lake Nasser would have been sufficient for six more months of irrigation. Experts were predicting a horrible catastrophe. Another dry year in Ethiopia, they forecast, and the eternal river would virtually begin drying up, with chaotic consequences.[2] On 10 August 1988 heavy rains began in Ethiopia, giving Egypt a last-minute reprieve. But had the two countries united in facing common challenges, such anxieties might have been spared and the Nile could have given life even when Mother Nature turned capricious.

Various plans to control the river were proposed during the twentieth century to offer solutions made possible by new hydrological information on the Nile. The British, who had occupied Egypt in 1882 and later the Sudan and most of the Upper Nile in 1898, sought to develop the most effective use of the Nile's water by regarding the Nile basin as an integral whole. To develop the Nile for Egypt, they needed to increase the amount of water by preventing waste, regulating the flow, and storing surpluses where evaporation was minimal. As early as 1904, Sir W. Garstin produced his "Report upon the Basin of the Upper Nile," designed to increase the flow from the Equatorial Great Lakes by cutting a canal through the Sudd. In 1946 a British hydrologist in the service of the Egyptian Ministry of Public Works, Harold Hurst, published "The Future Conservation of the Nile," proposing dams at the outlet of the Great Lakes and at Lake Tana in Ethiopia, which would provide reservoirs of minimal evaporation for overyear or "century" storage. In 1958 H. A. Morrice and W. N. Allen, British experts representing the government of Sudan, proposed dams and hydroelectric stations on the Blue Nile and the Baro in their "Report on the Nile Valley Plan." In 1964 the U.S. Bureau of Reclamation published the results of a five-year study ordered by the Ethiopians. "Land and Water Resources of the Blue Nile Basin: Ethiopia" envisioned twenty-six projects in Ethiopia, including four dams designed to turn Lake Tana and the Abbai's gorge into the primary all-Nile reservoir and to supply electricity and irrigation for Ethiopia while significantly enlarging and regulating the amount of water flowing to Sudan and Egypt.[3]

But for such all-Nile solutions to materialize, a unified multinational action was needed. In other corners of the globe, around other rivers, such unity and cooperation has been occasionally achieved. But the enormous, mysterious Nile, the home of humankind since its very beginning, has never experienced such human unity. No single political or cultural force has ever been able to control the entire basin. Islam failed in the seventh century to penetrate southward from Egypt beyond Aswan. Late-nineteenth-century European imperialism failed to subdue Ethiopia. Before, between, and after these periods no all-Nile unification of any sort has ever been achieved. The Nile system has remained a multicultural cosmos, a theater of ethnic diversity, of religious barriers, and of political dams.[4]

In this volume I will not address the stories of all the various riparian civilizations, nor will I elaborate on their multifaceted interactions. Rather, I confine it to Ethiopian-Egyptian cultural-political relations as seen from the perspective of the Nile. It is a long, multidimensional story, a unique case of inter-Eastern, inter-African dialogue between two ancient civilizations that have managed to endure, to undergo changes, and to survive. These are two history-oriented societies for which the memory of formative past events, the legacies of various chapters in their long dialogue, are still living sources of both identity and action. This is a story of mutual dependence, but it is also a story of broken eye contact.

"HISTORIC RIGHTS":
EGYPTIANS AND THEIR ETHIOPIAN DILEMMAS

Egypt and Ethiopia have no common border, but their histories have always remained interwoven. Their common story has culminated in various conflicts and crises, but beyond the dramas of strategic and political interests, there lay deeper dimensions of culture and identity.

For the Egyptians Ethiopia has always meant the source of their Nile. Although the extent of the Blue Nile as their main source of water became understood only in the early twentieth century, the rulers of Egypt from time immemorial realized that the floods were the gift of Ethiopia. Moreover, they were convinced (and so were many Europeans) that the Ethiopians were capable of obstructing the waters and the flow of the Blue Nile and its tributaries,[5] a theme that recurs throughout this history. Historically, the river produced an ever-developing world of anxieties and myths that, in themselves, went to the core of the Egyptian soul. Ethiopia in the Egyptian consciousness—and this is one major theme of this study—was important enough to become relevant even to the very essence of Egyptian self-perception. The concept of Ethiopia has been a meaningful "other" for centuries, an external being significant enough to influence attitudes stemming from the very definition of the "self." Indeed, the concept of Ethiopia in Egyptian eyes has continued to develop along with changes in the Egyptians' identity.

In my analysis of the Egyptian aspect, I shall concentrate on three relevant dimensions: the Islamic-Egyptian concepts of Ethiopia, the modern nationalist Egyptian concepts, and the Arab revolutionary concepts. All these identities were born during periods when Ethiopia was much on the Egyptians' agenda, as they interpreted the Ethiopian other as a reflection of the Islamic, Egyptian, or Arab self in their messages and legacies. Furthermore, their concepts of the Ethiopian other were as complex and varied as the Egyptian self-definitions. This is the very crux of my thesis. Just as Islam became rich and multifaceted as a comprehensive prescription for Muslims, so the multifaceted Islamic concepts of Ethiopia were developed. Christian Ethiopia was, from the very beginning of Islam to this day, a matter of intra-Islamic controversy. On the one hand, Ethiopia was the embodiment of evil and danger in the eyes of Islamic radicals. On the other hand, it was the positive, just, blameless neighbor for the moderates, a classical case of an accepted, legitimate other. This Islamic dichotomy regarding Ethiopia was created during the formative stage of early Islam, and it went on to reflect the continuous inner-Islamic arguments about Islam itself, arguments that are still just as heated, perhaps even more so, in Egypt today.[6]

When Egypt became the center of Islam, there followed another formative period of the Egyptian-Ethiopian dialogue. When medieval Egypt reached its historic peak during the time of the Mamluks (1250–1517), Ethiopia enjoyed its "golden era" under the new "Solomonian" dynasty (1270–1529). It was during that period of active interrelations that the Egyptian version of the Islamic concepts of Ethiopia, less abstract and much more practical, was reshaped.

In time, with the birth of modern Egyptian nationalism, much of the Islamic and Islamic-Egyptian dichotomy over Ethiopia was transmitted into the new, modern set of self-definitions. In the last quarter of the nineteenth century, when Egyptian history began revolving around new ideas of representative politics, as well as around a territorial concept of the Nile Valley as an historic entity, Ethiopia again became centrally relevant. Defeating the Egyptian army in 1876, the Ethiopians foiled the plan to connect the Red Sea coast with Khartoum and undermined the Egyptian chance to control the Sudan. This, in turn, began the countdown toward the fall of Egypt itself to British occupation.

In following decades Ethiopia was reinterpreted by the Egyptian nationalists in contradictory terms. In the eyes of the militants it became the uncivilized enemy and the brutal destroyer of the "Unity of the Nile Valley," a slogan and a goal of Egyptian nationalism during the first half of the twentieth century. However, it became also a friendly neighbor for the more liberal faction of Egyptian nationalists, a faction that captured the leadership in the 1920s. For them Ethiopia was a Coptic[7] Christian state, an anti-imperialist citadel, and a worthy partner in a region of diversity and pluralism. Indeed, as in Islam, this inner dichotomy among modern Egyptian nationalists reflected their different interpretations of politics, society, and culture.

Finally, modern, revolutionary Arab nationalism was born in the mid-1930s in the minds of a new young generation in Egypt and the Fertile Crescent. Again, it was a period during which Ethiopia, then facing Benito Mussolini's aggression, was much on the Egyptian agenda. Revolutionary Arabism, in its own formative stage, recycled some of the existing Ethiopian dichotomies and created its own. It perceived Ethiopia as a model for an anticolonialist struggle, but it also tended to adopt the more negative Ethiopian images of radical Islam and of militant Egyptianism. During its heyday in Egypt in the 1950s and 1960s, revolutionary Arabism's concepts of Ethiopia were behind many regional issues: the conflicts in Eritrea and between Ethiopia and Somalia, as well as the Israeli involvement in the Horn of Africa. They also had much to do with Gamal Abdel Nasser's Nile strategy, his blunt dismissal of Ethiopian relevance to the river's waters, and his decision to erect the Aswan High Dam.

By 1987–1988 it became clear that Ethiopia, as the main source of the Nile, could no longer be ignored. The Aswan High Dam was no final solution. It was a partial, one-sided Arab-Egyptian solution to a comprehensive all-basin issue. Compared to the all-Nile plans mentioned above, it is the wrong dam in the wrong place. Its price is today's Egyptian anxieties.[8]

Facing the possibility that Ethiopia may begin to construct projects that would reduce the amount of water in the Blue Nile, Egyptian policymakers continue to waver. As in the past, they must choose between threats, military intervention, and ethnic-religious subversion on the one hand or a friendly, appeasing dialogue with a potentially good and considerate neighbor on the other. In recent years, after the traumatic period of 1987–1988, their tendency seems to be toward the latter policy. In the

Egyptians' uneasy dialogue with the Ethiopians and in their public statements, the demand that the Ethiopians be prevented from using the waters is based on the concept of "historic rights," a concept perhaps as ancient as Egypt itself.

The Egyptians' legal argument for their exclusive rights to the Nile
waters is founded on precedence: Egypt has always used the waters of
the Nile without restriction. At least four of the major civilizations of ancient times—China, India, Mesopotamia, and Egypt—developed along
the waters of large rivers. The Egyptians maintain that the basins of such
rivers, the cradles of ancient cultures and states, should be seen as one
integrative theater in which use is determined not by geography or hy-
drology, but by human history. Moreover, they argue, the idea of the Nile
basin as an integrative entity of such a nature was confirmed by the international agreements signed during the twentieth century. The principle of historic rights was mentioned in the 1929 Egyptian [British]–Sudanese Water Agreement and reiterated in the Agreement for the Full
Utilization of the Nile Waters of 1959. In fact, Egyptian (and Sudanese)
exclusiveness with regard to the Nile waters was recognized by the
British in all their colonial agreements. Moreover, it was accepted by the
Ethiopians themselves, for in 1902 Emperor Menelik II agreed not to interfere with the flow of the river without British consent.

The moral dimension behind Egypt's "historic rights" is twofold:
first, Egypt has no other option to survive; second, Ethiopia has lived
without the Nile so far and presumably can do so in the future. In practice, however, the Egyptian interpretation of the "historic rights" concept
is becoming less acceptable. There is a growing realization that Egyptian
rights cannot exclude others. In the 1959 Nile Waters Agreement with
Sudan, Egypt quantified its rights, dividing the total annual amount of an
estimated 74 billion cubic meters: 55.5 billion for Egypt and 18.5 for
Sudan. In essence, the Egyptians recognized the Sudanese right to an
"equitable share." But Ethiopia was simply ignored, and the Egyptians
and the Sudanese concluded that any additional quantity that could be
conserved would be divided equally between them in accordance with
their "historic and established rights." Claiming to share the Nile waters
between them, Egypt and Sudan agreed to take joint action against any
upstream attempt to challenge their historic rights. Since 1987–1988,
however, it seems Egypt is more ready to accept Ethiopia as a legitimate
partner and neighbor.[9] In negotiating over the vital waters, Egyptian
leaders and public opinion makers have indeed resorted to the more positive concepts of Ethiopia, to images that were first created by early
mainstream Muslims, applied by the Mamluks, and reshaped by the pi-
oneers of liberal Egyptianism. In so doing, they are occasionally ready

to accept, albeit vaguely, the validity of the Ethiopian argument regarding the Nile waters, that of "equitable shares."

"EQUITABLE SHARES": ETHIOPIA AND THE MIDDLE EAST

The principle of "equitable shares" is indeed the polar opposite of "historic rights." According to scholar Robert Collins, it has been recognized in China and India for many centuries and has acquired a greater significance over the past 500 years with the development of the nation-state.[10] It was internationally defined in the Helsinki Accords of 1966 as a principle of "fair shares," ambivalent enough to leave much of the particulars to be negotiated by the parties concerned. The principle, however, is very clear as to the entitlement of every riparian country to a fair share of the waters of an international river and as to the obligation of all neighbors to accept the inviolability of these rights. In fact, nearly all international accords regarding international rivers are based on this principle. It was the imperialist British, the Ethiopians argue, who legally established Egypt's "historic rights," but they were never recognized by the independent African states. It is an unjust principle, the legacy of foreign intervention, long dead, like Emperor Menelik and British colonialism.

After centuries of internal wars and underdevelopment during which the Ethiopians did not have the resources to utilize the Nile, they are now determined to use it for Ethiopia. They are surely entitled to use a fair part for their enormous needs. Their country is no less populous than Egypt (it will soon become more so), and their infrastructure is less developed. At the very beginning of the twenty-first century, Ethiopia uses less than 1 percent of the Nile basin waters, while Egypt uses 80 percent. According to the World Bank in 1997, "the waters of the Nile probably constitute Ethiopia's greatest natural asset for development. . . . The development of the River Nile in Ethiopia has the potential to contribute significantly to poverty reduction, meet domestic power and food demands, and become a cornerstone of a future Ethiopian export strategy."[11] Could any government give it up?

Moreover, due to climatic changes during the 1970s and 1980s, the whole of northern Ethiopia is gradually drying up. The June–October rains that used to fall on northern Ethiopia, Tigre, Gojjam, Wallo, Bagemdir, and Gondar have been observed to be shifting to the center and the south. However, with the advent of the Tigrean leadership in 1991, the political center of gravity in Ethiopia has shifted to the north. The new regime in Addis Ababa introduced many revolutionary changes to the identity of Ethiopia, and doubtless it is also committed to the

development of northern Ethiopia, a region long neglected by its predecessors. But if Ethiopia, however lawfully and morally justified, begins diverting a significant amount of water from the Nile, the damage
to Egypt may prove irrevocable. The last time northerners led Ethiopia
in modern history (under Emperor Yohannes IV, 1872–1889) while
Egypt focused on the Nile (under Khedive Isma'il, 1863–1879), the
clash of interests quickly led to war.

Is this, then, a zero-sum game? Can these two countries reach a solution? Is there room for understanding and cooperation? Water experts
say that there is and that common efforts and diverse plans, implemented
in a spirit of goodwill, would be of mutual benefit in concrete terms of
irrigation, energy, and land erosion. We shall take them at their word, but
let us turn again to history, this time to the Ethiopian side. There—and
this is another major point in my argument—I think there is even more
room for optimism. Analyzing the Ethiopian views of the "self" and the
"other" may illuminate the "equitable shares" concept from a different
angle, thus opening up more constructive options.

If the waters of the Nile have meant life for Egypt, they have meant
something different for the Ethiopians. The part of the river in their own
territory gave no life, at least not in the material sense. The huge gorge
of the Abbai did not act as a bridge between people, as did the Nile in
Egypt, but divided them. The energetic, dramatic flow in the depths of
the gorge did not bring the water to the fields, but rather stole the precious liquid away. It also caused other damage, eroding the soil, killing
man and cattle. Yet the river was of great importance. For the Ethiopians
the Nile was primarily a major historical asset, their best card in their
desire to retain their most important connection with the Middle East.

Ethiopians have hardly identified themselves by the Nile. The Abbai
never really symbolized their territory or their history. Ethiopian identity, at least in terms of the dominant high culture and the state's institutions, was first and foremost Christian. Ethiopia's royal dynasty adopted
Christianity in the fourth century. Acquiring unique local features,
Ethiopian Christianity became the main source of political legitimacy as
well as a main reservoir of popular beliefs, traditions, and customs. Simultaneously, from the very outset, the Ethiopian Church linked itself to
the Egyptian Church of Alexandria and went on to rely on Christian
Egypt as the main external factor in building state and culture. The fact
that Ethiopia was a bishopric of the Egyptian Church until 1959 is a pivotal theme in this story. For sixteen centuries it went hand in hand with
the fact that nearly all the major elements of Ethiopia's canonical culture, in terms of political institutions, major languages, historic awareness, and national-royal ethos, were no less Eastern than African. From

its very beginnings Ethiopia was, at least in the eyes of its ruling groups, a part of the Middle East as well, and it remained so even after Islam unified the region and pushed Ethiopia to the sidelines.

Though surrounded by Islam, medieval Ethiopia managed to re-cover. During its so-called golden era (dating from the late thirteenth to the early sixteenth century), the country benefited dynamically from ac-tive relations on an equal footing with Egypt. However, traumatized by a sixteenth-century Islamic conquest, Christian Ethiopians developed a strong sense of siege, dreading a renewed Islamic offensive. It was be-cause of this that the Christian connection to Egypt and its Coptic Church, and to a lesser extent to Jerusalem as well, acquired added im-portance. For the Ethiopians Alexandria and Jerusalem remained the two corridors to the outside world, as well as the two outside sources of le-gitimacy for their Christian Ethiopian identity. The Ethiopian identity, in spiritual but also in concrete political terms, was therefore institutionally linked to—indeed, dependent upon—Egypt. This link meant both the re-ligious legitimacy of the imperial throne and salvation from the possi-bility of eternal Islamic siege. It also constituted a vital and active con-nection to the sources of Ethiopian culture and identity—to Eastern Christianity and, through it, to the greater Christian world.

The fact that Egypt was in a position to sever Ethiopia from the out-side world and undermine its political structure and its Christian culture shaped much of its history. If Ethiopia was the source of the Nile for Egypt, Egypt was the source of the *abun,* the Egyptian metropolitan bishop, for Ethiopia, the key to religious legitimacy for its whole politi-cal system. Yet Egypt was also the land of Islam, its very center in Ethiopian eyes. In that respect, Egypt embodied the greatest threat of Is-lamic usurpation of Christian Ethiopia. Ethiopians generally ignored the complexities of Islam, of Egyptian or Arab nationalism, and failed to see the positive concepts these identities possessed regarding Ethiopia. They were far more aware of, and sensitive to, the radical Islamic, militant Egyptian, and revolutionary Arab concepts of Ethiopia's illegitimacy. They perceived Islam, especially under Egyptian-Arab leadership, as eternally desiring their very annihilation. It was primarily for this reason that Ethiopia cherished the Nile as a weapon. Playing on Egypt's ancient fear that it could obstruct the Nile waters, Ethiopia sought to secure its ties with the East. Ethiopians wanted to deter Islam from renewing its assault by using their Nile card, and with it, in times of crisis, they man-aged to secure their bishop from Egypt.

The Ethiopians were not, however, merely Eastern Christians. They pursued other options as well, such as turning south to Africa to spread their culture and state, or endorsing a policy of isolation. Indeed, their

sense of uniqueness was perhaps the strongest dimension of their identity. Barricading themselves inside their mountainous citadel was often
believed to be Ethiopians' preferred approach to their existence. Yet the
connection they felt to Africa was also a major part of Ethiopian identity,
of its soul and self-image. Indeed, at certain times, particularly during
the late nineteenth century, the south proved a land of profitable expansion. However, while postcolonial Africa, experiencing a process of
emancipation, was the continent that provided Ethiopia with its historical seniority and political respect, the Middle Eastern option, though
usually far less friendly, remained throughout the most prominent external factor in Ethiopia's development—indeed, the main factor in terms
of both profit and danger. The Middle East, with Egypt as its center, was
a region of far greater significance and relevance, a region of which
Ethiopians were always suspicious, but one to which they always wanted
to belong.

Ethiopia's present demand for its "equitable share" of the Nile's waters
therefore marks merely a new chapter in a very long story. It is a renewal
of the Ethiopians' long-standing desire to retain their African-Ethiopian
identity while still belonging to the East. They aim, albeit reluctantly, to be
a part of the Middle East, to claim their share of this region's riches, to be
a player in a game of enormous potential and consequence.

ETHIOPIAN-EGYPTIAN DIALOGUE

In the following chapters I shall discuss the main concepts underlying
this multifaceted Ethiopian-Egyptian mutuality. Muslims, Egyptian Muslims, modern Egyptians, and Arab nationalists have developed a rich
reservoir of polarized Ethiopian images. The Ethiopians face their own
conceptual dilemmas vis-à-vis Egypt, its identities, and its strategies. On
both sides understanding of the "other," as is universally the case,
evolved from understanding and determination of the "self." I shall analyze this dialectical process of definition and redefinition as it unfolded
throughout history.

More specifically, Chapters 2 and 3 address the formative medieval
concepts. The initial dichotomy regarding Ethiopia was reflected in what
I define as two polarized, early Islamic concepts. One was of legal acceptance of Ethiopia, encapsulated in a saying attributed to the prophet
Muhammad: "Leave the Abyssinians alone." The other was one of total
delegitimization of Ethiopia as a Christian entity, manifested in the idea
of "*Islam al-najashi,*" a label I explain in Chapter 2. In parallel, the medieval dichotomy of Ethiopian concepts regarding Egypt was initially

reflected in a polarization mentioned earlier. On the one side, Ethiopians felt an urge to be affiliated with Egypt, and with the Middle East in general, a concept embodied in the institution of the "Egyptian *abun.*" On the other side, though, Ethiopians demonized the Islamic other, suspecting Cairo of being ever after the destruction of their country, a sense that was firmly formed in the sixteenth century and that I call the "Ahmad Gragn trauma," for reasons to be discussed later.

Chapters 4 through 9 are devoted to modern and contemporary developments. I shall discuss concrete Egyptian-Ethiopian relations that revolve mainly around the Nile, and I focus on the reinterpretations and modifications of these mutual images and concepts. As problems have become aggravated, greater efforts to develop an all-Nile debate have been made. In 1977 the Egyptians and the Sudanese began working on the formation of Undugu, an organization of Nile riparian countries that was to include Zaire, Rwanda, Burundi, and the Central African Republic. The Ethiopians, however, in accordance with their old strategy of letting the Egyptians sweat, preferred to participate as observers only.

The Egyptian-Ethiopian dialogue remains one of suspicion and threats, but my concluding chapter does contain elements of optimism based on recent developments. In 1992, for example, a new framework, TECCONILE, replaced Undugu and continued to host the annual Nile 2002 Conference. Although Ethiopia again avoided official membership in the organization, and although the "equitable shares"/"historical rights" debate is still lurking in the background creating political tension and potential crises,[12] at least the dialogue seems to have opened up. On 1 July 1993 Egypt and Ethiopia initiated an accord on Nile basin cooperation, agreeing that "the issues of the use of the Nile waters shall be worked out in detail through discussions by experts from both sides, on the basis of the rules and principles of international law." According to the Ethiopian interpretation, this was tantamount to Egypt's recognition of Ethiopia's rights to the Nile waters.[13] In February 1997 Addis Ababa hosted the Fifth Nile 2002 Conference, which was attended by hundreds of officials and scholars, including 163 Ethiopians and 16 Egyptians. As reflected in the published proceedings, the two sides are far from establishing a relationship of mutual trust. In fact, both sides are busy planning and mobilizing resources in pursuit of unilateral, mutually antagonistic Nile strategies.[14] But, evidently, there is a new readiness to listen and to recognize that psychopolitical hurdles, the product of a long history, must be addressed.[15] Such a readiness, I believe, represents an opening up to an understanding of the other—the dialectical chain I analyze throughout this book—and will remain the key for future success. The more the Egyptians and the Ethiopians liberalize their views of

themselves, the greater the chance for mutual understanding. With goodwill, say hydrologists, a win-win, all-Nile game can be developed. Leaders of both countries declare that this is their wish.[16] Attention to history
can provide a guide to the goal of all-regional, African, and Middle Eastern pluralism.

The history I present here is an attempt to follow a multidimensional
process stretching over sixteen centuries of vicissitudes and change. My
study weaves together three related themes: the political relationship between successive Egyptian and Ethiopian regimes; the involved story of
the connection between the Christian churches in the two countries; and
the way in which sharing the Nile system has influenced perceptions of
the other and played a role in both Ethiopian and Egyptian definitions of
national identity over time. Undertaking such a challenge, I can hardly
claim to have covered it all. I have tried to understand concrete political
issues in the context of their cultural backgrounds, but I could not render
full justice to each of these spheres. I followed much of the literature behind the international discourse and ended up more or less presenting the
Ethiopians' and the Egyptians' "official" mind-sets, the ideas of their
learned elite, and occassional "voices from below." It is perhaps easier
to properly present the relevant popular concepts in more focused studies.

NOTES

1. For general background information, see Waterbury, *Hydropolitics,* and
Collins, *Waters of the Nile.* See also Sa'id, *Nahr al-nil,* and Abate, *Water Resources Development.*

2. See Sofer, *Rivers of Fire,* chap. 2. See also *Al-Akhbar,* 8 March 1988;
Jerusalem Post, 29 June 1988.

3. For the main ideas and plans aired during the twentieth century, for their
failure to materialize, and for a warning that the continuation of one-sided policies by the governments concerned would lead to a major catastrophe, see
Collins, "In Search of the Nile Waters."

4. This is the main theme of Erlich and Gershoni's edited collection *The
Nile;* see mainly the introduction. See also Sa'id, *Nahr al-nil,* mainly chap. 8.

5. See Pankhurst, "Ethiopia's Alleged Control," pp. 25–37, and van Donzel,
"Legend of the Blue Nile in Europe," pp. 121–129.

6. The issue of Islamic and later of modern Egyptian nationalism's and Arab
nationalism's concepts of Ethiopia is a main theme of my book *Ethiopia and the
Middle East,* which also discusses Ethiopian concepts of the Islamic other. Some
of the ideas developed below were initially studied for *Ethiopia and the Middle
East.*

7. Although the Ethiopian Church was affiliated with the Coptic Church,
Ethiopian Christianity was not "Coptic." This issue will be addressed below.

8. See Collins, "In Search of the Nile Waters." More on the controversy
over the Aswan High Dam can be found in Chapters 8, 9, and 10 in this volume.

9. In 1988 the Center for Arab Studies in Cairo published a voluminous collection of articles by different authors reflecting this new spirit. See Markaz al-Buhuth, *Azmat miyah al-nil.* See discussion in Chapter 9.

10. See Collins, "A Nile Policy." I thank Professor Collins for generously sending me very helpful material.

11. See World Bank, "The World Bank, Ethiopia, and the Nile."

12. See Waterbury, "Is the Status Quo in the Nile Basin Viable?" and "Policy and Strategic Considerations."

13. See "Egypt Recognizes Ethiopia's Right to Nile Waters," *Ethiopian Herald,* 3 July 1993.

14. See details in World Bank, "The World Bank, Ethiopia, and the Nile," p. 12.

15. See the various contributions to the Ethiopian Ministry of Water Resources, *Fifth Nile 2002 Conference: Proceedings,* such as Abraham, "The Nile Issue," in which the author, a historian and a researcher for the Ethiopian Foreign Ministry, writes mainly on the Egyptians' need to overcome psychological barriers.

16. See details in World Bank, "The World Bank, Ethiopia, and the Nile," particularly quotations therein from Ethiopian prime minister Meles Zenawi (7 April 1998) and Egyptian minister of public works Mahmud Abu-Zayd (2 March 1998).

2

Christianity and Islam:
The Formative Concepts

THE ETHIOPIANS AND THE EGYPTIAN *ABUN*

Ethiopia arose as part of the East.[1] The fertile heights of the Horn of Africa attracted migrations and influences from nearby Arabia as early as the seventh century B.C. In later centuries cultural and trading ties were established with civilizations in the Nile Valley, primarily the Nubians and the Egyptians. Semitic languages, modes of economy, urban life, and other dimensions of ancient and early medieval oriental values went on blending and mixing with local elements. Together they formed the cultural basis for the Aksumite kingdom, an empire oriented around Africa, the Red Sea, and the Nile basin. As such, Aksum played an active role in the history of the Nile Valley to the west, as well as in the history of the Middle East during the first to seventh centuries A.D. Closely involved in the affairs of the Arabian Peninsula and a participant in the Byzantine-Persian rivalry, Aksum was a flourishing entity and the beginning of a very long story. It was then, amid the Aksumite dialogues with other oriental civilizations, that the basic Ethiopian institutions of state and culture were molded and formed; some of them have continued to adapt and endure to this very day. They were shaped in a long, multifaceted process, too lengthy for discussion here except to underline one major point of culmination: in the fourth decade of the fourth century, the early Ethiopian kingdom adopted Christianity. This was the third political entity in history, after Armenia (A.D. 301) and the Roman Empire under Emperor Constantine (in 312), to do so.   *early adopter*

The new Christian religion was to have a dual historical role. It would absorb and assimilate various local customs in its development, thus becoming the comprehensive prescription for the Ethiopian state,

15

culture, and lifestyle. It would also become the main, and soon the only, Ethiopian channel to the outside world.

Until the seventh century, however, the Aksumite Ethiopians still had other channels for international relations—political, diplomatic, economic, and cultural. Aksum conquered Yemen in A.D. 524–525, and Ethiopians ruled there for five or six decades (to around A.D. 590). Aksum also cultivated intensive commercial and social relations with such Arab towns as Mecca and the Red Sea ports. Ethiopian diplomatic missions reached other oriental capitals. Religious relations in themselves remained diversified, connected with the various centers of the East, then undergoing Christianization. The introduction of Christianity in the fourth century is attributed to two young brothers, Frumentius and Aedesius, who were rescued from a shipwreck while en route from India back to Syria, then taken to the Aksumite court. There they acquainted the royal family with Christianity and helped to administer the kingdom. In time Aedesius returned to the town of Tyre and told their story to the historian Rufinus Tyrannius.[2]

After the Council of Chalcedon in A.D. 451 in Syria, following the schism in oriental Christianity over the nature of Christ, nine Syrian monks who probably adhered to the minority Monophysite doctrine (the belief that Christ had one nature, both human and divine) fled to Ethiopia. The so-called Nine Saints, it is believed, spent the remainder of their lives there, laying the literary foundations of the rapidly growing Ethiopian Church. They were said to have translated the Scriptures into the Ethiopian language of Geez and established monasteries, turning monasticism into the main infrastructure of Ethiopian Christianity.[3] Sometime later, we are told (perhaps still in the fifth century), Ethiopian monks cemented their bond to the East by settling in Jerusalem. They established an Ethiopian community in the Holy City, adding a dimension to the strong biblical Zionist spirit of Ethiopian Christianity and national tradition and also beginning a story relevant to our main Ethiopian-Egyptian theme, a story still in progress. The Byzantine emperors themselves took an interest in the Christian empire on the Red Sea, and it was speculated that in the sixth century Ethiopia's Christians were in communion with the Catholic Church, perhaps even headed for a while by a bishop sent by the pope of Rome.[4]

The Bond with Christian Egypt

There was also a historical connection between Egypt and Ethiopia's Christianity, a more stable and meaningful bond than that between Ethiopia and the rest of the Middle East. When Aedesius returned to

Syria, Frumentius went to Alexandria to tell their story to Patriarch Athanasius. The patriarch then persuaded Frumentius to return to Ethiopia as a bishop of the Egyptian (later Coptic) Church. The year was most likely A.D. 333, and the new bishop for Ethiopia was given the special title of *abuna* ("our father" in Geez and Arabic) or *abun* (in Amharic). Back in Aksum, Frumentius, now renamed Abuna Salama,[5] was welcomed by the royal court and recognized as the head of the church. During his lifetime he worked closely with two kings and was referred to as Kassata Berhan, the "revealer of light." Abuna Salama's appointment began an enduring tradition, for when he died he was replaced by a new *abun* from Egypt, Abuna Minas.

Abuna Salama and Abuna Minas were thus the first in a chain of some 111 Egyptian *abuns,* the heads of the Ethiopian Church.[6] All of them, until 1951, would be Egyptian-born monks appointed to lead the Ethiopian Church by the Egyptian Coptic patriarch. The Church of Ethiopia would officially remain an extension of the Egyptian one, its "daughter," a bishopric of Alexandria,[7] until the days of Nasser and Haile Selassie. It was only in 1959, after sixteen centuries of meaningful mutuality, that the bond was broken when the Ethiopian Orthodox Church became autocephalous.

After the rise of Islam (A.D. 622) and its conquest of Greater Syria (A.D. 636) and of Egypt (A.D. 640), this fourth-century Egyptian-Ethiopian *abun* arrangement became vitally important. For the Ethiopians it was to remain practically their sole external channel for many centuries. As Islam worked to terminate the Ethiopians' political relevance to its domains (to be discussed shortly), it also managed to disconnect them from most of their other oriental Christian contacts. The Ethiopians considered the concept of the Egyptian *abun* vital to their claim of being part of the apostolic succession. They cherished this institutionalized dependency on the Egyptian Church as perhaps their only remaining token of affiliation with the Islamic-dominated Eastern world.[8]

For the Christians in Egypt the Ethiopian bishopric would become a major asset in their relations with Islam. They accepted Islamic rule in their country (in A.D. 641), and in return they were tolerated by the new rulers. Moreover, the Islamic governors of Egypt were happy to allow the continuation of their special ties with Ethiopia. In fact, they soon began usurping control of these ties, arranging things so that any Ethiopian request to the patriarch for a new *abun* would first be submitted to Egypt's ruler. The reason for this Islamic-Egyptian flexibility was quite obvious. Here was a contact with the land that held the source of the Nile floods. Indeed, upon his conquest in 640, 'Amr ibn al-'As, Egypt's first Islamic ruler, was greeted by a population dreading an

approaching disaster. In August the waters of the Nile refused to rise. Islamic legend has it that 'Amr rushed to send a letter from Caliph 'Umar
in Mecca to the river and that the Nile responded promptly, resuming its
regular flow.[9] Stories aside, the notion that the Ethiopians—*al-habasha,*
the people inhabiting the mysterious upstream country—had the power
to block the river had been long prevalent in Egypt. Though never tested
and proven, this assumption, as we shall see, was to shape history. In the
future, Egyptian correspondence regarding the Nile floods would be di-
rected to the Ethiopian court, and the Coptic religious leverage over the
Ethiopians would be appreciated by Egypt's rulers. In fact, this special
Ethiopian card was of crucial importance to the Copts in their long
struggle to maintain their position in Islamic Egypt. It would become an
even more important factor in the twentieth century.

After the Islamic conquest of Egypt the Copts acted to ensure their
position and guarantee Ethiopian dependency. Sometime in the mid-sev-
enth century there appeared a document falsely attributed to the Council of Nicaea of A.D. 325.[10] It canonized the nature of the Ethiopian-
Egyptian religious connection, stipulating that Ethiopia would be just
one bishopric of the Coptic Church and that no Ethiopian could become
an *abun.* In time this latter stipulation was inserted in the canonical literature translated from Arabic into Geez by Coptic scholars. Most notably it was enshrined when the Ethiopian legal code, the *Fatha Nagast*
(the Law of the Kings), compiled in 1238 by the Coptic scholar al-Safi
ibn al-Assal, was introduced (by Ethiopian tradition it was brought to
Ethiopia during the time of Emperor Zar'a Ya'qob, 1434–1468, and
translated into Geez during the reign of Emperor Yohannes I, 1667–
1682).[11] Article XLII of the *Fatha Nagast* reads:

> As for the Ethiopians, a patriarch shall not be appointed from among
> their learned men, nor can they appoint one of their own will. Their
> metropolitan is subject to the holder of the See of Alexandria, who is
> entitled to appoint over them a chief who hails from his region and is
> under his jurisdiction. And when the said metropolitan is appointed
> with the title given to the chief, he is not permitted to consecrate other
> metropolitans as the other patriarchs do. He shall only be honored with
> the name of patriarch, without enjoying the power of a patriarch.[12]

The institution of the Egyptian *abun* was of mutual benefit.[13] The
Copts gained respect in Egypt[14] and, occasionally, even actual Ethiopian
backing. When the Christians were persecuted in Egypt, the Ethiopians
threatened to block the Nile or retaliate by maltreating Muslims in the
Horn of Africa. The Copts continued to contribute to the development of
Ethiopian culture and state. Egyptian monks left their country and

helped spread monasticism throughout Ethiopia. Many of these Egyptian monks, along with their local Ethiopian colleagues and disciples, were behind the flourishing Aksumite period of translations of religious literature from Greek (and Syriac and Hebrew) into Geez. Together with the earlier work of the Nine Saints, they contributed to the creation of the early canon of the Ethiopian Church, numbering eighty-one books.[15] It was no doubt due to their influence, and of course that of the *abuns,* that by the eighth century the Monophysite doctrine was adopted by the Ethiopians. Christians who fled Egypt during periods of Islamic persecutions (such as the reign of al-Hakim, 996–1021)[16] entered the service of Ethiopia's kings. They provided valuable help in state organization and through their introduction of various technologies. There is no doubt that the Ethiopians derived their calendar, as well as the use of Greek letters for numbers, from the Copts.[17]

Most importantly, the Egyptian *abuns* attended and even administered the coronations of kings and provided patriarchal legitimacy to Ethiopia's rulers.[18] In fact, Ethiopia's political history of medieval times, indeed of later centuries as well, can hardly be separated from the history of the church and the story of the Egyptian *abun.*[19] In strictly political terms Ethiopia's history was a chain of volatile dramas, a game of endless rivalries and vicissitudes that were constantly energized by the nature of local geography and by the country's ethnic-regional diversity. Indeed, given those conditions, rulers and dynasties could hardly maintain political continuity in Ethiopia without the cloak of religious sanction. For an Ethiopian king to preserve power, or for a contender to challenge and replace him, the support of the *abun* was crucial. For the state to spread its control and build its loyalties, the network of monasteries and churches was essential.

After the rise of Islam and the decline of the Aksumites, the center of Ethiopian life shifted to the south. The Christian culture and institutions, detached from their Eastern connections, encountered the challenge of a renewed cultural transformation. In confronting the local Agaw ethnic groups with both their animist and Judaic traditions, Ethiopian Christianity, which already contained Judaic dimensions, proved capable of absorption and adaptation. The survival of Ethiopian culture was greatly due to the role of the church and its Egyptian connection, which also facilitated the process of political resurrection.[20] The Zagwe Agaw–Christian dynasty emerged around 1137, seeking legitimacy from the Christian-Egyptian connection. One of the first Zagwe kings sent a mission to Cairo to ask for a new *abun,* since the old one refused to recognize him as the new ruler.[21] In 1270 the Zagwe lost power, apparently due to the mediation of the church, which enabled the rise of the Solomonian dynasty. It was agreed that one-third of the kingdom's land should be ceded to the church for the maintenance of the *abun,* clergy, churches, monasteries, and monks. It was also reaffirmed that no native Ethiopian should be chosen as an *abun.*[22] Indeed, the new Solomonian emperors, particularly as of the time of the ascendancy of 'Amda-Zion in 1314, would further institutionalize their work with the Egyptian *abuns,* bringing the Ethiopian synthesis of church and state to its historic apex.

Voluntary Dependence

From the Ethiopian perspective there were obvious and very serious shortcomings to the situation. For a state so identified with Christianity to be a mere bishopric was a major compromise. On paper the Ethiopians could have up to seven bishops, but in practice the Egyptians saw to it (after the rise of the Solomonian dynasty)[23] that they had only one at a time. (Only fifteenth-century Emperor Zar'a Ya'qob managed to obtain two bishops.) The *abuns* were sent to Ethiopia under oath never to consecrate bishops in Ethiopia (a bishop who was not an *abun* was a *pappas* in Geez) or undermine the full Ethiopian dependence on Alexandria in any other way. Since only a bishop could consecrate a church and priests, and only priests could administer the sacraments, the very existence and spread of Christianity, a process upon which the entire empire really rested, was completely dependent on a limited church.

When an early tenth-century king, after some misunderstanding with Alexandria, dared to appoint an *abun,* the See of Alexandria reacted by refusing to send new *abuns* for nearly a century.[24] One of the last Aksumite kings (presumed to be named Sayfa-Ar'ad, 977–1005), facing destruction for other reasons as well, wrote to his Christian neighbor, the king of Nubia:

> [W]rite a letter on thy part to the father, the patriarch, in Egypt, to beg him to absolve us, and absolve our lands, and to pray for us that God may remove from us and our country this trial, and may grant to us that the patriarch may consecrate for us a metropolitan, as was the custom of our fathers. . . . I have mentioned this to thee, O brother, for fear lest the Christian religion pass away and cease among us, for six patriarchs have sat and have not paid attention to our lands, but they [the lands] are abandoned without a shepherd, and our bishops and our priests are dead, and the churches are ruined, and we have learned that this trial has come down upon us as a just judgement in return for what we did with the metropolitan.[25]

Abuns sent to Ethiopia were Arabic-speaking Egyptian Coptic monks, most of them already of advanced age, who were hardly prepared to meet the challenges of leading a church in a far-off country, particularly in a language they very rarely managed to master sufficiently. Since the appointment for life to Ethiopia was not that attractive (in Egypt there were sixteen archbishops and over 100 bishops), those sent were not always the very best Egypt could offer. Some were even said to have lacked basic education.[26]

As of the fifteenth-century reign of Zar'a Ya'qob, Ethiopian emperors—the de facto heads of the church—compensated themselves by relying on the Ethiopian head of the monastic system, the *echage,* but the damage to church and state was constant. The weakness of the institution of the *abun* and the frequent absence of the head of church resulted in the weakening of the entire priestly class. To avoid a shortage of clergy, young children were often consecrated as priests and deacons, though they received only a minimal education. Instead of institutionalized training, the priesthood became a practice of family tradition.

There were also several important ritual differences.[27] The Ethiopians adopted Monophysitism but incorporated it into their own particular version of Christianity. This Ethiopian blend was emphatically biblically oriented, containing customs such as circumcision on the eighth day, dietary prohibitions, ritual cleanliness, and observance of the Sabbath—clearly not compatible with Coptic traditions. The prayer texts, order of service, church music and iconography, musical instruments, and liturgical vestments were also different from those of the Copts. Though the sharp ritual differences created no serious theological rift between the two churches, they did cause periods of serious tension and led to endless disputations between the *abun* and the *echage,* or sometimes even the kings and emperors.[28]

Moreover, Ethiopia was not only a state that spread Christianity; it also confronted Islam in the Horn of Africa, an issue of central importance in our Ethiopian-Egyptian analysis. The *abun,* however, was imported to Ethiopia thanks to the goodwill of Islamic rulers. Prior to his nomination he was instructed by both sultans and patriarchs to not alienate Islam. In around 1080, for example, Abuna Sawirus arrived in Ethiopia with strict orders from the Fatimid Sultan al-Mustansir bi'llah (1036–1094) to look into the construction of mosques. Abuna Sawirus (like many of his predecessors and successors) tried to persuade his Ethiopian congregation to become monogamous and asked the patriarch to write to the king and the Ethiopians forbidding them to observe the customs of the Old Testament. He is said to have built seven mosques before he was imprisoned by the king. When the sultan heard that these mosques had been destroyed, he initiated reprisals against the Copts. Soon afterward the Nile waters went down and famine began. The disaster was quickly attributed to Ethiopian interference with the river, and the Coptic patriarch was duly sent to appease the king. The king then "ordered a large enclosed valley to be opened by the cutting of a dam. As soon as this was done the Nile rose ten feet in a single night and the whole land of Egypt was irrigated."[29] This episode[30] heralded a long cycle of threats and reprisals. Many Ethiopians, in any case, often suspected that the Egyptian *abun* cared for the building of mosques as much as for the building of churches.[31]

The most important shortcoming, of course, was the very fact of dependency on Egypt. The *abun*, embodying Ethiopia's Christian identity, was second only to the emperor. By tradition he would not only anoint the ruler, but also sit to his right, close enough to symbolize the unity of the cross and the crown. The fact that the Egyptian rulers were in a position to deny Ethiopia its religious head, a man of such political and spiritual centrality, was the main factor behind many relevant episodes. If the Nile, or the myth regarding the emperors' ability to block it, was the Ethiopian card, then the Egyptian card was the sultan's or the Coptic patriarch's ability to delay or avoid sending an *abun*. We shall consider some of these dramas below.

But if the flow of the Nile was the creation of nature, the dependency on Christian Egypt was in fact a voluntary Ethiopian undertaking. It is a unique case in Christian history—indeed, quite a curiosity. Why would a state of proven political validity, along with a church quite distinguished for its unique features, enter into and endure such relations? Why would it persist in maintaining this status, prescribed in a clearly fabricated canon, of a junior, underprivileged partner of a much smaller church, itself totally dependent on Muslims? Why would a medieval Ethiopian king (as recorded by an Egyptian chronicler)[32] eagerly await a letter from the Egyptian patriarch, which was supposed to arrive twice a year, and then listen to it read in public by the Egyptian *abun* as he stood solemnly in church on Sunday? Answering these questions here, at this point in the story, would be somewhat premature. By the end of this chapter, after Islamic attitudes and medieval Egyptian policies are discussed, these questions will become even more intriguing.

ISLAM AND ETHIOPIA: "LEAVE THE ABYSSINIANS ALONE"

The previous section looked at Ethiopia's initial affiliation with the East and introduced the institution of the Egyptian *abun*. This institution, I shall argue, would remain for centuries the embodiment of the Ethiopians' urge to retain this affiliation. But the more complex set of Ethiopian attitudes toward the oriental East can be better appreciated only after

Islamic and Egyptian-Islamic views of Ethiopia are brought to light. It was only after a long dialogue with Islam, primarily with Islamic Egypt under the Mamluk rulers (1250–1517), and then after a short yet traumatic conquest of Ethiopia by the Muslims of the Horn of Africa (1529–1542), that the Ethiopians' premodern concepts of Islam and the East were finally shaped. We shall analyze them at the end of the next chapter.

What, then, were Islamic concepts of Ethiopia, and was there a special Egyptian version of them?

As discussed below, Ethiopia was very important to Islam from its incipience. Middle Eastern Muslims developed a particularly articulate set of impressions of *al-habasha,* a term that encompasses Abyssinia, Ethiopia, and/or the Ethiopians. For most Muslims *al-habasha* became a very abstract idea of a mixed, half-black yet Christian "other," deserving special attitudes. This idea was dichotomous. On the one hand, Muslims totally delegitimized Ethiopia, declaring it a principal enemy of Islam; on the other hand, Ethiopia was cordially recognized, but only as a minor, distant neighbor. To the majority of Middle Eastern Muslims, Ethiopia was indeed an abstract other, a good theoretical case by which one could define and redefine the Islamic "self." For Egyptian Muslims, however, Ethiopia was equivalent to the main source of the Nile, a much more concrete vision. Yet the abstract Islamic dichotomy would always be available to the Egyptian Muslims, and they would readily use it whenever necessary to facilitate the arguments over the more practical dilemmas they had in regard to *al-habasha.*

"The First Hegira"

Ethiopia was the first case in Islamic history of foreign relations. When Muhammad and his small group of early followers, the *ansar* (helpers) or *sahaba* (friends), were persecuted by the leadership of Mecca in A.D. 615, the Prophet, in an hour of danger, told them to flee to Ethiopia and seek asylum with the *najashi,* the negus, the king of Aksum.[33] The Prophet, apparently, had a good knowledge of the nearby Red Sea–oriented Christian state that, as mentioned, had ruled in the southern Arabian Peninsula during the sixth century. There was an Ethiopian commercial quarter in Mecca, and Muhammad's nurse, who became his lifelong friend, Baraka 'Umm Ayman, was an Ethiopian. Many prominent Arabs of his time and of the late pre-Islamic period (including the famous poet, 'Antara ibn Rabiba) were of Ethiopian descent.

Muhammad had respect for the monotheistic culture of Ethiopia, and he probably even knew some Geez words. He told his followers: "If

you go to Abyssinia you will find a king under whom none are persecuted. It is a land of righteousness where God will give you relief from
what you are suffering." While Muhammad stayed behind, many of the
early Muslim converts fled by night to Ethiopia. A second wave (or perhaps it was a continuous flow) of Muslims followed somewhat later.
Their story would be recorded in Islamic history as "the first hegira,"
and they did indeed find shelter with the Aksumite negus, *al-najashi,*
Ashama ibn Abjar, as told by various Islamic chroniclers. The latter,
having heard from these Muslims about the new religion and being convinced by their leader, Ja'far ibn Abi-Talib, that Islam was affiliated with
and close to Christianity, rejected a demand by a Meccan delegation to
surrender them as traitors. The *najashi* (there is no *ashama* in Aksumite
records, and the king at the time was presumed by some traditions to be
called Negus Adriaz) then began corresponding with Muhammad in
Mecca and later (after 622) in Medina. According to all Islamic versions
of this story[34] (there are no others), *al-najashi* benevolently continued to
provide all sorts of vital services to the struggling Prophet, including arranging his marriage to a woman from a leading Meccan family, an important step on his road to salvation and success. Most of the Muslims
who found shelter in Ethiopia returned to Arabia years after the hegira to
Medina. All the Islamic sources also say that in the year 628, when
Muhammad sent letters to all the major rulers in the world asking them
to recognize him as the last messenger of God, they all declined, except
for his old friend the *najashi*. The latter, sources maintain, accepted Islam
and even sent his son to be educated by the Prophet. When *al-najashi*
died in 630, the Prophet prayed for him as for a departed believer.

This story of the first hegira led to the creation of the two contradictory Islamic views of Ethiopia. For in this formative episode the abstract concepts of both the legitimacy and the illegitimacy of *al-habasha*
were molded. They were to be recycled and reinterpreted, forever competing as the essence of Ethiopia and Islam to this day.

"Utruku al-Habasha": *The Acceptance of Ethiopia*

The first traditional view was to become the primary one and can be described as Islam's mainstream concept of Ethiopia. It is summarized in a
hadith, a saying attributed to Muhammad: *Utruku al-habasha ma tara-
kukum* (Leave the Abyssinians alone as long as they leave you alone).
According to this tradition, the Prophet's gratitude to the "righteous"
Ethiopian king who saved his followers, and perhaps himself and his entire mission,[35] reached such an extent that he was ready to recognize
Ethiopia, even though it remained a Christian entity. By uttering those

famous words, Muhammad in fact, many believed, exempted Ethiopia from the Islamic jihad. There were, to be sure, other populations that the Prophet ordered his followers to avoid (the Turks, the Nubians, and the Cypriots), but this was for practical military considerations and temporary in nature. For *al-habasha,* though, it was a matter of gratitude and grace and therefore permanently valid. In legal Islamic terms, it was argued, Ethiopia was to become the only "land of neutrality," a proclaimed state of political immunity positioned midway between the concept of the "land of Islam" and that of the infidels' "land of war."[36] This unique legal tolerance blended well with the abstract concept of Ethiopia as the embodiment of humanistic justice: a country accepted and praised, even though it was non-Islamic.

Over the centuries the Ethiopian model of a righteous and a legal other continued to resurface whenever Ethiopia was placed on the agenda. Moreover, it became, over time, a cardinal argument for the more moderate Muslims in their interpretations of Islam itself and its relations with the non-Islamic world. We shall follow the role of moderate Muslims in Egypt later. But for now it should be noted that the Ethiopian model that focuses on the benevolence of the Christian *najashi* in his hospitality to the Muslims is one of the more central arguments for those believers who would like to make Islam itself as politically flexible as possible. It serves, for example, Islamic leaders in Britain and the United States today, who thus justify their right to emigrate to a non-Islamic country and live under a non-Islamic government.[37]

The precedent of the Prophet ordering Muslims to go live under a non-Muslim regime and abide by its rules also served the moderate wing of the Islamic movement in Israel of the 1990s. These moderates maintained that they were fully ready to follow the line of the *sahaba,* provided, of course, that the Israeli government would be as righteous as the *najashi* had been.[38] In 1994 Anwar Haddam, one of the leaders of the Islamic Salvation Front, the Algerian underground opposition, fled and sought asylum in the United States. Interviewed by an Algerian correspondent, he said: "Clinton is like the king of Ethiopia in the dawn of Islam to whom the Prophet himself sent his followers to find shelter."[39] In 1996, when the Palestinian Authority, under Yasser Arafat, was established, there began a similar discussion among the learned men of the Palestinian Hamas Islamic movement. In a seventy-page booklet issued by their moderates, those advocating recognition of Arafat and cooperation with his non-Islamic administration, eleven pages were devoted to the recounting and analysis of the story of the Prophet and *al-najashi.*[40]

Was this acceptance of Ethiopia in humanistic terms also an invitation for it to be a partner in the history of the Islamic East? Throughout

Islamic history this famous hadith was brought up whenever Islam had cause to deal with Ethiopia. But apart from the abstract elements of grace and gratitude contained in the story, this concept basically meant only the sidelining of Ethiopia for all practical purposes. As long as the Ethiopians left the world of Islam alone and refrained from bothering it, Muslims were under obligation to tolerate their existence but not to befriend them. In fact, it might be argued that the essence of the message was rather to ignore Ethiopia.

Interestingly, it was not until the second half of the ninth century that the hadith was first put down in writing.[41] By that time early Islamic efforts to dominate the Red Sea (especially during the reign of Caliph 'Umar in 640) had been foiled. Later, when the center of Islam moved away from the Arabian Peninsula to far-off Damascus (the Umayyad dynasty, 661), and then to Baghdad (the Abbasids, 750), Ethiopia became quite irrelevant. The new Islamic dynasties were disconnected from the Red Sea (the little island of Dahlak, off the shore of Massawa, was occupied in 702, but it served as a prison rather than as a springboard to the Horn of Africa).[42] Distant, remote, and militarily inaccessible, Ethiopia was conveniently "left alone" and ignored. Christian Ethiopia remained more like an abstract concept: positive yet for the most part irrelevant. For some Muslims in the nearby Arabian Peninsula, *al-habasha* also became a hunting ground for the best slaves, another good reason to allow it to remain non-Islamic. "Leave the Abyssinians alone" was therefore far from being just a pure call for good-neighborliness founded on historical gratitude. It was no less a suggestion, bordering on an order, to disconnect, to ignore. Indeed, Islam, especially when led by non-Egyptians, isolated Ethiopia from the East, creating a buffer between it and the rest of the Christian world, and itself avoided relations. In time non-Egyptian Muslims seemed to lose all curiosity about the real Christian Ethiopia, and soon it was perceived as a mysterious land situated between the Red Sea and sub-Saharan Africa, the land of "the Sudan" (the blacks).

In medieval times the Sudan, stretching and spreading from the direction of sub-Saharan West Africa to the lower and western White Nile basin, became far better known to Islam. Indeed, many Islamic geographers searched there for the source of the Nile.[43] They showed little curiosity about the land of Ethiopia, and when they did, they were mostly interested in its Muslims. Arguably the greatest of them all, together with Marco Polo, the leading traveler of medieval times, was the Moroccan-born (1304) Ibn Battuta. An Islamic scholar of law, he spent three decades touring the greater Eastern world. He was curious enough to leave western Africa and to reach India and China in the Far East, the Central Asian steppe in the north, and tropical Africa in the south. He also spent much time in the Red Sea basin and visited Zeila in 1330. It was a period during which Ethiopia reached a political and cultural peak (during the reign of Emperor 'Amda-Zion) and had very significant relations and conflicts with both Egypt and the Islamic Zeila. But in his extensive writings the great Islamic traveler failed to mention Ethiopia at all. He practically bypassed the country and conceptually ignored it altogether.[44] In line with tradition he "left the Abyssinians alone."

However, with all due reservations, the tradition of leaving the Abyssinians alone was essentially a positive one, a unique case in Islam of accepting a politically sovereign "other." Moreover, Ethiopia's positive abstract image was, indirectly at least, strengthened by the Islamic tradition of glorifying Muslims of Ethiopian origins. The third person to answer the call of Muhammad was an Ethiopian slave in Mecca, Bilal ibn Rabbah. He was then freed and became the first muezzin, the one who calls Muslims to prayers. In time Bilal became an important Islamic hero and was buried in Damascus. According to another relevant prophetic saying, "The Khalifa [caliph] shall be of Quraysh, judicial authority shall be in the hands of the Helpers, and the call for prayers with the Abyssinians."[45] Indeed, the institution of the mosque became somewhat associated with "Bilal al-Habashi," or Bilal the Ethiopian. Hundreds of mosques the world over are named after him.[46]

Further, Bilal's story became the first proof of Islam's supraethnic, nonracist nature. In the vast literature produced over the centuries by Islamic purists working to defend this concept of purity, many other examples of Ethiopians joining Islam and preserving it in a pious spirit are discussed.[47] "Obey whoever is put in authority over you, even if he be a crop-nosed Ethiopian slave" was also attributed to the Prophet, emphasizing his universal, all-human message.[48] The righteous *najashi* himself, who, it was claimed, had himself become a Muslim, is also often mentioned as a case in point. As a whole, then, Ethiopia and Ethiopians constitute a major case for those who work to promote Islam as a benevolent universal message of tolerance and supraracial humanitarianism.[49]

"Islam al-Najashi": *Ethiopia's Illegitimacy*

In total contradiction to this rather positive image of Ethiopia, there existed throughout a very negative image. Ethiopia was also perceived by Muslims as the embodiment of evil and of barbarism. It was considered to be the country responsible for Islam's first failure, a Christian entity that blocked Islam in Africa,[50] and it remained a land that oppressed Islam. According to this concept, infidel Ethiopia deserved destruction and could be redeemed only by complete Islamization.

Ironically, the legitimacy for this negative view also stemmed from the initial story of the Prophet and *al-najashi*. Islamic radicals, those for whom Islam is intolerant of any politically sovereign "other," choose to concentrate on the end of that famous episode. Rather than remembering that the Ethiopians saved the *sahaba,* they focus on the contention that the king of Ethiopia, two years prior to his death, converted to Islam. As most Islamic sources agree, the *najashi* had to conceal his new faith, was persecuted by the infidel Ethiopians, and died lonely and miserable. Tradition also has it that he was betrayed by his Christian wife, Mariam. The *najashi,* claim the radicals, died as a Muslim, and Ethiopia, due to his conversion, was already a part of the "land of Islam." Rebelling against the Muslim king was therefore a *fitna,* an active act of heresy, and Ethiopia's return to Christianity was Islam's first defeat. Ethiopia was *Andalus al-'ula,* the "first Spain," a calamity Islam should never fail to redress. It was the duty and responsibility of Ethiopia's kings, it followed, to return to Islam. "*Islam al-najashi,*" the adoption of Islam by the rulers of *al-habasha,* was considered by Islamic militants to be a precondition to any dialogue with them.[51] This was a line the leaders of Egypt could never adopt but those of other Islamic countries occasionally did (such as a seventeenth-century imam of Yemen or the Sudanese Mahdi and his successor, the caliph, in the 1880s).[52] For the Islamic radicals Ethiopia was definitely not a "land of neutrality," but rather a classical "land of war," well deserving of a conquest in a jihad.

In the eyes of radicals Christian Ethiopia was not only the embodiment of an early sin. It was also depicted as an active and persistent enemy of Islam. First and foremost, they argued, Ethiopia oppressed Muslims in the Horn of Africa. The fact that Ethiopia maintained its hegemony, defeated and conquered local Islamic entities, and occasionally did force Muslims to adopt Christianity will soon be addressed in its medieval context. It also became a permanent theme in Islamic literature. If one is supposed to "leave the Abyssinians alone as long as they leave you alone," then one is obliged to fight them if they take the offensive. The record of Ethiopia fighting Muslims has grown over the centuries, and its assumed inherent aggression against Islam became a leading argument, especially in the twentieth century. Here I shall only mention the extensive writings of the important journalist, historian, and Syrian intellectual Shakib Arslan, arguably one of the most prominent all-regional Islamic-Arab public opinion shapers in the interwar period. When Mussolini threatened to invade Ethiopia in 1935, Arslan published dozens of articles in the Arabic press of all major Middle Eastern countries, recounting all the crimes Ethiopia had committed in oppressing Islam and supporting the Fascists' scheme to occupy Ethiopia and teach it a lesson.[53] This strong anti-Ethiopian line would be followed by Islamic radicals of Egypt, a discussion which we shall return to when relevant in later contexts.[54]

In their demonization of Ethiopia the radicals tended to portray the state as aiming to destroy Islam not only in the Horn of Africa, but also in the East at large. To prove this point, a pre-Islamic episode was brought forward and retroactively readdressed. In A.D. 570, the year Muhammad was born, Yemen was still in Aksumite hands. In that same year, according to the Quran (The Sura of the Elephant), the Ethiopian commander at that time, Abraha, led an army equipped with a number of elephants and approached Mecca. His intention, it was said, was to demolish the Kaaba, then a Meccan polytheistic shrine, when a miracle occurred and his army was stoned from the sky. "The year of the elephant" went down in history as the time the Kaaba was saved,[55] but from the perspective of the Islamic radicals, it was also proof that the Ethiopians wanted to destroy Islam. "The lean-legged Ethiopians, they will destroy the Kaaba" claims another famous ninth-century hadith,[56] engraving this tradition in Islam, to be recycled and repeated in both canonical and excanonical literature.

The Ethiopians, on their part, occasionally set off this Islamic fear. For example, according to a Coptic source, a late-eleventh-century Ethiopian king, hearing that Sultan al-Mustansir bi'llah, mentioned earlier, had threatened to destroy Coptic churches, wrote to him: "If you demolish a single stone of the churches, I shall carry to you all the bricks and the stones of Mecca, and I shall deliver all of them to you, and if a single brick is missing, I shall send to you its weight in gold."[57]

For Islamic radicals, too, the Ethiopians wanted to demolish more than the very heart of Islam; they particularly aimed to destroy all of Egypt. According to one age-old belief, Ethiopians would invade the country of the Nile and ruin it, while their fellow Copts, betraying their Muslim rulers, would sit passively by and watch.[58]

The demonic image of Ethiopians—to be sure, just one polar dimension of relevant Islamic concepts—has also percolated down to the sphere of popular culture. Over the centuries Egyptians (and other Middle Eastern Muslims), in their daily life, saw Ethiopians mostly as imported black slaves. The fact that behind them there stood a strong, proud, non-Islamic state, and that they were thus associated with the notion of such anti-Islamic and anti-Egyptian threats, only helped spread popular anti-Ethiopian racist attitudes. We shall address these attitudes in

Chapter 3 when discussing the literature of radicals, who fomented them. We shall also discuss the moderates, who worked to combat such negative images and to promote the concept of Ethiopia as a legitimate, neighborly "other."

NOTES

1. On the oriental aspects of Aksum see the three authoritative works on the subject: Hable Selassie, *Ancient and Medieval Ethiopian History;* Trimingham, *Islam in Ethiopia;* and Cuoq, *L'Islam en Ethiopie.* An emphasis on the oriental dimensions of Aksum was also the main thesis of the great Italian scholars Enrico Cerulli, Ignazio Guidi, and Carlo Conti Rossini, who led the field of Ethiopian studies in the first half of the twentieth century. For more on the African significance of Aksum and for more recent findings, see Munro-Hay, *Aksum.* For an integrative, succinct, and updated summary, see also Paul B. Henze, *Layers of Time,* chap. 2. It is a very careful background reading for most aspects of Ethiopia's historical and contemporary developments.

2. On Frumentius and Aedesius, as well as on the "Nine Saints" discussed below, see the summary and sources in Hable Selassie, *Ancient and Medieval Ethiopian History,* pp. 92–105, and Trimingham, *Islam in Ethiopia,* pp. 38–40.

3. Though the Nine Saints came from Syria, the rule of monasticism they introduced was that of St. Pachomius, a well-known monk and recluse of Upper Egypt. See Buxton, *Travels in Abyssinia,* p. 124.

4. Teklahaymanot, "The Egyptian Metropolitans." The ideas espoused by Dr. Abba Ayele Teklahaymanot, a Roman Catholic Capuchin father, have not been accepted by the establishment of the Ethiopian Orthodox Church.

5. Stuart Munro-Hay argues that the title of *abun* was introduced much later and reattributed to Frumentius, together with his moniker of "Kassata Berhan" (personal communication from Munro-Hay to author).

6. There are several lists of the Egyptian metropolitans of the Ethiopian Church (the most used one is Conti Rossini's list in the Accademia dei Lincei of Rome's collection (ms. no. 7, fols. 107–112). Here I rely on a reconstruction of the list by a modern Ethiopian historian of the church and its relations with Egypt; see Waldagiorgis, *Kagibts baityopya yatashamut papasat,* pp. 98–101. For a new historical interpretation by an Ethiopian religious scholar of the history of the Egyptian *abun* in Ethiopia, see Teklahaymanot, "The Egyptian Metropolitans," and his booklet *The Ethiopian Church.*

7. After 1045 the center of the Coptic Church moved to Cairo.

8. For the most up-to-date and authoritative history of the institution of the *abun* from the fourth century to the thirteenth, see Munro-Hay, *Ethiopia and Alexandria.*

9. See note 2 in Chapter 3 herein.

10. For the seventh-century forgery, see Meinardus, *Christian Egypt,* p. 371; Teklahaymanot, "The Egyptian Metropolitans"; and van Donzel, *Enbaqom: Anqasa Amin,* p. 3. The act of forgery was attributed to the thirty-eighth patriarch of Alexandria, Benjamin (623–662).

11. See Trimingham, *Islam in Ethiopia,* p. 25. Trimingham also summarizes the relevant works of Guidi and Conti Rossini.

12. Translation by Abba Paulos Tzadua, as quoted in Teklahaymanot, *The Egyptian Metropolitans,* p. 18. See also Hable Selassie, *Ancient and Medieval Ethiopian History,* p. 112. For another version of the Nicene pseudocanon, see Munro-Hay, *Ethiopia and Alexandria,* p. 17.

13. See Jones and Monroe, *History of Ethiopia,* pp. 47–53.

14. The Copts' Ethiopian dilemma will be discussed below in its various aspects. On the one hand, medieval Copts did their best to spread awareness in Egypt of their Ethiopian connection. Coptic writers were much behind the notion that Ethiopia was capable of both blocking the Nile and punishing Muslims in the Horn of Africa. On the other hand, they were also afraid that Egypt's Muslim rulers would not grasp the limitations of the *abun* and hold them responsible for whatever the Ethiopians did.

15. See Kamil, "Translations from Arabic" and "Al-Rahbaniyya fi al-habasha"; and 'Ashur, "Ba'd adwa' jadida."

16. See Trimingham, *Islam in Ethiopia,* p. 57. The issue of Coptic contributions to Ethiopian culture will also be addressed below in the discussion of the country's golden era.

17. Kamil, "The Ethiopian Calendar," p. 91; Hable Selassie, *Ancient and Medieval Ethiopian History,* p. 199.

18. For eleventh- and twelfth-century cases of Egyptian Copts fleeing to Ethiopia and making contributions, see Meinardus, *Christian Egypt,* pp. 375–376, 380–381. See also Budge, *History of Ethiopia,* p. 154.

19. See more on the institution of the *abun* in Munro-Hay, *Ethiopia and Alexandria,* pp. 36–44.

20. For a detailed analysis of related history, see Munro-Hay, ibid.; the role of the Egyptian *abuns* during the Aksumite period is discussed in pt. 2.

21. See Meinardus, *Christian Egypt,* pp. 378–379; Trimingham, *Islam in Ethiopia,* pp. 55–56.

22. See Bruce, *Travels to Discover the Source,* p. 173.

23. In all probability, there were more bishops during Aksumite and Zagwe times; see, for example, Meinardus, *Christian Egypt,* p. 379, and Teklahaymanot, "The Egyptian Metropolitans."

24. See Hable Selassie, *Ancient and Medieval Ethiopian History,* pp. 215–218, and Renaudot, *Historia Patriarcharum,* p. 283, as quoted by Teklahaymanot, "The Egyptian Metropolitans."

25. Hable Selassie, *Ancient and Medieval Ethiopian History,* p. 224; see also Munro-Hay, *Ethiopia and Alexandria,* p. 134, and Tamrat, *Church and State,* p. 41.

26. Meinardus, *Christian Egypt,* p. 390. (Meinardus wrote that Abuna Salama, a very important figure in Ethiopian history from 1841 to 1867, had been, prior to his appointment in Egypt, a twenty-two-year-old camel driver. According to other sources, however, he was educated at a school of the Church Missionary Society in Cairo).

27. See a summary in Jones and Monroe, *History of Ethiopia,* pp. 35–43.

28. For a discussion of a ninth-century crisis over circumcision between the *abun* and the king, see Meinardus, *Christian Egypt,* p. 375. For a dispute over the Sabbath and other crises, see below.

29. See Hable Selassie, *Ancient and Medieval Ethiopian History,* p. 248.

30. The story of Abuna Sawirus and the interference of the Fatimid rulers in the appointment and policy of the *abuns* in Ethiopia has been studied recently by

Emeri van Donzel; see his article "Badr al-Jamali." For this episode see also
Tamrat, *Church and State,* pp. 46–49; Trimingham, *Islam in Ethiopia,* pp. 64–65;
Meinardus, *Christian Egypt,* p. 377; and Munro-Hay, *Ethiopia and Alexandria,*
pp. 157–160.

31. See Teklahaymanot, "The Egyptian Metropolitans."

32. See 'Ashur, "Ba'd adwa' jadida." See also Munro-Hay, *Ethiopia and
Alexandria,* p. 204, quoting al-'Umari, *Ta'rif .*

33. The following section on Muhammad and the *najashi* is drawn primarily from chap. 1 of my *Ethiopia and the Middle East.* See also Hable Selassie,
Ancient and Medieval Ethiopian History, chap. 8, and Cuoq, *L'Islam en Ethiopie,*
chap. 2.

34. See sources in Erlich, *Ethiopia and the Middle East,* p. 6. In recent
years much has been published on the subject by Saudi scholars; for example,
Abu Bakr's *Ma'alim al-hijratayn ila ard al-habasha* (a very detailed account)
and Khattab's *Islam al-najashi.*

35. See an authoritative new study by an Israeli Muslim: Mansur, *Al-Hijra
ila al-habasha.* In his conclusion (pp. 257–258) Dr. Mansur summarizes his
main points: had it not been for the emigration to Ethiopia, the Islamic message
would not have succeeded; the emigrants could send vital financial help to the
Prophet; their survival and success inspired him to think of the second emigration to Medina; and the fact that the *najashi* received the Muslims worked to
convince Arab tribespeople to follow suit. For Mansur the first hegira was the
most important event in the history of Muhammad's Meccan period. See also Erlich, *Ethiopia and the Middle East,* chap. 1. In analyzing the episode Trimingham (*Islam in Ethiopia,* p. 45) uses a quotation from Muir's *Life of Mohammed:*
"If an Arab asylum had not at last offered itself at Medina, the Prophet might
happily himself have emigrated to Abyssinia, and Mohammedanism dwindled,
like Montanism, into an ephemeral Christian heresy" (p. 70).

36. See Khaddouri, *War and Peace,* chap. 12.

37. See, for example: Haddad, "The Challenge of Muslim Minorities";
Abou El Fadl, "Islamic Law and Muslim Minorities"; and Webman, "Maintaining Islamic Identity."

38. See Erlich, *Ethiopia and the Middle East,* p. 194, n. 44.

39. Quoted in *Al-Watan al-Arabi,* 11 February 1994.

40. Issued by "a group of religious learned men," the booklet was titled *Al-
Islam wal-musharaka fi al-hukm* (Gaza, n.d.).

41. In the *Sunan* of Abu Dawud, vol. 2, p. 133; Sulayman Abu Dawud died
in 888. See also van Donzel, "Al-nadjashi."

42. Erlich, *Ethiopia and the Middle East,* pp. 9–11.

43. See Levtzion, "Arab Geographers."

44. See Dunn, *Adventures of Ibn Battuta,* pp. 122–123.

45. See this and more on positive Islamic attitudes toward Ethiopians in
Ahmed, "Historiography of Islam."

46. In 1996 the Palestinian Authority contended that the Tomb of Rachel,
near Bethlehem, a most sacred place for the Jews, is also an Islamic mosque.
They named the place Bilal Ibn Rabbah Mosque, arguing that the seventh century Islamic occupiers of the land named the holy place after Bilal. See D. Ru-
binstein, "The Slave and the Mother" (in Hebrew), *Ha'aretz,* 9 October 1996.

47. See an extensive discussion in Lewis, *Race and Slavery.* See also Erlich,
Ethiopia and the Middle East, pp. 11–14.

48. Lewis, ibid., p. 34. For more traditions on the purity of Ethiopian Muslims, see, for example, a new edition of *Rasa'il al-Jahiz,* edited by Harun, mainly pp. 184–185; see also Fadl's new edition of Jalal al-Din al-Suyuti's (d. 1505) *Raf' sha'n al-hubshan.*

49. In 1974 the film *The Message,* narrating the life of Muhammad, was produced in the United States and starred Anthony Quinn and Irene Papas. The film forcefully carries the message of supraethnic, universal fraternity and focuses on the first hegira to Ethiopia. Two of its main heroes are the righteous Ethiopian king and Bilal al-Habashi. With Arabic dubbing, the renamed *Al-Risala* became a cult film, popularly shown all over the Islamic world, mostly on Ramadan nights.

50. See Trimingham, *Islam in Ethiopia,* p. xv.

51. See discussion and sources in Erlich, *Ethiopia and the Middle East,* pp. 16–19.

52. On seventeenth-century Yemeni-Ethiopian relations in this spirit, see Erlich, ibid., pp. 38–39; on the Mahdiyya and Ethiopia, see pp. 65–72.

53. See a detailed discussion in Erlich, ibid., pp. 95–126.

54. Two works of contemporary Egyptian Islamic radicals were also consulted for this chapter and contain important information: 'Aliyyan, *Al-Hijra ila al-habasha;* and 'Abd al-Halim, *Al-'Alaqat al-siyasiyya bayna muslimi al-zayla'.* Their concepts will be addressed in Chapter 9 below.

55. See Hable Selassie, *Ancient and Medieval Ethiopian History,* pp. 151–153. For a controversy over the dates see Trimingham, *Islam in Ethiopia,* p. 41.

56. The hadith was first collected in Muhammad al-Bukhari (d. 869), *Sahih al-Bukhari,* vol. 8, p. 12.

57. See van Donzel, "Badr al-Jamali," and Munro-Hay, *Ethiopia and Alexandria,* p. 157.

58. A rich variety of anti-Ethiopian beliefs, including those on the destruction of the Kaaba and of Egypt, is available in a book composed in Baghdad in 844: 'Abdallah Nu'aym ibn Hammad's *Kitab al-futan,* edited by Zakkar; see mainly p. 288 and the chapter titled "The Ethiopians' Invasions" (pp. 403–406). See also Zabiyan, *Al-habasha al-muslima.* The most radically Islamic anti-Ethiopian literature of the 1980s was published in Egypt and will be addressed in Chapter 9 below.

3

Medieval Prime:
The Legacies of the
Solomonians and the Mamluks

BLOCKING THE NILE: THE MYTH

Though Ethiopia became an abstract concept for most Middle Eastern Muslims, it remained a concrete issue for those residing in Egypt. The source of the waters and the life-bringing floods could hardly be "left alone." In fact, the very first Islamic ruler of Egypt, 'Amr ibn al-'As, had firsthand knowledge of *al-habasha*. Said to be of Ethiopian origin himself, 'Amr, while still a young member of the pagan elite of Mecca, had headed the mission to the court of *al-najashi,* asking for the surrender of the *sahaba* in A.D. 616. He was supposedly so impressed with the dialogue between the Ethiopian king and the early Muslims that he later returned to Ethiopia, where he presumably avowed his allegiance to Islam before the *najashi* himself, who acted as Muhammad's representative in accepting it.[1] 'Amr then became one of Islam's chief generals. Forced to deal with a failing Nile upon his conquest of Egypt in 640, 'Amr learned of the old Ethiopian-Copt connection.[2] His successors would make it their business to oversee the patriarch's appointment of the bishop of Ethiopia themselves.

For the Ethiopians Islam was not merely an abstract, alien, besieging sea that had moved its centers to far-off Damascus and Baghdad. They needed to address Islamic Egypt in order to obtain their *abun* and to build their Christian state. Moreover, as they moved their center southward following the fall of Aksum, the Ethiopians were about to collide head-on with Islam in the coastal and inland southern and central areas of the Horn of Africa.

The story of Islam in the Horn of Africa is significantly related to Ethiopian-Egyptian history throughout, although we cannot go into detail here. We shall have to confine ourselves to the fact that, beginning in the seventh century, Islamic communities were established first in coastal towns, such as Massawa, Berbera, Mogadishu, and notably Zeila, and then in the inland town of Harar. These urban centers flourished after the Fatimid rulers of Egypt (969–1171) worked to enliven their Red Sea commerce and established regular contact with the Muslims of the African coast. As a result, the activities of the Muslim merchants also increased in the Ethiopian highlands, and the Fatimids extended their protection to those inland traders.[3] "Thus there began the historic role of Egypt as the champion of Islam in Ethiopia, a position first assumed by the Fatimids, and which has characterized Ethio-Egyptian relations throughout the centuries."[4]

Islam then spread through southern Ethiopia among the Sidama and other local ethnic groups. The Muslims managed to establish various sultanates, which, by the sixteenth century, numbered fourteen, notably Shoa (the Makhzumi dynasty, 897–1285), Ifat (the Walashma' dynasty, 1285–1415), and Adal (also the Walashma' dynasty, 1415–1577). Unlike the unifying ethos of Ethiopian Christianity and of Middle Eastern Islam, the Islamic enterprise in the Horn failed to create political unity. Arabic spread mostly along the coast, but the inland groups, hardly developing urban centers, remained attached to and divided by their various languages and different traditions. They were slow to adopt Islamic urban institutions of education, law, and political unity. Their internal rivalries prevented the establishment of an all-Islamic state in the Horn and perpetuated Ethiopian hegemony. Both sides needed Egypt in the continuous struggle that began as Ethiopia moved southward, especially at the end of the eleventh century. The Muslims, often defeated, yearned for material and political support from Egypt. The Ethiopians, most often the victors, needed Coptic Christian inspiration and religious legitimacy for their kings.[5]

Sources for this history prior to the thirteenth century are meager. However, as illustrated by the episode in the 1080s mentioned above (i.e., the Fatimid ruler al-Mustansir sending the Coptic patriarch to Ethiopia to look into the resumption of the Nile's flow), religious and water affairs were already bringing new life to a dynamic Ethiopian-Egyptian dialogue. By the twelfth century there existed a multifaceted Ethiopian-Egyptian Christian-Islamic diplomatic cycle revolving around the cross, the crescent, and the Nile.

With the rise of the Zagwe dynasty in Ethiopia around 1137, there began a period of political and Christian revival.[6] The more the Zagwe kings established their hold on government in central Ethiopia, and the further they expanded southward, colliding with Muslims and pagans, the harder they worked to cement their relations with Egypt.[7] They wanted more bishops and exerted constant pressure on the patriarchs to send them. The Copts—ever fearful that, having more bishops, Ethiopia would be able, and eventually willing, to break away—proved inflexible. They allowed no more bishops and would adhere to their one-bishop policy until the late nineteenth century. It is believed that one of the Ethiopian kings (King Harbe, perhaps the fourth of the Zagwe rulers) was so frustrated that he sought to increase the number of bishops to seven and contemplated declaring his church autocephalous before he succumbed to tradition and the need to retain the oriental church connection.[8]

Egyptian Islamic rulers were evidently more open with regard to Ethiopian Christian necessities. Sultan al-Afdal, it is said, was not opposed to providing King Harbe with more bishops before he was persuaded by Patriarch Gabriel II to avoid it.[9] The Egyptian rulers' religious tolerance and generosity peaked when the great Salah al-Din of the Ayyubid dynasty (1169–1193) defeated the crusaders in the Holy Land and captured Jerusalem in 1187. In this hour of historical triumph he also returned the Ethiopian monks to their old houses and declared that Christian Ethiopians on pilgrimage to Jerusalem—usually by the overland route through western Eritrea, Qus on the Nile, and Egypt—would be exempt from the personal tax imposed on other pilgrims. It is believed that he ordered them to be treated as *dhimmis,* members of the protected non-Islamic communities residing within Islam. This supposed act of benevolence by the Egyptian ruler was to remain in effect until modern times.[10]

The Zagwe kings went on developing the "Zionist" biblical dimension of their political culture and adopted the myth that would lead to the rise of their successors, the Solomonians. The ethos of the Ethiopians as the legitimate successors of the Israelites was already a central theme at that time. The greatest of the Zagwe kings, Lalibela (circa 1190–1225), went down in history as the builder of the wondrous rock-hewn churches at the site named after him. He is traditionally said to have flown miraculously to Jerusalem, where Christ appeared to him and instructed him to build a new Jerusalem in Ethiopia. Lalibela churches were built as a model of the Holy City, and their construction, apparently assisted by Egyptian monks, took place not long after Salah al-Din had revived Ethiopia's contact with old Zion.[11]

Relations between the Zagwe and Egypt's rulers, however, were far from cordial. The latter, still facing the crusaders, were not always tolerant of their Coptic subjects, while the Ethiopians continued their policy of trying to defend their fellow Christians in Egypt. Moreover, Egyptian connections with the Islamic sultanates of southern Ethiopia had already become noticeable and were viewed with great suspicion by

Ethiopia, so much so that the myth of the Ethiopian threat to the Nile came into play. The great Lalibela, grateful because of Jerusalem, had become angry enough over Egypt's maltreatment of the Copts (during his reign many Christians were obliged to flee Egypt, seeking refuge at his court)[12] to consider diverting the Nile from its course toward Egypt. Legend has it that he refrained from doing so only because his advisers thought channeling the waters to the south or to the coast would help the Islamic sultanates there flourish.[13]

It is very doubtful that Lalibela, a great architect and builder, could have really interfered with the tumultuous river's course. It is also clear he had no control over the Blue Nile, located outside his dominions, but only over the Takkaze River.[14] What mattered was that in Egypt the Ethiopians' assumed ability to divert the Nile was already a working myth, one that was spreading across the country with the help of the Copts. In fact, the first Egyptian to write about it in Arabic was the Copt Jirjis al-Makin (d. 1273). In his book *Majmu' al-mubarak* he narrated the eleventh-century story about the Ethiopian king first diverting and then restoring the river to its old course.[15]

No less important was the fact that the Ethiopians (perhaps after the Coptic patriarch was sent to Ethiopia on a mission by al-Mustansir) learned about the Egyptians' fear and actually began playing upon it. According to tradition, they had another try at this myth during the period of the Zagwes. Their last king, Na'kuto La'ab, was also said to have contemplated diverting the Takkaze. He was furious at the Egyptians for failing to send a new *abun* and refusing to pay him tribute. He prayed to the Lord to stop the river and, according to tradition, was duly rewarded. Egypt, in any case, suffered three years and seven months of famine at roughly the same time,[16] during the age of the great Mamluk sultan, al-Zahir Baybars.

THE MAMLUKS AND THE SOLOMONIANS

In the mid-thirteenth century there began a long period of intensive Ethiopian-Egyptian relations that can safely be defined, from the modern perspective of the Nile, as the most formative one. Both states, perhaps coincidentally, reached their medieval prime almost simultaneously. They were also to lose it at practically the same time. The Mamluks ruled Egypt from 1250 to 1517, while Ethiopia's "golden era" under the early Solomonian emperors lasted from 1270 to 1529 (though some scholars date the actual start of this era at 1314, upon the ascension of 'Amda-Zion as emperor).[17]

The Mamluks, to be sure, had other external concerns and regional priorities. They headed the leading Islamic state of their time largely because the rest of the oriental East had been invaded and destroyed by foreigners—first by the crusaders, then, far more disastrously, by the Mongols. The Mamluk sultans, without exception, had their hands full preserving their power at home (their system of government prevented the establishment of hereditary dynasties) and facing these external threats. Though they defeated the Mongols in Palestine in 1260, they still had to focus their strategic interest on controlling and defending Palestine and Syria, as well as Egypt, from the later Crusades. They were also most successful in developing urban life in Egypt and Syria, including constructing mosques and Islamic schools, and they excelled in building both their military abilities and an elite military culture.

While rebuilding the centrality of Egypt, the Mamluks also became the leaders of Islam. After the Mongols destroyed Baghdad in 1258, an Abbasid caliph was proclaimed in Cairo in 1261. His successors remained there under Mamluk auspices throughout the Mamluk era, symbolizing the fact that Egypt had assumed the role of defender of Islam and had become its political, as well as its spiritual, capital.

Protectors of Islam in al-Habasha

This dual centrality—conducting an Egyptian-oriented policy combined with assuming responsibility for universal Islam—caused the Mamluks to look in the direction of the Horn of Africa and Ethiopia.[18] Because the overland routes to the Far East were blocked by the Mongols, the Red Sea now acquired added importance. More than their predecessors, the Mamluks developed the Red Sea trade and were quick to find useful partners in the Islamic communities along its African coast. The latter, with the help of the inland sultanates, tapped much of the regional Horn of Africa and the Ethiopian inland trade and connected it to Egypt.[19]

These followers of Islam were perceived by the Mamluks as the embodiment of the Muslim Ethiopians, the righteous successors of *al-najashi* and "Bilal al-Habashi." In fact, the Mamluks believed, at least as reflected by contemporary literature, that even the Arabic-speaking peoples of the coast—the inhabitants of Zeila, Massawa, and Berbera—were *habasha*. *Al-habasha* had long been for the Egyptians a term connoting the stretch of land between the Red Sea and the Nile Valley. To distinguish the Muslims of the Horn from the Christian *habasha,* the medieval Egyptians began calling these Muslims either "Zayla'un," after the town of Zeila, or "Jabarta" (the "burning land"), a tribute to the sultanate of Ifat.

As commercial relations flourished, so did the religious Islamic connection. In the Cairo *madrasa* of Al-Azhar, an institute of higher learning that the Mamluks transformed into the main center of Pan-Islamic intellectual life, a special wing was established for the Muslims of *al-habasha*. This wing, Riwaq al-Jabartiyya, was to become a major link between Egypt and the Muslims of the Horn of Africa, and it would even play an important role in twentieth-century developments. Most Islamic scholars of the coastal towns, as well as Harar, were trained at Al-Azhar. Some Muslim youngsters arriving from *al-habasha* remained in Egypt and gained prominence. Two of the leading *jabarti* scholars, for example, were the fourteenth-century Shaikh Fakhr al-Din 'Uthman bin 'Ali al-Zayla'i (d. 1342) and the sixteenth-century Shaikh 'Abd al-Rahman, the great-great-grandfather of the famous early modern Egyptian historian 'Abd al-Rahman al-Jabarti (d. 1822).[20]

But beyond these religious and commercial connections there developed a very important political dimension. The Mamluks assumed the role of protectors of "Ethiopian" Islam as it confronted Ethiopian Christian expansion. I shall mention, very briefly, some relevant cases, but it would be safe to state that during the Mamluk-Solomonian era a long, repetitive cycle of religious-political reciprocity gained momentum. As the Ethiopians fought with their Muslim neighbors in the south, the Egyptians threatened to take revenge on Egyptian Copts, and vice versa.

The Ethiopian "golden era," it is conventionally assumed, began when Amharic-speaking rulers replaced the Agaw-speaking Zagwe as leaders of the Christian state. The new rulers established a dynasty in 1270 that would bring Ethiopia to its historic prime. During this era—beginning more significantly in 1314 with the reign of Emperor 'Amda-Zion—the rulers gradually expanded the kingdom's boundaries until it included what is present-day Ethiopia's heartland, creating a vast empire. They assumed the title of emperor and established Ethiopia's set of classical political and cultural institutions. Much of their legacy was to last until the 1974 revolution and beyond. During this territorial expansion from 1314 to 1529, the rulers concentrated primarily on the south, with only two emperors venturing to the north, gaining temporary control over the territories of the defunct Aksumite kingdom. But the more their territorial ambitions moved away from the Red Sea, the more relevant Egypt became.

One of the reasons for this relevance, as mentioned above, was that as the Ethiopians fought with the sultanates of Ifat and Adal, they also collided with the Mamluks' patronage of the region's Muslims. Ethiopian victories over Islamic territories were closely monitored by Cairo and created tremendous anger. The other reason was that the Solomonian emperors were constantly intensifying their Christian connection to the Coptic Church as well as to Jerusalem. The emperors were always in need of more bishops to oversee the intensive process of Christianization in their newly occupied areas.

They also turned to biblical Jerusalem for further legitimation of their royal dynasty, claiming Solomonian origin by adopting and Ethiopi-anizing the ancient story of King Solomon and the Queen of Sheba. This claim of biblical, Zionist origins was even codified as a national ethos with the fourteenth-century recomposition from a number of sources of the *Kebra Nagast* (Glory of Kings) text. The importation of the legend, its translation from Arabic, and its adaptation into Ethiopian Geez were carried out with the help of Copts. Additionally, the Islamic Mamluk rulers of Egypt controlled Jerusalem and the Ethiopian pilgrimage route to Zion, a route constantly used by the Ethiopian Christian elite.

Another development of direct relevance to our story of the Nile was unfolding at this time. The great Solomonian rulers were about to establish contact with Christian Europe.[21] Perceiving themselves as de-fenders of Christianity, in terms not dissimilar to the Mamluks' patron-age of Islam, the Solomonian emperors were concerned with the lot of the Copts, who were experiencing difficult times, especially as Egypt confronted the threat of the later Crusades. Ethiopian emperors became the champions of Coptic security and welfare in Egypt, occasionally threatening the Mamluks with retaliation against Ethiopia's Muslims. At the same time, they also continued their ambivalent, multifaceted dia-logue with the Coptic Church itself. On the one hand, they were angry and frustrated by the patriarchate's inflexibility over sending more bish-ops. They continued deliberately to emphasize Ethiopia's unique tradi-tional religious elements that distinguished them from the Copts, such as observing the Sabbath and the rite of circumcision. On the other hand, their dependence on the Copts continued to grow. During this era the Egyptian-Christian connection became an even more central source of spiritual and technological materials. And amid the complex network of interrelations there was also the myth that Ethiopia's rulers could threaten the Mamluks with blocking the Nile.

THE NILE IN SOLOMONIAN-MAMLUK RELATIONS

As mentioned earlier, the last of the Zagwe kings was believed to have caused three years and seven months of famine in Egypt. The great Mam-luk Sultan al-Zahir Baybars (1260–1277), however, was apparently not impressed. He blamed the Ethiopians for abusing Islam and prevented the

Coptic Church from sending them an *abun*. When the first Solomonian emperor, Yekuno Amlak (1270–1285), came to power, he sent a letter of appeasement to Baybars in 1273 or 1274, praising the Egyptian, humbling himself, and asking for a "good, honest" *abun*. He also stated that he was protecting the Muslims under his rule and added a covert threat, noting that he had no less than 100,000 Muslim troops in his army.[22] When Baybars remained evasive about an *abun* and more blunt about the implied threat (writing "God has put a greater number [of horsemen] on the side of the Muslims"), Yekuno Amlak had to accept an *abun* from Syria, and Baybars retaliated by closing Jerusalem to Ethiopian pilgrimage. However, the appointment of a non-Egyptian *abun* quickly backfired on the Ethiopian ruler, as the legitimacy of the Syrian *abun* was questioned in all quarters.

In 1290 the new emperor, Yigba-Zion (1285–1294), assessing the overall accumulated damage, sent yet another letter to Egypt, addressing Sultan Mansur al-Qala'un (1279–1290) and offering a compromise: "I shall protect the Muslims throughout my kingdom and His Highness will do the same with the Christians of Egypt; so let us unite in mutual understanding and common action, and let us go on corresponding." Al-Qala'un then authorized the appointment of an *abun* and the reopening of the Ethiopian pilgrimage route to Jerusalem. The Syrian *abun,* together with his fellow Syrian monks, was probably expelled from Ethiopia.[23]

Al-Nasir Muhammad and 'Amda-Zion

This period of mutual appeasement did not last long. Sultan al-Nasir Muhammad (1309–1341) destroyed Coptic churches in Egypt, while a new Ethiopian emperor, one of the Solomonian greats, 'Amda-Zion (1314–1344), conquered Muslim territory. True to his nickname, the "Pillar of Zion" was a devout Christian and a crusader in spirit, successfully launching wars against the Ifat sultanate and overseeing the translation of numerous holy books with the help of Egyptian monks. (The *Kebra Nagast* was most likely introduced in his time.) One direction in which 'Amda-Zion led his Christian armies was toward Lake Tana. Until then the source of the Blue Nile had been inhabited by pagan peoples, such as the Wayto and the Gumuz. But 'Amda-Zion annexed Lake Tana to his kingdom and began building churches and monasteries on the lake's islands, sending his soldiers and monks down the Blue Nile to see to the Christianization of the land along the river's huge gorge.[24]

This was actually the first time that the Ethiopian state had obtained real control of the Abbai. But as we have already seen, the Egyptian belief that the Ethiopians could ruin Egypt by interfering with the Nile had long been in circulation. 'Amda-Zion's subsequent actions show that he immediately understood that the Abbai flowed into the Nile of Egypt, for he was quick to resort to the concept of blockade. Indeed, Ethiopia's blunt threat was communicated to Egypt in his letter to al-Nasir Muhammad, dated December 1325, in which 'Amda-Zion demanded that the Egyptian ruler "repair the damages he had inflicted on churches, and begin treating his Christians with honor and respect. He then threatened to destroy mosques in his country and block the Nile in a way that would prevent its flow to Egypt." According to Egyptian sources, the sultan was merely amused and dismissed the Ethiopian threat.

To complicate matters, the ruler of Ifat, Haqq al-Din, always in close contact with Egypt, invaded Ethiopia in 1328. Haqq al-Din captured land and burnt churches but was then undone by the swift retaliation of 'Amda-Zion, who invaded Ifat and took him prisoner. From 1332 to 1338 pleas from Ifat to Egypt for armies against the Pillar of Zion went unanswered. Instead, al-Nasir Muhammad ordered the Coptic patriarch to send a letter of appeasement to 'Amda-Zion. "The Ethiopians claim they were the guardians of the Nile," wrote the contemporary Egyptian historian Fadlallah ibn al-'Umari. "They say they allow it to flow only out of respect to the sultan."[25]

'Amda-Zion's son, Sayfa-Ar'ad (1344–1371), and his Mamluk counterpart, al-Nasir Hasan (d. 1361), went on exchanging threats and continued to retaliate by mutually maltreating Copts and Muslims (1354 was perhaps the worst year for the Copts in medieval times), which paved the way for the Ethiopians' warrior emperors Dawit (1380–1412) and Yishaq (1413–1429) and their Mamluk contemporaries, al-Zahir Barquq (1382–1389 and 1389–1399) and Barsbay (1422–1438). Again, this was a period of increasingly intensive and mutual enmity. Presumably, Dawit began his rule in 1381 by raiding Upper Egypt and "inflicting heavy blows on the Muslims." It was most probably a very short raid, for it is difficult to imagine an Ethiopian army marching so far in an inhospitable land. It was probably also the only incident of Ethiopian-Egyptian direct military contact in medieval times. According to Ethiopian tradition, the action was combined with actual Ethiopian interference with the Nile's flow. As noted by scholar Richard Pankhurst, a little-known version of the royal chronicles claims that Dawit held back the Nile when he heard that the patriarch in Egypt had been imprisoned.[26]

The traditional Ethiopian claim that Dawit blocked the river was apparently supported by the period's religious literature. Emperor Dawit was devoted to the ongoing enterprise of translations from Arabic into Geez by Coptic monks. During his reign (as well as that of his father, Sayfa Ar'ad), the Egyptian Abuna Salama III (1348–1388) was nicknamed "Meterguem" (meaning "the Translator") for his supervision of this literary enterprise. It was also during Dawit's reign that a collection of the Miracles of Mary, originating in Europe and transmitted and adapted by Coptic monks, was translated into Geez (the full translation and modifications were accomplished later). According to one of the 268 stories in the *Ta'amra Maryam,* the Ethiopian version of this collection, Dawit prayed to the Virgin before raiding Egypt. In reply she advised the emperor, in the name of God, to divert the Nile. The river is referred to in the legends as the "Abbay" or the "Geyon," the biblical river of paradise that flows through the land of Kush (Genesis 2:13). When the Egyptians saw that their waters had receded, they sued for peace and promised never again to be the foes of Christianity.[27]

According to perhaps more credible Egyptian sources, the raid resulted in Sultan Barquq forcing the patriarch to send a letter of warning to Dawit. Indeed, Dawit responded to Barquq in 1386, mixing respect with covert threats and offering a mutual protection agreement for Copts and Muslims. Dawit denied harming Ethiopia's Muslims and claimed that it was strange that there were those who contended that he had ordered his people to divert the waters of the Nile so that they would not reach Egypt. The two monarchs established workable relations, though Dawit continued to attack Ifat (especially in 1402), while the Copts in Egypt continued to suffer.[28]

Ethiopia of the Solomonian period was able to intensify its development due to the Mamluks' mistreatment of the Copts, which arose out of the suspicion that they were collaborating with the late European crusaders or with Ethiopia. During Dawit's reign, and even more so during the reign of Yishaq, Egyptian Copts fled to Ethiopia. One of them, Fakhr al-Dawla, formerly a prominent administrator in the Mamluk court, is said to have reorganized Yishaq's entire government, including the taxation system, along Mamluk administrative lines. He also taught the emperor to dress with "kingly splendor" and thus—for the first time in Ethiopian history—to distinguish himself from his people and nobles. Because of internal Mamluk rivalries, members of Egypt's Muslim elite were also forced to flee, some opting for the Ethiopian court. The former governor of the Qus area, Amir al-Tunbugha al-Mufriq, oversaw the modernization of Yishaq's army, including the introduction of "Greek fire."[29] These changes were most likely the reason Dawit and Yishaq were particularly successful in fighting the Muslims in the Horn of Africa. After Yishaq finally defeated Ifat by capturing Zeila in 1415, the Mamluk Sultan Barsbay retaliated, as he did when he came to power in 1422, by closing the Ethiopian monastery in Jerusalem. Yishaq lost no time in taking revenge on mosques and Muslims in Ethiopia, while Barsbay responded by threatening to harm the Copts in Egypt.

Yishaq, as the Egyptians were to discover, began building a Christian Ethiopian-European connection. Prior to his death he "wrote letters to the kings of the Franks urging them to ally themselves with him in order to eliminate Islamic power."[30] He established regular contact through a courier (a Persian merchant who was later captured by the Egyptians), for example, corresponding with Alfonso V of Aragon and Naples, calling on him to help fight the sultanate of Adal. In so doing, Yishaq connected with a medieval Europe still motivated by a crusader spirit and a fear of the rising Ottomans and now quite ready to discover Ethiopia.

After the fall of Acre in 1291, much of Europe's anti-Islamic zeal was focused on the hope of demolishing Egypt, which accelerated the circulation of a medieval European myth about Ethiopia and the Nile. It was widely believed that Prester John, a legendary priest, king of mysterious Ethiopia, was capable of diverting the river and of redeeming Christianity by destroying Egypt. According to Emeri van Donzel's analysis, this European legend spread during the fourteenth century and reached Ethiopia in the early fifteenth century. There, the European myth, imported by travelers and circulated through diplomatic ties, added a new dimension to the existing concept, born in eleventh-century Egypt, of diverting the Nile.

Zar'a Ya'qob and Jaqmaq

With the ascension of the greatest of the Solomonians, Zar'a Ya'qob (1434–1468), to power, the European-Nile connection became central to general Ethiopian strategy. Zar'a Ya'qob launched wars against Adal and strove to spread Christianity with the help of a united church. To advance this cause, he used his newly forged ties between the Coptic Church and the European Christians. When the churches of Rome and Constantinople, facing a new Ottoman-Islamic threat, formed an alliance at the Council of Florence (1439–1441), Zar'a Ya'qob and a delegation of Ethiopian monks arrived there from Jerusalem. (It was perhaps at the initiative of the Ethiopian Abbot Nicodemus rather than the emperor's.) This resulted in the opening of an Ethiopian monastery in Rome, as well as in improving Zar'a Ya'qob's ties with the Egyptian Coptic Church. The latter, itself besieged by suspicious Muslims in Egypt, also sent emissaries to Florence to speak for the Ethiopians. Moreover, for the first (and, for many centuries, the only) time, the Coptic patriarchate agreed to send a second bishop to Zar'a Ya'qob's court.

Perhaps this new Catholic European option and pressure on the patriarch helped Zar'a Ya'qob tighten his control over the *abun* at home. Traditionally, the Egyptian *abun* opposed those local Ethiopian monks and churchmen who sanctioned Saturday as the Sabbath, supporting

those who observed Sunday only. In 1450, however, Zar'a Ya'qob forced
the *abun* to accept the Ethiopian Church's unification of Saturday and
Sunday, as well as other Ethiopian characteristics.[31] But the new Coptic
flexibility toward the Ethiopians hardly helped them at home. When Sultan Jaqmaq (1438–1453) came to power, he renewed the Mamluks' attacks against crusaders stationed in Cyprus and Rhodes in the eastern
Mediterranean. He was especially angered by Coptic participation in the
anti-Islamic coordination effort at the Council of Florence and ordered
the Coptic patriarch to report any communication he received from Zar'a
Ya'qob. There followed a chain of anti-Coptic actions in Egypt, including new taxes and the burning of churches.[32]

In November 1443 a delegation from Zar'a Ya'qob handed this letter to Sultan Jaqmaq:

> From the righteous . . . Zar'a Ya'qob . . . king of kings of Ethiopia . . .
> to the noble, elevated Imam, the royal Sultan al-Zahir Jaqmaq, sultan
> of the Muslims and of Islam in Egypt and Syria. It is our goal to renew
> the understandings that existed between our predecessors. Let these un-
> derstandings remain preserved without interruption. You, may the good
> Lord save you, know well what the shepherd needs to do with his
> sheep. Our father the patriarch and our brothers the Christians, who are
> under your government and under your noble kingdom, are very few,
> weak, and poor. They cannot be more numerous than just one Islamic
> community in one of the regions of our country. And you, may the
> good Lord save you, are not aware of the Muslims under our govern-
> ment, that we are the rulers of their kings and we always treat them
> well, and their kings live with us wearing golden crowns and riding
> horses? And are you not aware, you and your Sultan, that the River
> Nile is flowing to you from our country and that we are capable of pre-
> venting the floods that irrigate your country? Nothing keeps us from so
> doing, only the belief in God and the care for his slaves. We have pre-
> sented to you what you need to know and you should know what you
> have to do.[33]

Zar'a Ya'qob's letter created little understanding. Jaqmaq responded
by sending an emissary bearing gifts and an evasive reply. When Zar'a
Ya'qob detained the emissary, Jaqmaq detained the patriarch in Cairo,
forcing him to write to the Ethiopian requesting the emissary's release.
Before his release, however, the Egyptian prisoner was taken to observe
Zar'a Ya'qob inflict yet another defeat on Adal's sultan, Shihab al-Din,
in 1445. When Jaqmaq wrote to the new Adalite sultan suggesting that
he make peace with Zar'a Ya'qob, the latter responded in 1449 that the
Ethiopian emperor had built a navy of 200 ships in preparation for an attack on Mecca and aimed to destroy the Kaaba. He further warned that
Zar'a Ya'qob was contemplating blocking the Nile.[34]

Zar'a Ya'qob brought Ethiopia's awareness of the Nile's political significance to its peak. He also added significant religious and cultural dimensions to this awareness by overseeing the completion of the translation and modification of the *Ta'amra Maryam*. This collection of legends included the Virgin Mary's advice to fight Egypt and Islam by diverting the Geyon, the Nile. Zar'a Ya'qob institutionalized the cult of Mary as preeminent among the saints of the Ethiopian Orthodox Church, and in 1441 he introduced the reading of passages from the *Ta'amra Maryam* as a major ritual on Sundays. The Nile legacy of the Virgin Mary, together with that of the entire Solomonian period, was to endure. The idea that the Geyon was part of Ethiopia's biblical heritage, that Ethiopia dominated its flow, and that Ethiopian control of the river was sanctioned by heaven remained part of the Christian Ethiopian ethos.[35]

Zar'a Ya'qob's and Jaqmaq's successors continued the same pattern, recycling this complicated international saga, though in a somewhat less dramatic manner. By the end of the fifteenth century, both countries had begun to weaken as they approached the end of the Mamluk period and of Ethiopia's golden era.

ETHIOPIAN CONCEPTS OF ISLAM AND EGYPT

From what has been said it becomes apparent that during this formative period, Egypt, in the eyes of Ethiopia, was far from being a distant, abstract country. Rather, the letters of Yekuno Amlak, Yigba-Zion, 'Amda-Zion, Dawit, and Zar'a Ya'qob to contemporary Mamluk sultans reflected concrete, businesslike concepts. The Ethiopian monarchs used the Nile myth (invented by the Egyptians themselves and magnified by medieval Europe) not to inflict a deathblow on a distant enemy, but to help strike a deal of mutual understanding with Egypt. They combined the threat with flattering aspirations for good relations. They needed Egypt to continue as the source of their Christianity, an aid in Ethiopia's spiritual, cultural, and judicial development, just as they wanted continued access to Jerusalem as the source of their royal Solomonian ethos and their special, Bible-oriented religious identity. (Indeed, the Mamluk period was one of prosperity for the Ethiopian community in Jerusalem.)[36] The Ethiopians also wanted Egypt to remain the major external source of their material and administrative modernization, and they wanted Egypt to refrain from supporting Islam in the Horn of Africa. Last but not least, they realized that the Nile myth was the key to building relations with Christian Europe.

It is central to my argument to compare this practical approach to Egypt and this Ethiopian yearning for partnership with the Mamluks, with contemporary Ethiopian attitudes toward the Muslims of Ifat and Adal. According to the royal chronicles, the leaders of Islam in the Horn were the ultimate embodiment of evil. For example, in the chronicle of 'Amda-Zion, his rival, Sabr al-Din, the sultan of Ifat (1328–1335), is described as "this rebel son of a viper, seed of a snake, son of a barbarian, from the origin of Satan" and an "enemy of righteousness who opposes the religion of Christ." As for the Muslims of the south and the coast, according to this chronicle, they are all "liars . . . hyenas, and dogs, sons of vipers and seeds of evil ones."[37]

The Ahmad Gragn Trauma

It was the Muslims of the Horn, long perceived by Ethiopia in terms of religious enmity, who ended the golden era and destroyed Ethiopia. The story of the Islamic conquest of Ethiopia from 1529 to 1543 has little to do with Egypt and is therefore beyond the present scope.[38] For our purposes it is useful to note that by the time the conquest occurred, Egypt had already lost its political independence, had become an Ottoman province (in 1517), and had no immediate connection to this historic event. A wave of Islamic revival in the Arabian Peninsula, itself related to the rise of the Ottomans, helped inspire an Islamic political revolution in the Horn of Africa. The various Muslim communities of *al-habasha,* consequently, were finally united under the religious and military leadership of Ahmad Ibn Ibrahim, nicknamed "Gragn," meaning "the Left-Handed." This new imam, helped by learned men from Arabia, managed to create an anti-Ethiopian jihad movement that, for the first time, sparked an Islamic revolution that united local Muslims of various ethnic groups and languages. Focusing his leadership on Harar, Ahmad Gragn led his armies into the heartland of Christian Ethiopia, occupying Shoa in 1529, Amhara in 1531, and then Tigre in 1535. Lebna Dengel, the last of the great Solomonians (1508–1540), was relegated to the status of a resistance fighter on the run as Ahmad Gragn conquered the entire country, with the exception of the Lake Tana islands and their churches. According to Ethiopian records, nine out of every ten Christians were forced to convert to Islam.

Ethiopia's salvation came after more than a decade of destruction and was related to its European connection. When the Portuguese discovered the sea route to India and settled there in 1510–1511, they also strove to control the Red Sea trade. Establishing contact with Ethiopia, their chief strategist in the East, Alfonso d'Albuquerque, envisioned the destruction of Egypt (still under Mamluk rule) by diverting the Nile. He was led to believe that by penetrating "a very small range" of Ethiopian hills, the Nile could be diverted to the Red Sea and Egypt would starve to death. In 1513 he even asked his monarch for workmen skilled in digging tunnels, but he was soon recalled home and his Nile illusion was abandoned.[39] The Portuguese connection with Ethiopia, however, was strengthened, especially after the Ottomans occupied Egypt and there began a long Ottoman-Portuguese rivalry for control of the Red Sea. A Portuguese mission remained in Ethiopia from 1520 and also worked to undermine the Ethiopian-Egyptian church connection. In 1538 one of the Portuguese was sent as an envoy to plead for help from Portugal, where he claimed to be patriarch of Alexandria and an *abun* of Ethiopia. Consequently, in 1540 some 400 well-trained Portuguese soldiers arrived to help the shattered Ethiopians reorganize. In February 1543 Ahmad Gragn was killed in battle and his armies quickly disintegrated. After further battles and bloodshed in 1577, the sultanate of Adal was finally destroyed by the Ethiopians, and the Muslims of the Horn of Africa were never to unite again.

Ethiopia's conquest by Ahmad Gragn was arguably the single most important chapter in Ethiopia's long history. The destruction of cultural assets and national pride was immense. The implications in terms of Ethiopia's concepts of Islam were far reaching. If the *sahaba* story was the formative episode for the Muslims' views of Ethiopia, Ahmad Gragn was the central figure in the Ethiopians' views of Muslims. The image of Islam as the main enemy of their Christianity was now engraved on their collective memory in theological terms as well. The religious enmity with Islam was reflected in the period's literature, most notably in a book written around 1532–1533 by the head of the Dabra-Libanos Monastery, the *echage,* Enbaqom (Habakuk). The book, *Anqasa Amin* (The Gate of Faith), written in Geez, was addressed to Ahmad Gragn himself, as though to persuade the Muslim invader to leave Ethiopia alone. Enbaqom's argument, a strong anti-Islamic polemic, was based on a profound knowledge of both Islam and Christianity (the author had been a Yemenite Muslim trader who converted to Christianity). It left a clear, comprehensive message of Christian moral and intellectual superiority over Islam for future generations of Ethiopians.[40]

No less important was the political-religious legacy of the conquest. From the sixteenth century to the present, the idea that Islam, once politically revitalized, could unite to destroy their national existence has been an integral part of the Christian Ethiopian consciousness. What could be called "the Ahmad Gragn trauma" seems to have been active ever since. It is the fear that Middle Eastern Islam, whenever it gains political, pan-regional momentum influencing events in the Horn, might bring about a local anti-Ethiopian Islamic unity. The Ethiopians have never feared a direct Middle Eastern invasion. Their concern has always been Middle Eastern ideological or material support for the local, otherwise politically fragmented Muslims in the Horn. In modern times not only political Islam but also secular revolutionary Pan-Arabism radiating from the Middle East would be perceived by Ethiopians in terms of this historical trauma.

Indeed, Egypt would be seen by Ethiopians as the capital of Islam and, in time, the capital of Arabism. Whenever Egypt behaved as such, the Ethiopian response would be one of suspicion, leading to either threats or avoidance and disconnection. Some relevant events will be discussed below. Yet the Mamluk period, marked by Egyptian Islamic leadership, also bequeathed the legacy of a pragmatic Egyptian state. As reflected in the various documents examined in this study, Ethiopians were often respectful of Egypt, differentiating between Egyptian uniqueness and the rest of Islam. Indeed, with Egypt as a source of spiritual and material progress, a key to both Eastern and (indirectly) Western Christianity, a state ready to negotiate with a non-Islamic, non-Arab neighbor on an equal footing, and a society with an identity based primarily on the centrality of the Nile, Ethiopians were eager for this mutually constructive connection.

THE MAMLUKS AND ETHIOPIA:
EGYPTIAN AND ISLAMIC CONCEPTS

How pragmatic was Mamluk Egypt regarding Ethiopia, and what were its perceptions of "the land of *al-najashi*"?

Judging by the actual policies of the sultans mentioned above, concrete Egyptian strategic interests were the guidelines. Although Egypt was the guardian of Islam and the patron of the Muslims of *al-habasha,* it never risked a war with Ethiopia, nor did it resort to the language of jihad. The Egyptians were apparently not unhappy to see the Solomonians constantly embroiled in internal wars, and they even encouraged local Muslims to participate in them. But they seemed to have played their game carefully, occasionally restraining Ifat and Adal from drifting toward all-out collision. When the Muslims, under Ahmad Gragn, finally engaged in their united holy war against Ethiopia, it was after the Mamluks had lost their power and disappeared from the Ethiopian scene. Indeed, it is not unreasonable to speculate that had Egypt remained the major Islamic power in the Red Sea region, a comprehensive Islamic-Christian conflict would never have been ignited.

Moreover, the Mamluks proved relatively pragmatic in their policy vis-à-vis the Copts. Given the fact that they were facing the later European Crusades and that the spirit of the time was still that of Christian-Islamic animosity, the Mamluks' anti-Coptic actions seldom went too far. In fact, it seems quite clear that the Mamluk sultans were appreciative of the Coptic-Ethiopian connection and the leverage it gave them over Ethiopia. They also knew how to use this leverage to advance their regional interests. As we have observed, they constantly played their patriarchal card against the Ethiopian Nile card, and they did so very skillfully.

Between al-Maqrizi and al-Suyuti

The Mamluk period, especially the fifteenth century, saw a great revival of historiography in Egypt. The vast literature produced at that time dealt with Egypt and the East, and much of it has been thoroughly studied by modern scholars. It also contained, however, a significant Ethiopian dimension, which has been but partially studied.[41] From the texts surveyed for this study, it is evident that many of the leading scholars of Mamluk Egypt never really "left Abyssinia alone." Rather, they expressed real curiosity and made it their business to inform their public about *al-habasha*.

Of the relevant historians, only a few shall be mentioned here. The first to devote substantial portions of his writings to Ethiopia was the fourteenth-century historian Shihab al-Din ibn Fadlallah al-'Umari (d. 1348). His encyclopedic book of Mamluk history, *Masalik al-absar fi mamalik al-amsar* was written between 1342 and 1348, a period that had just witnessed the conflicts between 'Amda-Zion and Sultan al-Nasir Ibn Qala'un (and the beginning of Sayfa-Ar'ad's conflict with Barquq). Yet despite the heated atmosphere (e.g., 'Amda-Zion's victories over Ifat, his threats regarding the Nile, and the destruction of Coptic churches in Egypt), al-'Umari tried to get the facts right. He based his chronology not only on evidence gathered from Zeila, but on Coptic sources as well. In doing so, he relied primarily on his communications with the patriarch, from whom he learned about Ethiopia and the Ethiopian versions of the Ethiopian-Egyptian saga.[42] However, in his writings al-'Umari repeated al-Makin's version of the eleventh-century story of the Ethiopians' blocking and subsequent freeing of the Nile. He thus contributed significantly to the recycling of that myth.[43] Yet al-'Umari also claimed that 'Amda-Zion had secretly converted to Islam and managed to retain his kingship only by concealing his conversion.[44] He thus also recycled the old "*Islam al-najashi*" story, the main argument used by Islamic radicals to negate Ethiopia's legitimacy. In applying it to one of the great advocates of Christianity, al-'Umari once again exposed Islam's conceptual duality regarding Ethiopia.

The next to concentrate on *al-habasha* was Shihab al-Din al-Qalqashandi (d. 1418), whose comprehensive book *Subh al-a'sha fi sina'at al-insha'* contains many relevant passages written in the same documentary spirit (al-Qalqashandi also quoted al-'Umari's tale about 'Amda-Zion's conversion to Islam,[45] as well as al-Makin's story about the Ethiopians' diversion of the Nile).[46] He was closely followed by the prolific and famous Ahmad bin 'Ali al-Maqrizi (d. 1441), who, in his four comprehensive histories of the period, covered Ethiopian-Egyptian relations up to the reigns of Yishaq and Barsbay, including the destruction of Ifat by the Ethiopians. Al-Maqrizi also wrote two smaller treatises focusing on this subject matter. One, titled *Irathat al-umma bi-kashf al-ghumma* (Crying over the Nation on the Revealing of Agony), dealt with the water system of the Nile and described periods of famine in Egypt caused by rainfall shortages in Ethiopia;[47] the other, *Kitab al-Ilmam bi-akhbar man bi-ard al-habasha min muluk al-Islam* (The Book of the True Knowledge of the History of the Muslim Kings in Abyssinia), was written in 1435–1436 and became the most quoted Egyptian source on the Mamluks and *al-habasha*.

The *habasha* who really interested al-Maqrizi and his contemporary Muslim Egyptian scholars were naturally the Muslims of the Horn. *Kitab al-Ilmam* is mostly devoted to the people of the Ifat and Adal sultanates, who constituted "one community of the Islamic nation in the land of *al-habasha* who fight in the name of God against those who stand against him and deviate from his way."[48] Describing Christian Ethiopia in his first chapter, al-Maqrizi was far from being an admirer. He told his readers about people who lived in straw shacks, walked around half naked, ate raw meat, were organized primitively, and owed much of their progress to Egyptian advice given by Fakhr al-Dawla, al-Tunbugha al-Mufriq, and others. Identifying with the Muslims of the Horn, al-Maqrizi depicted the Christians as fanatical zealots who would even kill fellow Christians who were not of the Coptic-Ethiopian persuasion. At one point he called Emperor Yishaq's men "devils." Nevertheless, the book is clearly appreciative of Ethiopia's wealth, including, emphatically, its water and its role as the source of the Nile. The book is also very appreciative of the might and the power of Ethiopia's emperors. In discussing them, al-Maqrizi mentioned the traditional Islamic title of *al-najashi*, but he did not raise the issue of "*Islam al-najashi*." In fact, he resorted more frequently to *al-hati*, the Arabic word for *atse*, a title of the emperors of Ethiopia. He claimed Egyptians were unfamiliar with Ethiopia and should learn about it. More significant is the fact that in *Kitab al-Ilmam* (as well as in his more comprehensive book *Al-Suluk fi ma'rifat duwal al-muluk)*, al-Maqrizi tried to analyze the Ethiopian-Egyptian conflict in concrete, rational terms. In his narrative the Ethiopians were not always the guilty party. They often launched their wars against the Muslims of *al-habasha* as reprisals for Egyptian maltreatment of the Copts. Similar explanations were also offered by other Egyptian historians, like al-Nuwayri (d. 1331) and al-Sakhawi (d. 1496).[49]

Perhaps the most significant book reflecting Mamluk Egypt's concepts of Ethiopia is Jalal al-Din al-Suyuti's *Raf' sha'n al-hubshan*. Although written at the end of the fifteenth century (al-Suyuti died in 1505), after more than 200 years of active conflict, it remained true to its title: The Raising of the Status of the Ethiopians.[50] Like his predecessors, the great al-Suyuti also concentrated on the *habasha* Muslims and hardly mentioned the Christian state of his era. The book was not intended to be a political history, but rather a call to preserve Islam as a supraracial religion and culture. Al-Suyuti's main concern was to emphasize the equality of the blacks within the Islamic nation,[51] and he did so by gathering nearly all he could find on the Ethiopians in Islamic tradition and writings.

He divided his 110 chapters into seven sections. The first three contain prophetic sayings, references to Ethiopians in the Quran, and the influence of Geez on the language of Islam's holy book. A longer and very detailed fourth section is devoted to the story of the *sahaba* and the *najashi*. Al-Suyuti's emphasis is clearly on the historical importance of the Ethiopian king's rescue of the Prophet's followers and how this first hegira paved the way for the great hegira to Medina and victory of Islam. A fifth, equally long section narrates the stories of thirty-five Ethiopians who distinguished themselves as good, pious Muslims. Its longest chapter (or subsection) is devoted to the *najashi* (after which comes a chapter on Bilal ibn Rabbah). The *najashi* subsection begins with a long discussion of his road to power in his father's court, continues with quotations from his correspondence with the Prophet, and ends with his recognition of Muhammad as the messenger of God and the latter's prayers for him as for a departed, distinguished Muslim. A smaller, sixth section surveys the general evidence in Islamic tradition regarding good Ethiopian qualities. The book's concluding section is devoted to various issues, one of which is the Nile. Al-Suyuti confines himself to quoting a tradition in which "the reason for the rising tide of the Nile in Egypt is heavy rain in the land of *al-habasha*." The last section also addresses mythical concepts of future catastrophes and contains short quotations about the destruction of various places all over the world. According to one such tradition, Egypt will be destroyed due to the drying up of the Nile. According to another, Mecca will be destroyed by the Ethiopians.

respected

Apart from these indirect, hidden implications, there is nothing negative about Ethiopia and Ethiopians in al-Suyuti's entire book. (He also issued a short version of it titled *Azhar al-'Urush fi Akhbar al-Hubush*.) In fact, all the materials usually used by Islamic radicals to "prove" Ethiopia's illegitimacy, primarily the *"Islam al-najashi"* argument, are presented by the author in detail, but he clearly refrains from giving them an anti-Christian-Ethiopian interpretation. The message of the book was the strengthening of the pan-humanistic, universal essence of Islam by showing Islam's complete acceptance of dark-skinned *habasha* Muslims. However, it clearly implied that such an enlightened Islam was also more tolerant of non-Islamic peoples and that Ethiopians in general were human beings with good qualities.

Al-Suyuti's book was not unique in kind. Back in the late twelfth century *The Lightening of the Darkness on the Merits of the Blacks and the Ethiopians,* by Jamal al-Din Abu Faraj ibn al-Jawzi (d. 1208), had preached the same ideas of ethnic equality among Muslims. As analyzed by Bernard Lewis, such literature was to be produced and reproduced in order to protect Islam from existing popular racist tendencies.[52] All throughout the centuries *habasha* slaves were considered the best merchandise in the markets of the Middle East. The popular image of them as racially inferior slaves, then, persisted in Egypt and the Islamic East (the Arabic word *habsh* means a mixture, and in popular usage it connoted a mixed ethnic origin, partly black, partly brown). In early-twentieth-century Cairo, as we shall see in Chapter 5, would again combat this popular image. He would resort to the same traditional arguments and the same old Islamic-Ethiopian issues in his attempt to promote tolerant, universally supraethnic, humanistic Islam.

The fact that during the Mamluks' time such a moderate version of Islam was preached by such a leading historian attests to the pragmatic nature of that Egyptian regime. In 1517, however, the Mamluk period came to an end. The Ottoman occupiers of Egypt turned the country into one of their many provinces, ruled by a new imperial elite answerable to policy dictated from far-off Istanbul. For a short while the Ottomans maintained an interest in the Red Sea. They clashed, as mentioned earlier, with the Portuguese on the route to India; they captured Yemen and gave some aid to Ahmad Gragn. After the fall of Gragn (1543) and their final defeat in the contest for the sea route to the Far East (1555), the Ottomans decided to entrench their forces along the Red Sea coast. In 1557 they landed in Massawa and established the "Province of Ethiopia," which stretched roughly over today's Eritrean coast. Because this sparked a war of attrition with the Ethiopians, and because the Ottomans themselves were engaged elsewhere and had lost much of their Mediterranean navy in 1571, the entire enterprise was conducted from Egypt. In December 1578, however, the last Ottoman Egyptian ruler of the Ottoman province Habesh was defeated in the highlands by Sersa Dengel, the Ethiopian emperor. The Ottomans then left a small garrison in Massawa and appointed a local dignitary as their representative. They would never again try to control areas in the Horn of Africa.[53] Egypt, itself reduced to a mere province, would "leave the Abyssinians alone" for the next three centuries.

NOTES

1. Guillaume, *Life of Muhammad,* p. 484; Munro-Hay, *Ethiopia and Alexandria,* pp. 103–104.
2. On 'Amr ibn al-'As and the *najashi,* see Jalal al-Din al-Suyuti, *Raf' sha'n al-hubshan,* p. 7 and pt. 4, and Erlich, *Ethiopia and the Middle East,* pp. 7–8. On his sending a letter to the Nile, see *Aja'ib al-Makhluqat* (The Marvels of the Creation), a Turkish text in a manuscript dated 1685 in the Bibliotheque Nationale, Paris (Ms. Or. Suppl. Turc 1063. fol. 26b). See also the jacket of Erlich and Gershoni, *The Nile.* See more in Butler, *The Arab Conquest,* chap. 14 and app. E: "Some say that 'Amr was in Abyssinia at the time of his conversion, which was brought about by Ja'far ibn Abi Talib" (p. 201).
3. Van Donzel, "Badr al-Jamali."
4. Tamrat, *Church and State,* p. 46.
5. For summary and references see Erlich, *Ethiopia and the Middle East,* pp. 25–28.
6. The following is based mainly on Tamrat, *Church and State,* pp. 53–64.
7. See Negash, "The Blue Nile as Bait."
8. Hable Selassie, *Ancient and Medieval Ethiopian History,* pp. 251–254.
9. See Meinardus, *Christian Egypt,* pp. 378–379.
10. 'Ashur, "Ba'd adwa' jadida."
11. See van Donzel, "Ethiopia's Lalibela." On the Egyptian influence and contribution to Lalibela's enterprise, see also Gervers, "The Mediterranean Context."
12. Meinardus, *Christian Egypt,* p. 380.
13. Perruchon, *La Vie de Lalibala,* pp. xx–xxviii.
14. See Pankhurst, "Ethiopia's Alleged Control," pp. 25–37.
15. Van Donzel, "Badr al-Jamali."
16. Conti Rossini, *Storia d'Etiopia,* p. 310; Pankhurst, "Ethiopia's Alleged Control."
17. For a summary of Ethiopian-Egyptian relations during the period under discussion, see Abir, *Ethiopia and the Red Sea,* pp. 19–96.
18. The following section on the Mamluks and the Horn of Africa is based on 'Abd al-Halim, *Al-'Alaqat al-siyasiyya bayna muslimi al-zayla';* Qasim, "'Alaqat misr bil-habasha fi 'asr salatin al-mamalik"; 'Ashur, "Ba'd adwa'

jadida"; Wiet, "Les Relations Egypto-Abyssines"; and Cuoq, *L'Islam en Ethiopie,* chaps. 5–6.

19. See Tamrat, *Church and State,* pp. 72–89.

20. 'Ashur, "Ba'd adwa' jadida."

21. Tamrat's chapter 7 in *Church and State,* "Early Contact with Christian Europe (1380–1460)," analyzes Ethiopian-Egyptian relations in this context.

22. See full text of the letter in Munro-Hay, *Ethiopia and Alexandria,* pp. 196–197; for Baybars's response see p. 199. See also Tamrat, *Church and State,* pp. 126–127.

23. See Tamrat, ibid., pp. 69–72; Trimingham, *Islam in Ethiopia,* pp. 61–69; Pankhurst, "Ethiopia's Alleged Control," p. 29; 'Ashur, "Ba'd adwa' jadida," pp. 16–20; Qasim, "'Alaqat misr bil-habasha fi 'asr salatin al-mamalik," pp. 66–67; Hecht, "Ethiopia Threatens to Block the Nile"; and Munro-Hay, *Ethiopia and Alexandria,* pp. 199–201.

24. See Henze, "Consolidation of Christianity," and Tamrat, *Church and State,* pp. 189–196.

25. Trimingham, *Islam in Ethiopia,* pp. 70–73; Pankhurst, "Ethiopia's Alleged Control," p. 29; Meinardus, *Christian Egypt,* pp. 382–383; 'Ashur, "Ba'd adwa' jadida," p. 26 (quoting 'Amda-Zion's letter from al-Nuwayri's *Nihayat al-arab*); and Qasim, "'Alaqat misr bil-habasha fi 'asr salatin al-mamalik," p. 27.

26. Pankhurst, "Ethiopia's Alleged Control," quoting Guidi, "Due nuovi manoscritti," p. 360.

27. Cerulli, *Il libro etiopico;* Six, "Water, the Nile, and the *Ta'amra Maryam.*"

28. Qasim, "'Alaqat misr bil-habasha fi 'asr salatin al-mamalik," pp. 68–70; Trimingham, *Islam in Ethiopia,* pp. 73–75.

29. 'Ashur, "Ba'd adwa' jadida," quoting al-Maqrizi, *Kitab al-Ilmam.*

30. Van Donzel, "Legend of the Blue Nile."

31. For background and details see Tamrat, *Church and State,* chap. 6.

32. 'Ashur, "Ba'd adwa' jadida"; Qasim, "'Alaqat misr bil-habasha fi 'asr salatin al-mamalik"; Pankhurst, "Ethiopia's Alleged Control"; and Trimingham, *Islam in Ethiopia,* p. 76.

33. 'Ashur, "Ba'd adwa' jadida," pp. 38–39. See also Plante, "The Ethiopian Embassy."

34. 'Ashur, "Ba'd adwa' jadida."

35. Six, "Water, the Nile, and *Ta'amra Maryam.*"

36. Pedersen, "The Ethiopian Community in Jerusalem."

37. Quoted in Erlich, *Ethiopia and the Middle East,* p. 27.

38. The following section is based on Erlich, *Ethiopia and the Middle East,* chap. 3: "The Trauma of Gragn and the Diplomacy of Habesh."

39. Van Donzel, "Legend of the Blue Nile"; Pankhurst, "Ethiopia's Alleged Control."

40. See Van Donzel, *Enbaqom: Anqasa Amin.* For Enbaqom's attitudes toward Muslims and Islam, see the analysis in chap. 7 of that text. Enbaqom's text made no mention of Egypt.

41. All the works referenced thus far, particularly 'Ashur's and Qasim's articles, are based on research in Mamluk-era sources. The most extensive study of these sources is 'Abd al-Halim's 1985 book, *Al-'Alaqat al-siyasiyya bayna muslimi al-zayla' wa-nusara al-habasha fi al-'usur al-wusta.* His rather radical Islamic interpretations of these sources will be discussed below in Chapter 9.

42. 'Abd al-Halim, ibid., p. 5.

43. Van Donzel, "Badr al-Jamali."

44. Munro-Hay, *Ethiopia and Alexandria,* p. 105, quoting Gaudefroy-Demombynes's edition of Ibn Fadl Allah al-'Omari's *Masalik el Absar fi Mamalik el Amsar,* p. 32.

45. Munro-Hay, ibid., p. 105.

46. Van Donzel, "Badr al-Jamali."

47. 'Ashur, "Ba'd adwa' jadida," pp. 1–2.

48. Al-Maqrizi, *Kitab al-Ilmam,* p. 2.

49. See 'Abd al-Halim, *Al-'Alaqat al-siyasiyya bayna muslimi,* p. 39.

50. See Fadl's edition of al-Suyuti's text. The interpretations of Dr. Fadl, an Azhari scholar, will be discussed below.

51. See Lewis's discussion of al-Suyuti in his *Race and Slavery;* see also my discussion on the subject in *Ethiopia and the Middle East,* pp. 11–14.

52. See Lewis, *Race and Slavery,* pp. 33–35.

53. For a fuller discussion see Erlich, *Ethiopia and the Middle East,* pp. 33–40.

4

Modern Rediscovery
and Fatal Collision

For three centuries Ethiopian-Egyptian relations lost much of their significance to both sides. After the shock of the Islamic conquest in the sixteenth century, Ethiopia experienced difficulties in reunification. It continued to face enormous new challenges, notably the sixteenth-century invasion of the Oromos, the settlement of many of them in the very heartland of Ethiopia, and the eighteenth-century conversion of many of the latter to Islam. The emperors, roving about or retiring to their newly built seventeenth-century capital of Gondar, proved unable to impose any central authority. The church, torn by rival monastic movements and by renewed theological disputes, fell under the influence of European Catholicism, and its Coptic ties were nearly severed. However, the connection survived, and as Ethiopia drifted deeper into political disarray during its "era of the princes" (1769–1855), the significance of the Egyptian *abun* was reemphasized as perhaps the most meaningful connection to the outside world. During the eighteenth century, moreover, the Middle Eastern Ottoman world of Islam, now centered in distant Istanbul, continued to "leave the Abyssinians alone." Post-Renaissance Europe also evidenced little curiosity about Ethiopia, for the Prester John legend, part of the long-defunct crusader ethos, had been practically forgotten. The Ethiopian elite was too busy with fratricidal wars to think of the Nile as a card in international relations. The myth about diverting and blocking the river was maintained primarily by local tradition, visiting travelers, and European scholars.[1]

With the demise of the Mamluks and the Ottoman conquest, Egypt fell under a new leadership that was much less concerned with the Nile. The river, to be sure, remained the hub of local economy and popular culture, but in terms of political strategy, Egypt was reduced to a province of the greater Ottoman Empire. As of the early sixteenth century,

59

Cairo was no longer a capital with political authority, nor did Egypt have a foreign policy of its own until the last quarter of the eighteenth century. Egypt's rotating provincial administrative rulers sent by Istanbul, or its local Turkish-oriented elite of Mamluk origin, were now members of a pan-regional Ottoman society more than they were Egyptians. They had hardly the time, interest, or abilities to invest in Egypt's infrastructure, let alone the effort needed to rid Egypt of its ancient dependence on the Nile's annual flood. Though Cairo under the Mamluks, a center and a capital in itself, had attributed importance to the regions up the river and along the Red Sea, Ottoman Cairo paid little attention to these areas.

In the early nineteenth century, however, Egypt regained its unique political identity as a Nile country. Under a new dynasty of independent rulers, a new Nile-centered economy and society were reborn, and Egyptian strategic interests in the areas up the Nile were accordingly resurrected. Renewed Egyptian interest in Ethiopia would reach its peak in the 1870s and produce one of the more influential chapters in Egypt's modern history, which would also lead to Egypt's fall in 1882 to British occupation.

Ethiopia was also undergoing fundamental changes during the formative second half of the nineteenth century as it struggled to reestablish imperial authority and revive its Christian identity. In the process the medieval past would repeat itself. The more Ethiopians worked to modernize their state, the more Egypt became centrally relevant to Ethiopia.

MUHAMMAD 'ALI AND TEWODROS II: REESTABLISHING EYE CONTACT

The founders of modern Egypt and modern Ethiopia—Muhammad 'Ali Pasha (1805–1849) and Emperor Tewodros II (1855–1868), respectively—lived in different periods. Yet it seems valid to compare them. The former would put Ethiopia back on Egypt's agenda and would begin to face a relevant strategic dilemma that Egyptian policymakers still face today. The latter would also revive, modify, and pass on a medieval Ethiopian dilemma, the conflict between the Ahmad Gragn trauma of suspicion and enmity with political Islam and Ethiopia's traditional interest in benefiting from workable relations with Egypt and the East.

Muhammad 'Ali resurrected Egypt as an independent entity and a Nile country. Originally a provincial Ottoman administrator, he amassed power as a political sovereign and, unlike the Mamluks, established a hereditary dynasty that lasted until the mid-twentieth century. He became famous as a great modernizer, first and foremost by terminating

Egypt's ancient dependence on the Nile's floods. The network of dams, barrages, and irrigation canals built during his rule made possible the introduction of cotton as a major export crop and the ensuing centralization of agriculture, economy, society, and authority. By modernizing control of the river in Egypt itself, Muhammad 'Ali transformed the Nile country into a mighty state, capable of raising a powerful army and conducting regional strategy. One dimension of this modern Egyptian regional strategy was what can be called a new "Upper Nile option."

In 1820–1821 Muhammad 'Ali dispatched his army to conquer the Sudan. His men occupied much of that country and in 1830 established the new city of Khartoum, where the Blue and the White Niles converged. Sudanese resources, manpower, and minerals were sought to strengthen Egypt's modernization enterprise, and Egyptian missions were commissioned to discover and map new areas in the vast land of the Sudan.[2] Though the story of Egyptian administration in the Sudan is outside our present scope, its main significance, from our perspective, lay in the fact that for the first time in recorded history, Egypt occupied most of the valley of the White Nile. Taming the floods at home and controlling the Sudan was a new combination that ushered in a new era. In the seventh century Egypt's Muslim rulers had been defeated by the Christian Nubians, and none of their successors, until Muhammad 'Ali, had managed to cross the political-cultural "Nubian dam" at Aswan. (The Mamluks managed to impose rulers on the Nubian kingdom several times and even convert them to Islam.)[3] By removing this obstacle and by annexing the Sudan to Egypt, Muhammad 'Ali seemed to have fulfilled, retroactively, the ancient Egyptian claim to historical rights to the entire river. The ancient dependence on, and identification with, the Nile now acquired new political reality. For the moment, during Muhammad 'Ali's reign, it was little more than a strategic development. By the beginning of the twentieth century, however, it would become the conceptual framework for Egyptian nationalism.

The Upper Nile and Middle Eastern Options

But if Muhammad 'Ali opened up the Nile Valley to Egypt and its coming modern identity, his main interest still lay elsewhere. This great ruler, a Turkish-speaking officer born in Albania, was still more of an Ottoman than an Egyptian, and his primary goal throughout remained that of attaining hegemony in the Ottoman East. In 1831 he felt ready to begin working toward this goal. His modern army occupied Syria and challenged the sultan. In 1833, having defeated the main imperial army, the pasha of Egypt would have done away with the Ottoman dynasty and moved the imperial Islamic center to Cairo had Britain and France not stopped him. Though still focused on this theater, on Egypt's Middle Eastern option, on settling in and administering Palestine and Syria, Muhammad 'Ali had time, for a while, to resume his interest in the Upper Nile option.

New Egyptian missions were dispatched during the 1830s to explore areas in the Sudan and administer its tribes. One such mission, sent in 1838 and personally inspected by the pasha himself,[4] traveled up the Blue Nile and reached Ethiopian territory. By that time Egyptian administrators and Ethiopian chiefs had already been engaged in hostilities along the newly created border area. At one point in 1838, and perhaps in connection with the Blue Nile mission, Egyptian forces penetrated deep into Ethiopian territory from Gallabat. The incident moved the French to warn the pasha not to invade Ethiopia, and the latter replied that he had never intended to do so.[5] Indeed, he was already concentrating on his coming showdown with the Ottomans. In June 1839 his army routed the Ottomans in northern Syria and forced the road to Istanbul wide open. Again the British intervened to save the Ottomans, and in September 1840 they landed in Beirut and forced the Egyptian army to pull back and return to Egypt.

Aging and frustrated, the pasha began neglecting his reforms at home. With the demise of his Middle Eastern option, he showed renewed interest in the Upper Nile option during his last years. His men in the Sudan would not penetrate central Ethiopia again, but they seemed to have marked the area of the future Eritrea as a vital corridor to the Sudan. It became clear to the Egyptians in the Sudan that their land route from Egypt along the river was too difficult. In order to control the Sudan, it became vital to gain a foothold in the Red Sea port of Massawa and then obtain control over the convenient land route from there to Khartoum. In 1840 the Egyptians established the town of Kassala, midway along this route, and in 1846 leased Massawa from the Ottomans.[6] They also began overseeing the conversion of local tribespeople to Islam, a process begun by the Egyptian al-Mirghani family, which spread popular Sufi Islam among the Banu 'Amir and other clans in the 1820s. Kassala became the Egyptian-sponsored headquarters of the Mirghaniyya Sufi order, which continued to spread Islam and aided the strategic Egyptian cause in the entire Sudan, with an emphasis on the Kassala-Massawa area, part of the future Eritrea.

Muhammad 'Ali's priorities were not in the Nile basin but in the Middle Eastern arena. He definitely did not focus on Ethiopia. The fact that Ethiopia was the main source of the Nile had not yet been discovered, and after the completion of the new irrigation system, Egypt's ancient dependence on Ethiopia for the floods was substantially eased. The Christian country, still lacking an imperial authority and torn by internal rivalries, was hardly in a position to interfere with the Blue Nile, and in any case, the medieval myth about diverting the flow had long been forgotten. Ethiopia was part of Muhammad 'Ali's agenda in the context of controlling the Sudan. The theory that the pasha of Egypt contemplated the conquest of Ethiopia's heartland (and was deterred only by the Europeans)[7] seems unconvincing.[8] In fact, he even ignored a most tempting invitation from within rival-torn Ethiopia to meddle in its internal affairs. Ras 'Ali II, perhaps the strongman of central Ethiopia from 1831 to 1853, was an Oromo leader who had only outwardly embraced Christianity to facilitate his all-Ethiopian ambitions. He corresponded with the Egyptians in the Sudan and also wrote to Cairo advising Muhammad 'Ali to avoid sending an *abun* to replace Abuna Qerilos, who died in 1828. His letters to the Egyptian ruler make it clear that Ras 'Ali considered himself a Muslim sultan of *al-habasha* and pinned his hopes on Egyptian intervention.[9] Muhammad 'Ali, however, avoided any such action and in 1841 finally authorized a new bishop. Abuna Salama, aged twenty-two, would become a pivotal figure in the unfolding saga of Ethiopia's Christian revival.[10]

By indicating the importance of the Massawa-Kassala strip to Egypt's hold on the Sudan and by spreading Islam throughout the Sudan and Eritrea in the service of Egyptian interests, Muhammad 'Ali set the stage for future developments. By dispatching the *abun,* he also revived the Egyptian government's interest in the old Egyptian-Ethiopian Christian connection. His successors, Egypt's political leaders up to Gamal Abdel Nasser, would be, like the Mamluks in their time, very appreciative of this precious political card. However, a new chapter, far less happy, now began unfolding in the very core of the Coptic-Ethiopian connection.

In 1838, while Jerusalem was still under Egyptian control (1831–1840), nearly the entire Ethiopian community in that city perished in a plague. By that time the "golden era" of vibrant Ethiopian pilgrimage had long since subsided, and the few remaining Ethiopian monks lived in a shabby corner on the roof of St. Helena's Chapel, a part of the Church of the Holy Sepulchre complex. They called their corner Dabra Sultan, better known by its Arabic name, Deir al-Sultan, meaning "the monastery of the ruler." Neglected by their fragmented motherland during the "era of the princes," the Ethiopian monks lived on the charity of Armenian fellow Monophysites[11] and shared the keys to the roof courtyard with the Copts, the monks of the adjacent Monastery of St. Anthony. After the Ethiopians perished in the 1838 plague, the Copts obtained the

Egyptian governor's permission to burn the Ethiopians' belongings and library. When the Egyptians were forced to leave in 1840, the restored Ottoman administration allowed the Ethiopians to return. The Egyptian Copts, however, claiming they had always owned the premises, were ready to accept them as guests only, without sharing the keys.[12] Subsequent Ethiopian efforts to reclaim ownership over their humble portion of Jerusalem, a source of their Christian as well as national identity, would bear no fruit before 1970. The dispute over the keys would mar relations between the Ethiopian Church and its mother Coptic Church in Egypt for decades. It is still going on.

Muhammad 'Ali claimed the Sudan as part of Egypt, a fulfillment of its historical rights over the Nile. In so doing, he reestablished contact with Ethiopia and revived both Christian and Islamic dimensions of the old relationship. Tewodros II, Ethiopia's first reformer, would also renew Ethiopian interest and policy vis-à-vis Egypt. His dilemmas, like those of Muhammad 'Ali, remain relevant to this very day.

Tewodros and Egypt

Though related to Ethiopian provincial nobility, Tewodros had to make his way up the ladder of power the hard way. He ascended through *shift-net,* or sociopolitical banditry, an integral, virtually legitimate institution in Ethiopia's political culture. A *shifta* would often defy existing authority, not in order to depart from or challenge the sociopolitical code, but rather to acquire enough nuisance value and gain enough attention to be recruited into the upper echelon. Combining *shiftnet* with a political marriage and other arrangements, Tewodros managed to ascend to the imperial throne itself. He then undertook to build a centralized state,[13] perhaps consciously modeled after Muhammad 'Ali's Egypt. But he was far less successful than the Egyptian, and after reaching his peak in 1860–1862, he began losing ground to regional actors. His efforts to strengthen centralization of the country by obtaining technical aid and know-how from Europe met with indifference. Frustrated, he imprisoned European missionaries and aroused the wrath of Britain. Isolated and mentally depressed, besieged in his capital of Magdala by an invading British army, Tewodros committed suicide in April 1868.

Tewodros's story, a formative chapter in the country's modern history, has attracted Ethiopians and historians of Ethiopia. Because of the manner in which he died, many have preferred to see him as a defender against Western involvement; some have even portrayed him as a xenophobe. More valid, however, is the view that he wanted to institutionalize his relations with the outside world, considering them essential to his centralization enterprise. In this context one should also examine his Egyptian and Islamic policies.

Here again can be discerned a conceptual dualism that has its roots in the medieval past. On the one hand, Tewodros II saw himself as a Christian warrior facing an Islamic siege. Born Kasa Hailu, he chose Tewodros as his imperial name upon his coronation in 1855. Tewodros was the name of a legendary medieval king who had been expected to redeem Jerusalem by defeating Islam.[14] In his correspondence with the Europeans he portrayed himself as a crusader holding off Islam and the "Turks"—namely, the Egyptians—and in domestic affairs he treated Ethiopian Muslims as though they were about to produce a new Ahmad Gragn.[15] Tewodros, no doubt, envisioned a European-Ethiopian anti-Egyptian alliance and was deeply frustrated by British, French, and German policies of friendship toward Cairo.[16] On the other hand, recent studies show that he was not just a self-imagined Prester John. In his correspondence with the Egyptians he rather emphasized a desire to create a constructive dialogue. In 1847, while still an ambitious *shifta* prince on the Ethiopian-Sudanese border, he sent several letters to the Egyptian authorities in the Sudan with offers of friendship. In his letters he even tried to imply that he was a proponent of Islamic culture.[17] Twenty years later, on 13 March 1867, a year before he ended his life as a frustrated reformer king, he wrote again to the Egyptian governor-general of the Sudan, dismissing a complaint about a border incident and asking that his letter be conveyed to Khedive Isma'il, the ruler of Egypt (1863–1879): "I wish friendly relations with you, in amity."[18]

For twenty years Tewodros's drama had an important Egyptian dimension. A main figure during this period was Abuna Salama. A talented, forceful person, he had become integrated into Ethiopian society and culture, and during the 1840s he had worked hard to rescue the church from its fragmentation during the era of the princes. He also stemmed the growing influence of Catholic missionaries in Ethiopia, working closely with Tewodros in both enterprises. However, when Tewodros tried to centralize taxation and obtain control over the church's assets, he and Abuna Salama collided. The relationship between the emperor and the *abun* was undoubtedly one reason for Tewodros's failure.[19] It was perhaps natural for a non-Ethiopian to look after the interests of the church, placing church interests above those of Ethiopia's national modernization. The conservatism of the Egyptian *abuns* would remain a factor in modern Ethiopian history.

In his effort to attract European attention to his state-building enterprise, Tewodros naively tried to revive the defunct Prester John myth, doing his best to persuade the British and French to help him fight Islam.

Immediately after his coronation, a rumor that the Egyptians were about to invade Ethiopia from the Sudan spread, but Sa'id Pasha (1854–1863) had nothing of the sort in mind. Instead, he sent the Coptic patriarch, Cyril IV, on a friendship mission to Tewodros. It was the first time in modern history that the head of the mother church paid a visit to Ethiopia, but Tewodros was apparently unimpressed. When the patriarch suggested that Egyptian officers help train Tewodros's army, he aroused the emperor's suspicions; when he asked to review imperial forces, he was detained, together with Abuna Salama, and forced to remain in Tewodros's court for an entire year (December 1856 to November 1857).[20]

Perhaps the best way to make sense of Tewodros's Egyptian policy is to readdress the inherent dichotomy: Ethiopia's fear of political Islam and its simultaneous need to be part of the East. In the final analysis we must believe Tewodros's statements about desiring cordial relations with Egypt, provided, of course, that these relations were based on material aid and not religious subversion. In detaining the patriarch, Tewodros behaved exactly as he would with European missionaries at a later date. He took hostages to gain attention, to connect with the outside world, not to isolate his country. Acquiring nuisance value in order to join systems, not to isolate himself from them, was, after all, his formative *shifta* experience.

YOHANNES AND ISMA'IL: GURA AND GRAGN

In 1869, one year after the death of Tewodros, the Suez Canal was inaugurated, ushering in the beginning of a new chapter in the story of Egypt and Ethiopia. Both countries embarked on a collision course that would result in a war in 1876, an event of far-reaching consequences for each and for the nature of their modern relations.[21]

In both countries the last thirty years of the nineteenth century, as well as the Ethiopian-Egyptian issues of that time, have been extensively researched and described. Here I will make do with a brief analysis, leaving more room for later implications, the impact of the period on the Ethiopian perception of modern Egyptian nationalism, and the influence it had on Ethiopian policy regarding the Nile during the first half of the twentieth century.

Isma'il, the Nile, and Ethiopia

Khedive Isma'il, Muhammad 'Ali's grandson, continued Egypt's development in nearly all areas. Unlike his grandfather, however, he did not have a Middle Eastern option. The Western powers would no longer allow Egypt to divert its ambition and abilities to the Middle East, nor would Egypt attempt it again prior to Nasser's era. But instead of exporting Egyptian reforms to the East, the khedive could import resources from Europe. Investing borrowed money in Egypt's infrastructure, Isma'il not only brought the country's cotton economy to its peak, he also accelerated the directing of Egyptian society toward new, Western-oriented values and institutions. Moreover, forging ties with Europe in nearly every aspect, he focused his foreign strategy on the greater Nile Valley. An African empire of the Nile, according to Isma'il's vision, was both a source of prestige and power and a ticket of admission to the European club of nations he so admired. Egypt's Nile empire, thought Isma'il, would be approved by the powers, particularly Britain. In October 1867, prior to facilitating the British military mission against Tewodros, he wrote to the Ethiopian emperor. In a long letter filled with praise of British might, Isma'il advised Tewodros to release his hostages quickly, before the powerful Europeans could do to Ethiopia what they had done to the much more powerful India and China.[22]

A few of the relevant reforms instituted by Isma'il, "the impatient Europeanizer," should be mentioned. In the area of higher education he established a law school (1866–1868) based on the French legal code and staffed by French professors, an institute that would turn into a hothouse for future modern nationalists. He hired European and American military officers, adventurers, and geographers to overhaul the armed forces and administration. In culture he helped create a cosmopolitan atmosphere revolving around a renovated Cairo, rebuilt as a close imitation of Paris. Altogether he oversaw the rapid transformation of Egypt into a state and society modeled on Western institutions and representative bodies, among them one of direct relevance to our story: the organization of a new, modern secular wing of the Coptic community.

Modernizing Egypt had already begun to open up new opportunities for the Copts. They would benefit from modern education and excel in the new state administration and economy. Many Copts had been recruited by Muhammad 'Ali and gained new status by entering his service. In the later, more Western-oriented period of Sa'id Pasha and Isma'il, educated Copts quickly became part of the new urban elite. In early 1874 a group of young Coptic laymen demanded that the community's assets no longer be administered by the clergy alone and should be used for the benefit of the needy as well as for the promotion of general education. Under the leadership of Butrus Ghali Pasha, a group of Coptic laymen appealed to Isma'il, asking his permission to establish a *majlis milli,* or community council. The new body was authorized by

Isma'il (on 5 February 1874).[23] The *majlis milli,* perhaps the first manifestation of modern Coptic life, was the embodiment of the educated
youth's desire to be accepted by modern Egyptian society. In time this
modern wing of the Coptic community would develop its own Ethiopian
ideas, quite different from those of the patriarchate, the Holy Synod, and
the Coptic Church establishment.

Focusing on the Upper Nile option, Isma'il began reinvesting in the
Sudan in 1865. The khedive continued development of the Nile irrigation system in Egypt and took a personal, daily interest in its various
projects. For him Egypt was to stretch over the entire Nile Valley, and
absorbing the Sudan was the prime object of his imperial vision. However, with the opening of the Suez Canal, the Red Sea area became also
a target for Egyptian expansionism. This was not an entirely new sphere
of ambition, for the Mamluks (and their predecessors) had been closely
involved in the local medieval Islamic sultanates of Ifat and Adal. In
1865, the year of his renewed interest in the Sudan, Isma'il requested and
renewed the Ottoman authority over Massawa and Suakin (which had
lapsed upon the death of Muhammad 'Ali). Then, beginning in 1870,
after the canal was opened, the entire Somali Red Sea coast, from Zeila
to Cape Guardafui, was captured by Egyptian military missions. One of
these missions, commanded by Ra'uf Pasha, completed the enterprise in
1875 by conquering Harar. Reporting to Isma'il, the chief of staff of the
Egyptian army wrote on 16 October 1875: "I am sure that Egypt under
the rule of Isma'il will constitute one unified government from the
Mediterranean to the Equator, and that the kingdom of Harar will reach
the highest stage of welfare and progress in the East after Egypt."[24]

Occupying the historic capital of Ahmad Gragn, Isma'il appeared to
adhere to the old Mamluk legacy of a pan-regional Islamic leadership.
Scholars from Al-Azhar's Riwaq al-Jabartiyya were sent to institutionalize Islamic law and studies in the town. The Egyptians in Harar sent
missions to spread Islam by both the sword and the book among the
Oromos of the vast regions surrounding the city and far beyond. Their
action had a tremendous impact on the history of the Oromo clans of
southern Ethiopia, a subject that cannot be adequately addressed here.
The intensive Egyptian-initiated spread of Islam from Harar accelerated
the final collapse of the Oromos' sociopolitical system based on age
groups (*gada*) and facilitated its replacement by individual authoritarianism. This process (which had begun long before the Egyptian involvement) weakened the Oromos at the time imperial Ethiopia was
about to expand into their territories.[25] During the nine years of their
presence in Harar, the Egyptians, numbering more than 14,000 men,[26]
worked also to modernize the town, including constructing a modern

hospital. They strove to make Harar an example of Egypt's progressive civilization,[27] for it was primarily through their modern progress, and in the name of Egypt's historic rights over the Nile (rather than in the name of Islam), that Isma'il and his men legitimized their African enterprise.

Yet the success of this vision depended not on Harar, but on Massawa. Sudan, the White Nile basin, was the heart of Isma'il's African empire, and its development could hardly be advanced without a railroad from Massawa, via Keren and Kassala, to Khartoum. In 1871 Isma'il sent his Swiss employee Werner Munzinger to Massawa; Munzinger occupied Keren one year later. He began developing the area and making plans for a railway. He also continued to make contact with the local tribes, some already influenced by the Mirghaniyya's Islamic mission in Kassala. By 1875, the year Harar was captured, Egypt seemed to be in control of the strip from Massawa to Kassala, the future Eritrea, ready to connect the Red Sea with the Sudan and stabilize a whole new empire. But then Egypt collided with Ethiopia.

Tigrean Concepts and Egyptian Defeat

It was a fatal coincidence that as Isma'il built his African-Nile-Egyptian empire, Ethiopia also turned again toward the Red Sea. In 1872 Emperor Yohannes IV was crowned in Aksum, ending four years of turmoil. He had been a prince from northern Ethiopia who helped the British in their 1867–1868 campaign against Tewodros II. As the British were leaving, they decided to help the country recuperate under a more moderate authority, and they left Yohannes with enough arms to build up his power gradually and gain superiority in Ethiopia.

During his first four years in power, Emperor Yohannes IV worked hard but flexibly to restore order, offering the promise of relief from his predecessor's revolutionary centralization. Himself a pious Christian, he had married a Muslim woman (who died in 1871)[28] and developed a dialogue with the Oromo Muslim community of central Ethiopia. Yohannes IV was the first Tigrinya-speaking emperor, and he brought to the throne the Tigreans' culture, vision, and concepts of Ethiopia. According to this set of values, Ethiopia was in fact a land of diversity, a home to many peoples and languages. The Tigrinya language itself is essentially Semitic, closer to Geez than the dominant Amharic. While the Amhara rulers of Ethiopia had traditionally striven for cultural integration and political centralization, the Tigreans preferred, for the most part, to maintain their separate, exclusive identity, though they aspired to regain their leadership of a rather diversified Ethiopian world. True to this philosophy, Yohannes did not seek the creation of a centralized government but was happy to recognize and legitimize the actual autonomy of the various provincial rulers. He recognized the ruling dynasty in the central province of Shoa, now led by Negus Menelik (who would become Emperor Menelik II in 1889), as kings and did the same with the ruling family in Gojjam, the land of the Blue Nile.

But the fact that the emperor was a Tigrean also meant that the very center of Ethiopian politics shifted northward to the province of Tigre, as well as to the area inhabited by Tigrinya speakers north of the Mareb River, called the *"Mareb melash,"* highland of Eritrea. When Yohannes came to power in 1872, the Egyptian effort to gain control over the same land, the middle of their vital Massawa-Khartoum line, was already in full swing. There was little room left for compromise. The Egyptians in Massawa bought the loyalty of several Tigrean family leaders and *shiftas* in the highland *Mareb melash,* and Yohannes's diplomatic appeal to the indifferent British went unanswered. By 1875 the scene was set for a showdown.

After occupying Harar two new armed Egyptian missions penetrated Ethiopian territory. A small force, headed by Munzinger, was to reach Menelik in Shoa and cooperate with him in destroying Yohannes. En route, however, the group was annihilated by the Afar people. A second force, 3,000 strong, set out from Massawa simultaneously in order to capture the area from the highlands to the Mareb River. On 15–16 November 1875 this force met with Yohannes's army in Gundet and was virtually wiped out.

When the news reached Cairo, Isma'il prepared for a full-scale war. An invading army of 15,000 men, under the command of Ratib Pasha, along with a team of U.S. mercenaries headed by General W. Loring, returned to Eritrea. On 7–9 March 1876 they were maneuvered out of their fortifications at Gura by Yohannes's generals and overwhelmingly defeated. Of the 5,200 Egyptian soldiers who launched the attack, only 1,900 managed to return. Those who escaped the massacre were taken prisoner and released only after negotiations were conducted and a treaty signed in which the Egyptians agreed not to reenter the highlands. A recent Egyptian study based on extensive archival work has estimated the total number of Egyptians killed in Gundet and Gura to be 8,500.[29]

The Egyptians remained in Massawa and Keren. They fortified their new Egyptian-Ethiopian border and for the next eight years conducted a war of attrition with the restored Ethiopian government in Eritrea. Yohannes's general, Ras Alula, the hero of Gura, was now charged with confronting the Egyptians. He based his headquarters in the village of Asmara, turned it into a thriving provincial capital, and took his revenge on the local Tigreans who had collaborated with the Egyptians. He also laid claim to Keren and its surrounding area, raiding and taxing its tribes frequently as the Egyptian garrison locked itself in town and watched helplessly.

The Ethiopian victory at Gura in 1876 was arguably one of the most important events in the history of modern Egypt. It was a turning point not only from victory to defeat, but from authoritarianism to nationalism as well. By regaining control over Eritrea, the Ethiopians foiled the Egyptians' goal of connecting their Red Sea ports to the Sudan. It was this failure (more than the Mahdiyya revolt in the Sudan five years later) that shattered Isma'il's dream of a Nile empire. In fact, the Egyptians had all the resources and international legitimacy in 1876 to build a greater Egypt if they could only maintain a smooth connection with the Sudan. But this was not to be, nor would Ethiopia's part in this loss be forgotten in Egypt's collective memory, as will become evident. Additionally, the huge, immediate financial losses caused by the Gura defeat worsened an already deteriorating balance of payments and ushered in the beginning of direct European interference in Egyptian affairs. It also convinced the British, hitherto at least indirectly supportive of the Egyptian enterprise in Africa, that Egypt could hardly maintain its own independence or live up to its financial commitments, much less run an empire.

The Gura defeat began the rapid countdown toward Egypt's fall into British hands in 1882.[30] It can also be considered the point at which early modern Egyptian nationalism was born. For it was in witnessing the Gura calamity firsthand that Amir Alai (Colonel) Ahmad 'Urabi, a Massawa-based officer in charge of supplies, began his protest movement. Already frustrated by Isma'il's preference for Westerners as generals and administrators, this talented son of an Egyptian peasant blamed the U.S. mercenaries for the defeat. He thought that Egyptian commanders, more patriotic and no less efficient, could have won the day. Returning to Egypt, he and other veterans of the Gura defeat (notably 'Ali al-Rubi, Ahmad 'Abd al-Ghafar, and 'Ali Fahmi)[31] coined the slogan "Egypt to the Egyptians." Challenging both the khedive's dependence on foreigners and growing French-British control of Egypt's economy and debt, they launched the 'Urabi revolt.[32] In his memoirs Ahmad 'Urabi would describe the entire chain of subsequent events—the early uprising, the 1879 removal of Isma'il by the Europeans, the deepening crisis, and the British conquest of Egypt in 1882—in a chapter titled "The Ethiopian Campaign."[33]

Yohannes IV and Islam

The battle of Gura was no less important for Ethiopia than it was for Egypt. It initiated a period of external victories, but also one of retreat to traditional structures and values. For the next twenty years, until March

1896 and the final victory at Adwa against the Italian imperialists, Ethiopia would experience formative events that would influence its history as well as its relations with Egypt to this very day.

In facing Isma'il's 1876 challenge, Yohannes seemed to have lost his early religious flexibility and reactivated the memory of "the Ahmad Gragn trauma." His actions and words are evidence that Ethiopia could not and would not view Isma'il in terms other than that of a religious enemy. Regardless of Isma'il's motives and methods, the moment his men invaded Ethiopian territory to undermine its government and recruit local Muslims, the Ethiopians responded as though he had embarked on an Islamic holy war.

Yohannes's call to arms in 1876 to defend Christian Ethiopia took the shape of a crusade against invading Muslims. J. Spencer Trimingham summarized the words of a European eyewitness: "It was in fact the first time in centuries that the Abyssinians as a whole responded to a call to protect their land and faith, and the clergy were the most potent instruments of propaganda. The popular movement was such that even Menilek, who the previous year had been intriguing with Munzinger, felt he ought to send his complement of troops."[34] According to the account of another, Egyptian, eyewitness, there were some 4,000 priests and monks in Yohannes's camp in Gura, all praying together with their emperor.[35] Yohannes and the clergy surrounding him now regarded the Egyptians in terms similar to those of 'Amda-Zion depicting the Muslims of Ifat or to medieval Ethiopian descriptions of Gragn. The Egyptians were now "the tribe of the Ismaelites . . . wicked and apostate men."[36] Beginning in Gura, Yohannes's policy was marked by a strong anti-Islamic element as he aimed at converting all the Muslims of Ethiopia to Christianity.[37]

One contemporary Ethiopian source quoted Yohannes's justification of his coercive Christianization: "I shall avenge the blood of Ethiopia. Gragn Islamized Ethiopia by force, fire and sword."[38] His policy vis-à-vis Ethiopian Muslims now included harsh measures, such as the destruction of mosques and the construction of churches. Many Amharic- or Tigrinya-speaking Muslims—now called "Jabarties" after the old name of Ifat—in towns such as Gondar and Aksum were forced to convert. Others fled by the thousands to nearby Sudanese territory. The more powerful Oromo Muslims of the central highlands and the Wallo and Yadju regions presented a major problem. They were militarily strong, and many of them had participated loyally in Yohannes's army, constituting its main cavalry. Nevertheless, Yohannes was now determined to convert them en masse. In May and June 1878 he summoned Ethiopia's prominent figures to a religious council in Wallo. Two of the major local Oromo chiefs were also summoned. According to an Ethiopian chronicler,

Yohannes told them: "We are your apostles. All this [Wallo and the central highlands] used to be Christian land until Gragn ruined and misled it. Now let all, whether Muslim or Galla [Oromo], believe in the name of Jesus Christ! Be baptized! If you wish to live in peace preserving your belongings, become Christians." It is estimated that by 1880 some 50,000 Jabarties and 500,000 Oromos had been forced to renounce Islam and convert to Christianity.

Yohannes went on to rule Ethiopia until 1889, but his anti-Islamic obsession constantly undermined his leadership. His coercive methods ruined his relations with the central Oromos, as well as his chance to develop and urbanize the areas under his direct government. Urban development in Ethiopia was usually possible due to Christian-Islamic co-existence and the irreplaceable contribution of Muslim traders. The seventeenth-century emperor Fasiladas had built Gondar, complete with a thriving Muslim quarter. Yohannes's contemporaries, including some of his provincial vassals, did initiate urbanization in the periphery. Ras Alula built Asmara in the 1880s, Menelik established Addis Ababa in 1886, and Ras Makonnen was appointed over Harar in 1887, restarting the Egyptian development enterprise and quickly turning it into a source of modern power. All three of them did this by cultivating good relations with local Muslims. Yohannes, however, failed to build a real capital. He had his urban bases in three small northern towns and remained essentially a roving emperor, with all the natural consequences of this for modernization and power. When he died, the central Oromos quickly turned to Menelik, and rural Tigre would not recuperate in terms of Pan-Ethiopian political leadership prior to 1991.

The Ahmad Gragn trauma also prevented Yohannes from applying a more flexible foreign policy. When Isma'il sent his British employee, the famous Colonel Charles Gordon, himself a devout Christian, to negotiate an agreement over Eritrea, Yohannes declined to meet with him. He was ready to deal with the British but not with an (albeit British) envoy of the Muslims. Only after the British occupied Egypt was Yohannes reluctantly ready to negotiate a deal. In accordance with the Hewett Treaty of June 1884, he undertook to help relieve the Egyptian garrisons besieged in eastern Sudan by the Mahdists, in return for the areas of Keren and lowland Eritrea (with the exception of Massawa). Thus, in opening a new front with the powerful Islamic movement and state in the Sudan, Yohannes again failed to see Islam in terms other than a two-dimensional enemy. When the Mahdi (d. 1885) and his successor, the caliph, wanted to avoid conflict, they resorted to the prophetic *utruku* message, hinting that they preferred to sever relations. Yohannes, however, was slow to respond. When he finally seemed to grasp the complexity of Islam, its various

nuances regarding Ethiopia and the options thus available, it was too
late. He died on 9 March 1889 fighting the Mahdists in a battle no one
really wanted.[39]

Yohannes's victory at Gura was remembered by Egyptian nationalists, especially the militant ones, for undermining the Egyptian control
of the vital Red Sea–Nile route and thus thwarting Egyptian unity with
the Sudan. His subsequent anti-Islamic policy would also be remembered. By not leaving Islam alone and by maltreating Muslims, Yohannes
played into the hands of the modern Islamic radicals. Literature produced
by such circles in twentieth-century Cairo portrayed Ethiopia as an ever-
hostile crusading state and featured Emperor Yohannes IV prominently.

The Gura battle, however, also began a period of Ethiopian victories. For reasons outside the scope of our present study, Ethiopia proved
a very resilient political culture, capable of mobilizing forces by traditional methods to defend its independence. The Ethiopians went on defeating the Egyptians, the Mahdists, and the Italian representatives of
imperialist Europe. Moreover, by obtaining modern firearms in sufficient
quantities, Ethiopia could not only defend itself against aggressors from
the north, but also expand into new territories to the south. While
Yohannes fought his defensive wars, Negus Menelik of Shoa was free
to occupy all the areas that today constitute Ethiopia south of Addis
Ababa. In doing so, he also conquered Muslim peoples, including the
newly converted southern Oromos, and notably, as mentioned earlier, the
old Islamic capital of Harar. As Emperor Menelik (1889–1913), he
proved far more flexible toward Islam, even allowing one entity, Jimma,
which capitulated in time, to retain full Islamic autonomy. He also improved relations with the Mahdiyya by resorting to sophisticated diplomacy and avoiding war. By doing so, Emperor Menelik accumulated
enough power to raise a huge army against the Italians. When the latter,
exploiting the demise of Yohannes, occupied Eritrea and declared it an
Italian colony in January 1890, they penetrated deep into Tigre in 1895
and sought to dominate the entire country. But in March 1896, exactly
twenty years after Gura, the Ethiopians under Menelik defeated the Italians in nearby Adwa. Their victory, a rare case of an oriental, African
people defeating and humiliating a European power at a time of imperialist dominance, would be carefully noted by the Egyptians.

Yohannes should be given credit for his "Tigrean" decentralist approach. His recognition of the various local rulers, notably Menelik,
made possible Ethiopia's defense in the north and expansion in the
south. This formula allowed Ethiopia to survive late-nineteenth-century
imperialism. It was mostly his lack of sophistication regarding Islam that
prevented him from rebuilding an Ethiopia focused on the "Aksumite"

north and reoriented to the Red Sea. However, in our context Yohannes must be remembered for yet another issue: the Ethiopian-Egyptian *abun* connection.

Immediately after the battle of Gura Yohannes eliminated Abuna Atnatewos. The Egyptian *abun* in Yohannes's camp was suspected of sympathizing with the enemy. In fact, he did establish contact with a prominent Egyptian prisoner, to whom he confided his contempt for the emperor. He mocked the Ethiopians and said he missed Egypt. He asked the Egyptian for a cigarette and smoked it secretly, saying that Yohannes had forbidden smoking and would have declared him an infidel if caught.[40] According to one Ethiopian source, he was killed in action; according to the memoirs of a European missionary, he was strangled.[41]

Yohannes, however, perhaps because he did not insist on political centralization, considered the church and its unity to be a main pillar of his state. For a while he toyed with the medieval idea of importing Armenian or Syrian bishops, but after further consideration and Isma'il's demise, he decided to renew the Egyptian connection. He sent his envoys to Egypt demanding the appointment of four bishops. In November 1881, for the first time since the days of Zar'a Ya'qob, the Coptic patriarchate was ready to send more than one. Patriarch Cyril V, perhaps sensing the turmoil in Egypt and respecting the victorious Ethiopians, agreed to Yohannes's request.[42] The four Egyptians left for Ethiopia but not before they had signed the customary written commitment never to work for the appointment of an Ethiopian *abun*.[43]

In Ethiopia Yohannes kept Abuna Petros in his court as the metropolitan prelate, dispatched Abuna Luqas to the kingdom of Gojjam, and sent Abuna Matewos to Negus Menelik in Shoa (Abuna Marqos died soon after arrival). Abuna Matewos crowned Menelik as emperor in 1889; two days later Menelik wrote to Abuna Petros announcing he was no longer the metropolitan prelate. Faced with this fait accompli, Alexandria had to endorse the change a year later, and Abuna Matewos would serve as the metropolitan prelate of Ethiopia until 1926.

Abuna Matewos was to be perhaps the most important *abun* in modern times. Completely integrating into Ethiopian culture, he proved loyal to Menelik and became one of his closest associates and advisers. He played a significant role in nearly all the major events of his long period in office, including the conquest of southern Ethiopia and the Christianization of most of its elite, the establishment of Addis Ababa as a modern center, and the victory over the Italians culminating in the battle of Adwa in 1896. After the death of Menelik in 1913, he was deeply involved in the struggle between the elite of Shoa and Menelik's proclaimed heir, Lij Iyasu, who was said to have converted to Islam. After the deposition of Iyasu in 1916, Abuna Matewos served under Empress Zawditu (1916–1930). During her reign, until his death in late 1926, he was one of the country's strongest men. In the spirit of his predecessors he was a religious conservative leader throughout and the chief rival of a new modernizing prince, Ras Tafari, heir to the throne in 1916 and the future Emperor Haile Selassie.

NOTES

1. For a discussion of the Nile as viewed by Europeans, see the following four essays in Erlich and Gershoni, *The Nile:* Arbel, "Renaissance Geographical Literature and the Nile," pp. 105–120; van Donzel, "Legend of the Blue Nile," pp. 121–130; Dirar, "The Nile as a Gateway," pp. 139–149; and Pankhurst, "Ethiopia's Alleged Control," pp. 25–38.

2. On Egypt's geographical enterprise in the greater Nile Valley, see Nasr, *Juhud misr al-kashfiyya.*

3. See Ayalon, "The Spread of Islam."

4. Trimingham, *Islam in Ethiopia,* p. 115.

5. See Abir, "Origins of the Ethiopian-Egyptian Border Problem"; Dombrowski, *Ethiopia's Access to the Red Sea,* pp. 44–48; and Harraz, *Iritriya al-haditha,* pp. 35–53.

6. For a discussion of Muhammad 'Ali's relations with Ethiopia, see Abir, *Ethiopia: The Era of the Princes,* pp. 95–137, and Rubenson, *Survival of Ethiopian Independence,* pp. 115–120.

7. See Trimingham, *Islam in Ethiopia,* pp. 115–116.

8. This is also the conclusion of Sven Rubenson in his *Survival of Ethiopian Independence,* see mainly p. 99. Rubenson's book contains the best documented analysis of Ethiopian-Egyptian diplomatic relations during the nineteenth century.

9. See Ras 'Ali's letters to Muhammad 'Ali in Rubenson, *Acta Aethiopica, Vol. 1,* pp. 94–97; see also Eshete, "Une Ambassade du Ras Ali en Egypte."

10. Meinardus, *Christian Egypt,* pp. 389–390.

11. During the "era of the princes" the position of the *abun* was weakened, as was the connection with Egypt. In 1803–1815 and again in 1828–1841, there was no *abun* from Egypt, and some Ethiopian rulers and clergymen thought of severing ties with Alexandria and seeking patriarchal authority and legitimacy from the Armenian Church.

12. For a detailed history, see Cerulli, *Etiopi in Palestina.* For the story of the nineteenth-century Deir al-Sultan, see Pedersen, *History of the Holy Community in the Holy Land* and *The Ethiopian Church and Its Community.* See also Suriyal, *Mushkilat dir al-sultan bil-quds.*

13. The question of Tewodros as a modernizer or just a mere autocrat in pursuit of absolutist centralism has aroused much discussion but is beyond the realm of this discussion. For more on the issue see Bekele, "Kassa and Kassa."

14. Trimingham, *Islam in Ethiopia,* p. 117.

15. See analysis and sources in Erlich, *Ethiopia and the Middle East,* pp. 48–52.

16. See a succinct analysis in Pankhurst, *The Ethiopians,* chap. 8.

17. Rubenson, "Shaikh Kassa Hailu."

18. Pankhurst, "Unpublished Letter of King of Kings."

19. On the work and activities of Abuna Salama in Ethiopia, see Crummey, *Priests and Politicians,* pp. 85–91, 141. See also Meinardus, *Christian Egypt,* p. 390, and Zewde, *History of Modern Ethiopia,* pp. 31–35.

20. For the most detailed and authoritative discussion of Tewodros's relations with the Egyptians, see Rubenson, *Survival of Ethiopian Independence,* pp. 172–287, esp. pp. 208–223; see also Harraz, *Iritriya al-hadidha,* pp. 53–59. For a new Egyptian analysis of Tewodros see Muhammad, *Thiyudur al-thani imbiratur ithyubia.*

21. The sections below on Isma'il and Yohannes are based on two of my previous studies: *Ras Alula and the Scramble for Africa,* chaps. 1–7; and *Ethiopia and the Middle East,* pp. 53–72. For the best diplomatic analysis see Rubenson, *Survival of Ethiopian Independence,* pp. 288–384.

22. The full text of the letter is in Sarhank, *Haqaiq al-akhbar fi duwal al-bihar,* pp. 298–300.

23. Meinardus, *Christian Egypt,* pp. 21–25.

24. Quoted in Sabri, *Misr fi Ifriqiya al-sharqiyya,* p. 73.

25. For a discussion see Jalata, *Oromia and Ethiopia,* pp. 22–29. See also Trimingham, *Islam in Ethiopia,* p. 121.

26. Sabri, *Misr fi Ifriqiya al-sharqiyya,* p. 72.

27. Ibid., pp. 71–76.

28. Trimingham, *Islam in Ethiopia,* p. 122.

29. Bayumi, *Mawsu'at al-ta'rikh,* p. 147. This volume is the most detailed and up-to-date study of the Egyptian military enterprise in the Horn of Africa during the 1870s.

30. See al-Rafi'i, *'Asr Isma'il,* p. 152.

31. Rif'at, *Kitab jabr al-kasr,* pp. 74–75.

32. Bayumi, *Mawsu'at al-ta'rikh,* pp. 148–150.

33. 'Urabi, *Kashf al-sitar 'an sirr al-asrar,* pp. 30–50.

34. Trimingham, *Islam in Ethiopia,* p. 121, quoting Rohlfs, *Meine Mission nach Abessinien,* p. 62.

35. Rif'at, *Kitab jabr al-kasr,* p. 65.

36. Erlich, *Ethiopia and the Challenge of Independence,* chap. 5. The chapter, titled "A Contemporary Biography of Ras Alula: A Ge'ez Manuscript," was first published in *The Bulletin of the School of Oriental and African Studies* in 1976, with the Geez text translated by Roger Cowley. See Erlich, *Ethiopia and the Challenge of Independence,* for an Ethiopian description of the period reflecting attitudes toward Islam, the Egyptians, and the Sudanese Mahdiyya.

37. See details and an important analysis in Caulk, "Religion and State."

38. The quotes attributed to Yohannes in this paragraph are in Caulk, ibid.

39. See Erlich, *Ethiopia and the Middle East,* pp. 65–72.

40. Rif'at, *Kitab jabr al-kasr,* pp. 64–65.

41. Lamlam, *Ya'atse Takla-Giyorgisna ya'atse Yohannes tarik;* Massaia, *I miei trentacinque anni di missione nell'alta Etiopia,* p. 177.

42. Meinardus, *Christian Egypt,* p. 391.

43. Tafla, "The Father of Rivers."

5

Nationalism and Mutual Perceptions

By the end of the nineteenth century, modern Egyptian nationalism had emerged under British occupation and began to revolve around the renewed territorial and historical concept of the Nile. As this new sense of modern Egyptian identity began molding and providing new meanings for Egyptian society and politics—from the internal role of the Copts to a new conceptual geographical framework of "Unity of the Nile Valley"—the modern rediscovery of Ethiopia left its marks. The old image of the land of the Blue Nile was reinterpreted by modern Egyptianism as it recycled medieval Islamic and Mamluk dichotomies. It also modified these old legacies in the spirit of its own rising liberalism.

But while Egyptian nationalism was molded by a sense of defeat and occupation, late-nineteenth-century Ethiopia experienced victories. Emperor Yohannes IV's victory over Khedive Isma'il's army in 1876 began a period of great military achievements that culminated two decades later, in March 1896, with Emperor Menelik II's victory over the Italians at Adwa. Ethiopia would enter the twentieth century amid this unique experience of rebirth and victory. During the first third of the twentieth century, as a new generation of Ethiopians were reshaping their nationalist consciousness, the Blue Nile played a major role in their interaction with the outside world. Egypt, in their eyes, conquered by the British, was rendered nearly irrelevant as a Nile country. It would remain, however, as important as ever, a source of both religious identity and modern progress.

THE ETHIOPIANS AND THE NILE, 1902–1934

Chapter 3 discussed Ethiopia's medieval perception of its ownership of the Nile River. In a recent study one of Ethiopia's leading historians,

79

Bairu Tafla, analyzes the Nile in Ethiopian literature.[1] He tells us that the Abbai, meaning "big" (the *abbay wanz,* the big river) in the classical language of Geez, was also popularly referred to as "the father of rivers," with *abbawi* in Geez meaning "fatherly." The big, fatherly river was a main factor in Ethiopia's culture and history. The awesome, mighty, lengthy gorge was personified and admired, feared and loved.[2] The symbolism of the Abbai, representing nature's superiority, was reflected in an infinite number of tales, proverbs, poems, novels, and private names. Together with Islam and the Red Sea, Tafla concludes, the river was the factor that guided Ethiopia's foreign relations in the direction of the Middle East rather than Africa. From the ancient and early medieval formation of Ethiopian culture and statehood to the decisive confrontations in the second half of the nineteenth century, the Nile connected Ethiopia to the Middle East, primarily to Egypt, transforming Egypt into the important "other" that contributed so significantly to the shaping of the Ethiopian self. Medieval and premodern Ethiopians, Tafla asserts, considered the Egyptians to be their only partners in possession of the great river.

It is therefore, perhaps, ironic that from the last decade of the nineteenth century until World War II, Egypt, in the sense that it was *the* Nile country, became quite irrelevant in Ethiopian eyes. The Abbai, however, was to become a pivotal factor in Ethiopia's fateful dialogue with Western imperialism, as well as an important factor in the internal Ethiopian struggle between centralization and regionalism. As Ethiopia underwent the major transformations of the early twentieth century, the Blue Nile, Ethiopia's property, acquired new, modern nationalist significance. But for a long while the river lost its importance as a link connecting the histories of the two countries. Occupied by the British, Egypt lost its control over the upper river, and the Egyptians themselves lost contact with its real sources.

During the reign of Menelik II, 1889–1913, Egypt's direct significance as regards Ethiopia was diminished in other aspects too. Abuna Matewos lived long enough (until late 1926) to render the issue of a new appointment by Alexandria quite irrelevant. The old Islamic Egyptian-Ethiopian relations also seemed to relax. During the period up to 1898 Ethiopia conquered many Islamic peoples, but under Menelik's leadership, occupation and annexation were conducted without overt crusading zeal; Cairo, in any case, was in no position to lodge an Islamic protest. And Jerusalem, too, was no longer a real issue in Ethio-Egyptian relations.

The Holy City, to be sure, though far away, remained very meaningful. While the revival of Ethiopian statehood revolved around military victories and territorial expansion, traditional and religious concepts were not pushed aside. On the contrary, they were thoroughly transmitted and integrated into Ethiopia's modern identity and nationalism. Jerusalem, both because of its biblical Christian legacies and because of its royal Solomonian Ethiopian ethos, had been much on the minds of Tewodros II and Yohannes IV. The latter began reinforcing the Ethiopian community in Jerusalem, but his relations with Islam did not allow him to launch a major initiative. Menelik, in contrast, confident and victorious over European imperialism, could work for Ethiopia's status in Jerusalem. He did so with all his might, but his Islamic counterpart was now the Ottoman sultan in Istanbul, not an Egyptian khedive. Menelik's dialogue with Sultan 'Abd al-Hamid II during the early 1900s (the latter, worried by Italian encroachment in Tripolitania, sought an alliance with Menelik) yielded Ottoman authorization for new Ethiopian churches and buildings in Jerusalem.[3] The Ethiopian community in the city expanded as pilgrimage via Egypt continued. The issue of the keys to Deir al-Sultan, however, still held by the Egyptian Copts, remained. These keys, together with the overall issue of an Egyptian *abun,* would be placed on the Ethiopian-Egyptian agenda by Ras Tafari, though not before 1924.

A new development made Egypt even more important to Ethiopia. Cairo's modern Coptic community, led by the new *majlis milli,* took renewed pride in a strong, independent Ethiopia. Coptic intellectuals now took it upon themselves to modernize Christian relations with Ethiopia, particularly in a field open to them for the first time: education. The first modern elementary school in Addis Ababa, inaugurated by Menelik in 1908, was staffed primarily by Egyptian Copts led by Salib Hanna. It was a modest beginning with significant consequences.

Paradoxically, however, Ethiopia could now ignore Egypt in terms of the Nile. After the British conquest of the Sudan in 1898–1899 and their defeat of the Mahdist state in the name (and with the resources) of Egypt, England refused to reunite the two countries. Their enforced separation of Egypt and the Sudan will be addressed further in the context of Egyptian nationalism. It is mentioned here because the new masters of the greater Nile Valley, the British, initiated an all-Nile strategy that had a direct bearing on Ethiopia. They did so, conducting an intense, critical dialogue with Ethiopia, in the name of the British government of the Sudan. Both England and Ethiopia would keep the Egyptians out of the all-Nile picture for at least three decades.

The history of the Anglo-Ethiopian Nile dialogue, which lasted from 1902 to 1935, cannot be retold here in detail,[4] but its British dimension should be summarized briefly. As the British completed construction of the (first) Aswan Dam in 1902, they dispatched an envoy to Menelik. In an agreement reached in 1902 the latter undertook not to construct "any works across the Blue Nile, Lake Tana or the Sobat, which would arrest the flow of the waters into the Nile, except in agreement with His Britannic Majesty's Government and the Government of the Sudan." A British mission was permitted to survey Lake Tana that same year and reported that a dam at the lake, the source of the Blue Nile, would be an optimal enterprise, would be easy to build, and would create the best reservoir possible. From that moment the British vision of an all-Nile system under their control focused on the idea of a Lake Tana dam. Their interest in the project became a major goal after World War I, when the prices of Sudanese and Egyptian cotton skyrocketed and a new survey of Lake Tana in 1920 established the overwhelming quantitative significance of the Ethiopian waters. British strategists were prepared to do almost anything to secure an agreement with Ethiopia regarding the dam. They worked relentlessly, resorting to various incentives, from promising generous financial subsidies to offering to cede the British-controlled Somali port of Zeila (the old Islamic capital of medieval Ifat!) to Ethiopia (an offer made in 1922).

The British were also ready to consider military occupation of western Ethiopia (especially in 1913 and 1917) and coordinated their efforts with colonial counterparts in the region. In 1906 they signed a tripartite agreement with the Italians and the French, securing their recognition of the Lake Tana region as a British sphere of influence. In December 1925, frustrated by Ethiopian procrastination, the British signed an agreement with Mussolini. Although Ethiopia had become a member of the League of Nations in 1923, the two European powers ignored Addis Ababa and agreed to support each other's interests in Ethiopia. Ras Tafari lodged a protest with the League and in 1927 asked an American company to plan an Ethiopian dam at Tana. By the early 1930s, amid the global economic crisis and the collapse of cotton prices, the British slowed their efforts, many of them now convinced that their long-term, all-Nile interests would be better served through an understanding with Mussolini rather than with Ras Tafari, crowned Emperor Haile Selassie in 1930.

Ethiopia's reluctance to cooperate with a British all-Nile scheme originated in its own perception of the river. The Blue Nile was indeed an integral part of Ethiopia, but it played a different role for Ethiopia than it did for Egypt. Whereas the river was the source of life for the Egyptians, a creator of human harmony, a unifying bridge, the Abbai for the Ethiopians was a formidable obstacle. According to Tafla, whose above-mentioned essay summarizes the role of the Nile in Ethiopian literature, the huge gorge, that awesome phenomenon of nature's might, brought no waters to the fields, but rather stole Ethiopian waters away. The "father of rivers" did not bridge people but divided them.[5] Crossing the Blue Nile was quite an operation before 1933, the year the first all-weather bridge was erected over the gorge. Prior to that year the entire land surrounded by the Abbai's loop, the province of Gojjam, was virtually isolated from the rest of Ethiopia in the rainy season, July through November. During the rest of the year crossing the Abbai usually meant either swimming or using boats made of cow skin and straw.

The people of Gojjam considered the Abbai a protector and a symbol of their local autonomy. Sandwiched between the otherwise more powerful Shoans of the south and the Tigreans of the north, they often called themselves "the river's children"[6] and sang about its bounty: ". . . as long as the Abbai is our river, whoever rules is not our concern."[7] In 1882 Yohannes legitimized Gojjam's autonomy by recognizing the head of the leading local Amhara family as a negus, or king. Emperor Menelik managed to curb Negus Takla-Haimanot's power and demote his son to a *ras,* or duke. By 1920, however, after Menelik's death, this son—Ras Hailu Takla-Haimanot of Gojjam—managed to solidify his autonomy. Defended by the gorge of the Abbai, he overtly defied the central government and the authority of the regent, Ras Tafari.

After the death of Menelik in 1913 and until the coronation of Haile Selassie in 1930, Ethiopia's internal affairs revolved primarily around the struggle between the central government, itself divided and rival torn, and the leading regional families. The British, for their part, did their best to cultivate Ras Hailu; some even considered the option of helping him secede in order to sign a Tana dam contract with him. Ras Tafari, meanwhile, worked for the centralization of government around his own personal authority. His goal was to achieve this through intensive modernization, and for this purpose he needed British money and, in particular, the port of Zeila. But Tafari remained suspicious of the British throughout and felt their Tana enterprise would cause the whole of western Ethiopia to fall under British rule. Indeed, according to the British plan, the dam was to be linked by a new road from Khartoum, not from Addis Ababa, as Tafari had envisioned.

This issue also complicated the struggle within the Ethiopian capital itself, as the more conservative members of the elite resisted the negotiations, fearing that modernization would help Tafari gain control and arguing, among other things, that the dam would destroy the churches on Lake Tana's islands, precious evidence of Ethiopia's medieval glory that had escaped Ahmad Gragn's destruction. (One of Tafari's major rivals, Ras Gugsa Wale, was married to Empress Zawditu. An opponent of the dam, he was also governor of the province of Bagemdir and controlled Lake Tana itself.) Prior to 1926 Tafari, who had led the British to believe he wanted to make diplomatic progress, had no real power to finalize matters. But by 1930, after he won control of the capital and gained superiority over the regional lords of the north, the global economic crisis and the British-Italian dialogue had already changed the game.

Tafari, crowned Haile Selassie I, tried in vain to interest the British in an internationally (and primarily American-) financed and Ethiopian-controlled Tana dam. He organized a Nile conference in 1933, but the British barely responded. He tried again in May 1935, this time in a desperate effort to mobilize international help in order to confront Mussolini. But it was too late. The Fascists, with their dreams of an African oriental empire, considered the Lake Tana area a major target for their future Italian colonization enterprise.[8] Moreover, they thought to use the Blue Nile as leverage against the British and as a means to realize their dream of a Mediterranean empire. Their conquest of Ethiopia in 1935–1936 was to be a fateful global event.

The long and futile Anglo-Ethiopian dialogue over a possible Tana dam left some intriguing what-ifs in its wake. What if an agreement had been reached? Could Ethiopia of the 1920s have maintained its territorial integrity, or would it have lost its western region to the British? Would Mussolini, given such British involvement, even have contemplated or carried out the conquest of Ethiopia? What would have been the all-Nile hydropolitical picture today had a dam in Lake Tana been erected at that time? Would the Aswan High Dam still have been built in Egypt? Would Ethiopia still have had to struggle for an "equitable share," or could it have dominated the distribution of the Nile's waters? All of these questions remain unanswered. One point, however, can be made from our perspective: for more than three decades the Egyptian public and leaders were not properly informed about this cardinal Nile issue. In fact, it was only in 1929, when the British oversaw the Egyptian-Sudanese Water Agreement, that the Egyptian government was introduced to the Anglo-Ethiopian dialogue. But this was too late. As in the medieval past, the Ethiopians were masters of the Nile. As in the past, however, the Nile was to them less a matter of water than a crucial card in international relations.

EARLY EGYPTIAN NATIONALISM AND ETHIOPIA

We have surveyed very briefly the role of the Nile in shaping Ethiopia's relations with the world during the early twentieth century. To Egypt during that same period, the Nile was the very heart of the country's self-redefinition. Modern Egyptian nationalism, which had its first manifestations in the Ahmad 'Urabi revolt, culminated in the 1920s, revolving around the concept of the Nile Valley as the theater of unique Egyptian history.[9] This Egyptian nationalism offered new prescriptions for the essence of society, politics, and culture and, much more important to us, redefined the role of the Copts in all these spheres as well. Moreover, by defining the rebirth of the Egyptian nation in the territorial concept of the Nile Valley, modern Egyptian nationalism made the land of the Blue Nile, "the Nile's heights," even more relevant.

During the period from 1840 to the 1950s, for all intents and purposes, Egypt lost its strategic Middle Eastern option. When new generations of educated young people began developing Egypt's modern identity around the turn of the century, their own formative memories and experiences consisted of the collapse of Isma'il's dream of an all-Nile African empire, the British occupation of their country, and Britain's imposed separation of Egypt from the Sudan in 1899. Although Isma'il had failed to assert Egypt's historical rights over the entire Nile, the modern nationalists remained loyal to this concept. "Unity of the Nile Valley"—emancipating an Egypt that stretched all along the White Nile—remained their goal and slogan until the rise of Gamal Abdel Nasser.

Indeed, during the entire first half of the twentieth century, the territorial definition of the Nile Valley competed successfully for the Egyptian soul with the Pan–Middle Eastern, supra-Egyptian dimensions of religion and language. A more Western-oriented, liberal faction of Egyptian nationalists led by Ahmad Lutfi al-Sayyid saw a unique "Egyptian personality" molded for thousands of years by the unique geography of the Nile. A somewhat competing school, led first by Mustafa Kamil, accepted the centrality of the Nile's historical role but also integrated Egyptian identity with the wider circles of pan-regional Islam and Arabism. We shall address aspects of this internal identity struggle below and discuss it where it has a bearing on Egyptian-Ethiopian relations. Here we shall analyze the early-twentieth-century images of Ethiopia as reflected in the new prisms of modern Egypt.

Egyptian Army Officers and the Memory of Gura

When Egypt suffered its defeat at Gura at the hands of the Ethiopians in 1876, Egypt's modern nationalism had not sufficiently developed to be able to respond. The new politically aware and informed sector was still too small to shape public opinion. Judging by the Egyptian press in existence at the time, the entire disastrous collision with Ethiopia was kept from the public. For example, *Al-Ahram,* a daily newspaper, was established in 1876, its first issue appearing not long after Gura. Yet this crucial strategic defeat and later events along the Egyptian-Ethiopian border in Eritrea up to 1884 were practically ignored, at least by *Al-Ahram*. It was only after Ethiopia's victory against the Italians in Adwa, in March 1896, twenty years after Gura, that the first manifestations of modern curiosity about Ethiopia could be discerned. By that time not only had an Egyptian press mushroomed, but the modern production of books in general, their wide distribution, and their increasing impact on the rapidly growing educated public had begun. Some of the relevant writings during the period from 1896 to 1908, in which modern Egyptian nationalism underwent a transformation from initial ideas into political movements, will be discussed below.

Not long after the battle of Adwa, two books written by army officers appeared in Cairo in 1896–1897. The first, by Amir Alai Isma'il Sarhank, inspector of the military schools in the small Egyptian army, was titled *The Truthful News About the Countries of the Seas*.[10] It gave a detailed history of Egypt's nineteenth-century foreign relations, including two sections about Khedive Isma'il and Ethiopia. The first section described how Isma'il helped the British destroy Tewodros II; the second described his defeat at the hands of Yohannes IV in Gura and the disastrous consequences of the defeat. The narrative of the book was factual, with little value judgment of the Ethiopians. One point, however, was significant: the author completely avoided any mention of Adwa.

Ignoring such a significant victory by a close neighbor over European imperialists in Egypt's own backyard was even more blatant in the second, more relevant book published in Cairo in late 1896: *Overcoming the Calamity in Release from Captivity,* by Muhammad Rif'at, secretary of the Egyptian army's 1876 expedition to Ethiopia that had been shattered at Gura.[11] The book is a detailed document narrating the Gura story from the Egyptian point of view and following the actions of this high-ranking officer. On the fateful day of 9 March, he was captured by the Ethiopians, spent time as their prisoner, and then served as a mediator-translator in the negotiations leading to the release of prisoners and the Egyptian withdrawal from the Eritrean highlands. It was perhaps the first book on Ethiopia and Ethiopians published in Egypt since al-Suyuti's late-fifteenth-century *Raising the Status of the Abyssinians*.

During his short time in captivity and over the course of the following twenty years until the book was written, Rif'at acquired a detailed knowledge of Ethiopia. His writing reflected a clear duality. On the one hand, his attitude toward his Ethiopian captors was quite positive. He described the Ethiopians' pure, innocent religiosity and their tolerance (pp. 65, 80). As a prisoner, for example, he was free to talk to Muslim Ethiopian soldiers about Islam (p. 73). He described the Ethiopians' military ability and organization in positive terms, similar to those used by

Ahmad 'Urabi in his description of Gura (published much later, in 1929). Rif'at also portrayed Emperor Yohannes, as well as some of his aides, as reasonable, even kind (pp. 41, 55, 61, 79, 85). There is an air of sympathy throughout the book. However, the work also contains a great deal of contempt and cultural paternalism as it consistently depicts un-civilized customs and manners, lack of cleanliness and poor hygiene, the consumption of raw meat (pp. 80–82), a total lack of mutual trust among Ethiopians (pp. 17, 26, 81), and their general cruelty (pp. 46, 50–53). The book is replete with descriptions of how the Ethiopians murdered Egyptian prisoners, not even having mercy on a Christian Copt (p. 53). Other prisoners suffered mutilation and all sorts of humiliation.

Rif'at himself, he admitted, was too moderate to be mobilized by Ahmad 'Urabi and the other Gura veterans who led the earlier Egyptian movement (p. 102). Yet his writing seemed to reflect what Egyptian army officers, in their version of a more militant Egyptian nationalism, felt toward Ethiopia. They were inclined to remember Gura, the shame-ful, disastrous defeat at the hands of mysterious semibarbarians. They retained the concept of Ethiopia as a land that, rather than being subject to Egypt's civilizing mission, was responsible for thwarting Egypt's all-Nile dream and for the destruction of an Egyptian empire stretching over the Somali and Eritrean coasts. The Egyptian army officers, perhaps re-cycling in their humiliation a modicum of the old popular anti-Ethiopian attitudes, wanted to forget Adwa and avoided crediting Ethiopia, where they themselves had failed, for stemming and defeating Western imperi-alism (an experience that Boutros Boutros-Ghali would call "the Somali syndrome" in 1997).[12]

Coptic Intellectuals and the Glory of Menelik II

Not so the Copts. The modern faction of the Coptic community was now fully ready to embrace victorious Ethiopia. After the British occupied Egypt acceptance of Copts in general Egyptian affairs increased. In 1894 Boutros Ghali, the founder of the *majlis milli* (and grandfather of Boutros Boutros-Ghali), was appointed foreign minister and held the post until 1908, when he became prime minister. In 1895 Tadrus Shenudah established a daily newspaper, *Misr* (Egypt), which, together with his new Misr Press, further strengthened Coptic awareness of, and participation in, modern Egyptian nationalism.[13]

The more religious faction of the Coptic community naturally re-mained less involved, as well as less sympathetic toward Ethiopia. Its mood could be discerned in late 1896, in the aftermath of Adwa, when Monsignor Qerilos of the Catholic Coptic Church returned from Ethiopia.

He had been asked by the Italians to mediate for the release of their prisoners and upon his return gave a lecture to the Egyptian Geographical Society. This "Lecture on Ethiopia" was published in December 1896.[14] The monsignor, unlike the officer Muhammad Rif'at, did not ignore the fact of Ethiopia's victory. But he told the story of the Italian prisoners as if he were an Italian observer, very emphatically reflecting the same message contained in Rif'at's book: Ethiopia's cruel mistreatment of innocent prisoners.

But modern Copts clearly had a different Ethiopia in mind and were happy to spread this awareness in Egypt as a useful card in their own integration. In 1906, a very important year in the history of Egyptian nationalism, Ramzi Tadrus, an editor of *Misr,* published his book *Ethiopia's Present and Future.*[15] Very detailed, the book was the product of a systematic study of the available primarily European sources. It contained information on dozens of issues and a basic introductory survey of Ethiopia. Though far from being completely accurate, the spirit of the entire book was one of admiration. Early in the book Tadrus wrote that he had three aims. The first was to acquaint the Egyptian public with Ethiopia. "Though it seems to be far off," he said, "it should always be in our minds and hearts, and not only because of our religious connections and geographical proximity. We should reach a stage of comprehensive cooperation and mutual help with Ethiopia." Second, the study of Ethiopia, he wrote, was a lesson in an oriental nation's awakening and triumph, an important lesson to all Egyptians. Ethiopia, he declared, was an oriental kingdom that had succeeded more than any other oriental nation. Third, Ethiopia should be connected with Egypt. Its vast potential in economy, tourism, and culture should benefit Egypt and help it advance (pp. 4–5).

In later chapters Tadrus singled out the field of modern education as one of the areas in Ethiopian society most in need of attention, an area in which Egypt's ability to contribute was significant. But it is the Egyptians, he wrote, who should learn the meaning of patriotism and unity from the Ethiopians. His main hero, of course, was the victor of Adwa, Menelik II (whose picture graces the cover of the book). Tadrus narrates Menelik's reforms in various fields and concludes: "To put it succinctly, Emperor Menilek is one of the great kings of the world today, one of the mightiest in terms of power, ability, wisdom and righteousness" (p. 16). Tadrus also devoted a chapter to Ras Makonnen, Menelik's chief political aide and Ethiopia's modernizer of Harar (and the father of Ras Tafari), as well as to other figures, including Abuna Matewos. In a chapter devoted to Ethiopia's Muslims, the *sahaba-najashi* story is briefly told, with an emphasis on the Ethiopian king's rescue of Islam. The medieval religious wars are also discussed, but there is no mention of Yohannes's anti-Islamic campaigns. In recent times, Tadrus stated, Ethiopian patriotism had dissolved the differences, and Christian-Islamic relations in Ethiopia were good.

The last chapter (pp. 163–170), titled "Her Present and Her Political Future," is again a tribute to Ethiopia's ability to retain its independence and an analysis of its place of honor among the family of nations. It ends with a section subtitled "The Black Peril," which equates Ethiopia to Japan: "If we compare the Ethiopians with the Japanese we see that the latter, after they opened their country to Europe, made cultural progress, became modernized and reached the highest level in the whole world. It is also possible for the Ethiopians to find the road which can lift them higher and higher, until Ethiopia reaches the level of Japan, for her men do not lag behind the Japanese in brightness, resourcefulness, cleverness, and wisdom, and they are even superior to them in bravery." Concluding a book with such a passage was significant in 1906, for Japan's victory over Russia in 1905 had a tremendous impact on Middle Eastern and Islamic publics and gave a boost to modern Turkish, Persian, Arab, and Egyptian nationalist movements. The example of the modernized oriental Japanese beating Europeans inspired many to challenge both traditionalism and European involvement. Mustafa Kamil, the charismatic leader of Egyptian nationalism, published his book *The Rising Sun* in 1905. Ethiopia's victory at Adwa, no less a drama of European defeat, was hardly noticed at the time. In 1896 these nationalist movements were not yet ripe enough to be inspired, and Ethiopia could hardly have served as a model for modern progress. Modern Copts, however, were now more than curious. They were fully ready to recycle the message of their medieval ancestors, that of a powerful Ethiopia, their Christian ally, a state able, if necessary, to punish Islam and Muslims. Ramzi Tadrus's book would be thoroughly studied by new generations of Copts, who would do their best to modernize the Coptic-Ethiopian bond and would continue to spread knowledge of Ethiopia in Egypt.

Islamic Modernists and the Legacy of al-Suyuti

Yet what of Egypt's Muslims? Were they ready to recognize a new Ethiopia? From the evidence gathered for this study, it is apparent that most of them, at the beginning of the twentieth century, were prepared to do so. During the first third of the century, most Islamic leaders in Egypt were moderate, working to modernize Islam and make it as compatible as possible with the new spirit of emerging liberal, parliamentary nationalism. Only with the rise of Islamic militancy during the 1930s would the image of Ethiopia as an enemy of Islam and the radical "*Islam al-najashi*" anti-Christian approach find supporters in Egypt.

The person who spearheaded the moderate Islamic concept of Ethiopia was the leader of modernist Islam, Muhammad Rashid Rida. Born in Lebanon, he became the disciple of the great Egyptian Islamic modernizer, Muhammad 'Abduh. After he moved to Cairo in 1897, Rida founded a journal, *Al-Manar,* as well as a movement named Al-Salafiyya (Return to the Founding Fathers), which preached Islamic reformism and modernism through inspiration from and new interpretations of Islam's early days. In this he followed in the footsteps of 'Abduh, but he added to Islamic modernism a generous dose of anti-Westernism. It was probably this combination that led Rida to celebrate the Ethiopian victory of Adwa and Italy's humiliation.

In the first issue of *Al-Manar* in 1897, not long after Adwa, an article appeared titled "Al-Habasha." It began as follows:

> In the nineteenth century the sword built two great empires: the German empire and the Ethiopian empire. If the victory over the French [1870] united the Germans, the victory of the Ethiopians over the Italians in the battle of Adwa gave Menelik the leadership of Ethiopia, and made him the king of the united empire. The Ethiopians are an oriental nation that was awakened by the roar of the Italian cannons. They rose from their deep sleep and stormed the gates of modernization. The day is not far, maybe fifty years from now, that Ethiopia will equal Japan in power, formidability, and glory. And when Ethiopia reaches the level of Japan it will be a second sign that the oriental peoples are ready to march forward toward progress and prosperity, that they are capable of reorganization, and they are able to stabilize themselves in spite of what their rivals say.

The rest of the article presented an interview with Menelik's adviser, and it then mentioned that Muslims in Ethiopia were still discriminated against and that this issue would be solved only when Ethiopia made more progress on the road to modernization.[16]

Though Rida was probably disillusioned with Ethiopia's pace of modernization later on and wrote no more in this spirit, his support was ongoing. He would become the father figure of the *Jam'iyyat al-shubban al-muslimin* (young men's Muslim associations) in the 1920s, which would spearhead support and aid of Ethiopia in its struggle against the Fascists in 1935. The leader of modernist Islam in Egypt died at the end of that year but not before he had come forth to defend Haile Selassie and attack Mussolini.

In 1902–1903 a 324-page book was published in Cairo by Ahmad al-Hifni al-Qina'i titled *The Beautiful Diamonds in the History of the*

Ethiopians,[17] reflecting the renewed concepts of mainstream Islam. The book was officially endorsed by the establishment of Al-Azhar, where the author was a teaching member. No less than six of the most prominent Islamic scholars and leaders of the great *madrasa,* including the Shaikh al-Azhar himself, wrote lengthy introductory notes praising the book and its author. The book may even have been commissioned by this Islamic institute of higher learning, for the author appears to have been aided by a team that helped him exhaust the Al-Azhar library. Virtually all Islamic sources on Ethiopia, from the early writings about the days of the Prophet to the Mamluk and Ahmad Gragn eras, were consulted and quoted. In addition, some of the modern European literature on Ethiopia was used to update the chapter "History of the Ethiopians."

The book, however, hardly lived up to its name. Apart from the long introductory chapter that dealt with Ethiopia's contemporary history, the rest was merely the story of early Islam's meeting with that Christian land. The main inspiration behind the book, the author himself wrote, was al-Suyuti's *Raising the Status of the Abyssinians.* Indeed, apart from containing minor incidents of indirect criticism, the essence of the book (in line with the twelfth-century book of Ibn al-Jawzi mentioned in Chapter 3, *The Lightening of the Darkness on the Merits of the Blacks and the Ethiopians*) was a tribute to Ethiopia and Ethiopians in classical Islamic style and terms. The story of the dialogue between Muhammad and the *najashi* and the latter's rescue of the *sahaba* was pivotal in sending a double central message: that Muslims should gratefully accept Ethiopia's historic role and legitimate sovereignty and that Ethiopian Muslims had made a very positive contribution to Islam, adding to its purity and humanism. In making this dual point, al-Qina'i followed the traditional mainstream Islamic view that the *najashi* had converted to Islam, but he urged that the fact that the *najashi* was not followed by his peoples should not be held against them. The author returned time and again to the hadith of "Leave the Abyssinians alone as long as they leave you alone" and explained Ethiopia's survival accordingly:

> Allah in his grace fulfilled what *al-najashi* Ashama hoped for when he said "May God let it be that Ethiopia will stay well as long as this book [a Quran he is said to have hidden from his people] stays with them." In fact, if you look at the history of the nations, especially those situated in close proximity to the center of the Islamic religion, you will not find any state that has kept its internal independence and its freedom from foreign control but Ethiopia, from the beginning of Islam to the present. And why is it, if not because of Ethiopia's reconciliation with Islam and the Muslims, a concept that only the Ethiopian king understood at that time, and not other kings such as Khosrau, Qaysar, al-Muqauqas, and others whose kingdoms were destroyed. (Pp. 13–14)

It is clear throughout that al-Qina'i did his best to paint a very favorable picture of Ethiopia, avoiding any of the negative Islamic concepts he had surely come across in his readings and combating any racist anti-Ethiopian images still circulating in public. He mentioned the Ethiopians' pre-Islamic threat to the Kaaba but passed no judgment. He made no issue of *"Islam al-najashi"* in the sense that the country was already a part of the land of Islam and therefore its return to Christianity offensive. He made little of Ethiopia's destruction of the medieval Islamic sultanates and of Ahmad Gragn's holy war against Ethiopia. His interpretation of Islam and Ethiopia in history was loud and clear: the Ethiopians were dear brothers and legitimate neighbors.

In his introduction he mentioned three reasons why his fellow Muslims in Egypt should cherish the notion of Ethiopia: first, because of their shared pre-Islamic past and general cultural and ethnic affinity: "Their country is among the oldest countries in the world after Egypt. It has an importance for Egypt which came from neighborly relations and the fact that both countries excel in their long existence, [which began] even before the Greeks or the Romans or any other country" (p. z). The second reason was due to Islamic history, following the arguments presented above. The third was modern history. Both Egyptians and Ethiopians, together with other peoples of the East and Africa, face European imperialism, aggression, and conquest, he said. In this respect Ethiopia is a model for self-emancipation: "Every nation has a period in which it wakens from sleep and frees itself from its shackles, and takes control of itself and of others" (p. b). "Now it is the time in which the Ethiopian nation is going through an awakening, and therefore it deserves our intellectual attention" (p. j).

The introduction to *The Beautiful Diamonds in the History of the Ethiopians* also includes a long section on the modern collision between Khedive Isma'il and Emperor Yohannes. In al-Qina'i's opinion, the man to blame was none other than the overambitious Egyptian. Isma'il, he wrote, attacked Ethiopia out of greed and because he thought he could defeat it. Egypt paid dearly for this mistake. Though al-Qina'i did not say so directly, his message regarding that fateful chapter comes across clearly: Isma'il did not "leave the Abyssinians alone" and was punished accordingly. Further, it was the khedive and his aggression that inflicted a disaster on Ethiopia's Muslims, for it was in response to his invasions that Yohannes launched his anti-Islamic campaigns. However, the persecution of Muslims in Ethiopia came to an end when Menelik came to power (p. 22).

Like Rida and Tadrus, al-Qina'i also admired Menelik, "the beloved *najashi*" (p. 22), praising him both for dealing justly with Islam and for defeating the Italians at Adwa. "The memory of that defeat, which everyone talks about, is still strong in Italy to this day. . . . [I]t brought about great appreciation of Menelik in European eyes" (pp. 25–26).

Al-Qina'i's book is often referred to by later twentieth-century Egyptian authors. His overall message, though strongly couched in traditional Islamic terminology, was quite compatible with the liberal essence of that era's modern Egyptianism. Yet it was soon replaced as the most-quoted work on Ethiopia in Egypt and the Arab-Islamic world by another book that carried the same message but in modern style and language. *The Voyage to Ethiopia* by the Syrian Sadiq al-Mua'ayyad al-'Azm was published in Cairo in 1908.[18] The author was a member of a leading Damascene family who became a general in the Ottoman army. In 1904 he was sent by Sultan 'Abd al-Hamid to Ethiopia in response to Menelik's overtures regarding Jerusalem and a visit to Istanbul by Ras Makonnen. The Ottomans, as mentioned earlier, had become interested in an independent Ethiopia, especially as they began clashing with the Italians. Sadiq al-'Azm spent several months in Ethiopia. Upon his return to the Ottoman capital near the end of 1904, he published his story in Turkish. In 1908 his two cousins, Haqqi and Rafiq al-'Azm, close associates of Rashid Rida in Cairo, issued an Arabic translation of *The Voyage*.

The 312 pages of the book all praise Ethiopia and its emperor, Menelik II. The Ottoman visitor made his way from Jibuti to Harar, crossing the newly occupied Muslim-inhabited areas of southern Ethiopia. His vivid descriptions of what he saw attested to the benevolence and tolerance of the Christian king. Harar, by his record, was a thriving center of Islamic learning, the home of a large and a prosperous Muslim community. Harar's community leaders and its Islamic scholars and judges were grateful to Ras Makonnen, their governor, for their religious freedom. The same was true of Jimma, the Muslim autonomous principality in the southwest. The brother of its sultan and his sons came to meet the Ottoman envoy. Riding their decorated horses, they were dressed like proud Muslim princes and proved their knowledge in Islamic literature. The Islamic community in Addis Ababa was somewhat less happy. Its leaders complained that there was no mosque nor a Muslim cemetery in the capital. But as the author raised the subject with the emperor, the latter was quick to promise the construction of a main mosque, to be named after Sultan 'Abd al-Hamid.[19]

A chapter of *The Voyage* and an appendix were devoted to the history of Muhammad and the *najashi*. Al-'Azm's emphasis was exclusively on the positive aspects. Though he mentioned the alleged conversion of the *najashi* to Islam, he never used it to undermine Ethiopia's legitimacy. On the contrary, his Ethiopia was a Christian land yet a "land of justice," and Menelik was a modern *najashi*, equally enlightened and noble:

> He [Menelik] then asked me about the historical relations between Ethiopia and the Muslim world, and I started telling his highness in general and in detail on the connection and the exchanging of presents between the Prophet and the *najashi* Ashama, and how the refugees found the best of shelters in Ethiopia, and how many followers of our master Muhammad were Ethiopians. . . . It all made the emperor very happy and he said he wanted the good relations to continue for ever, and that he loved his fellow Muslim Ethiopians like he loved the Amhara without distinction. (P. 230)

Al-'Azm was far from being a blind admirer. He wrote about the cultural tension between Christians and Muslims and mentioned the anti-Islamic atrocities of Yohannes IV. But he described Yohannes's oppressive measures as a reaction to Sudanese-Mahdist aggression and remarked that they were "contrary to the spirit of religious freedom prevailing in this country" (pp. 176–177). The last chapter of *The Voyage* was dedicated to a long analysis of the 1896 Ethiopian victory over the Italians at Adwa (pp. 277–313). It powerfully radiated the notion that Ethiopia was not only a just, benevolent country, but a strong one as well.

The Voyage to Ethiopia became the standard work on Ethiopia in Egypt for many decades. It was written in modern Arabic (Rafiq and Haqqi were to be the founders, together with Rashid Rida, of one of the first modern parties of Arab nationalism in Cairo), and it appealed to the modern educated public. As such, it may be considered of seminal importance. It helped recycle the positive dimensions that Islam had developed regarding Ethiopia and transmitted them to new generations of Egyptian nationalists. Only in 1935 would a book on Ethiopia competing in popularity with *The Voyage* be published in Cairo. *Islam in Ethiopia* by Yusuf Ahmad would reflect the new spirit of the 1930s and, as we shall see, would return to the same Islamic traditions and sources to recycle and transmit their anti-Ethiopian elements.

RENEWED DIALOGUE, FRUITLESS CORDIALITY, 1924–1934

In 1924 the old Egyptian-Ethiopian dialogue was reactivated. It was a year of great hopes for both nations. In Egypt the Wafd Party, the moving factor behind Egyptian parliamentarian nationalism, won the first constitutional elections. In January Sa'd Zaghlul, its charismatic leader, formed his cabinet, popularly known as "the people's government," which lasted until November. It was perhaps the finest year in the history of Egyptian liberalism.

In terms of Ethiopia, 1924 was also a year of great promise in national history, for Ras Tafari, Ethiopia's modern innovator, had just scored a major success. Against strong conservative opposition at home, he led the process of Ethiopia's admission to the League of Nations in September 1923. Tafari, unlike most members of the elite, had little illusion that Ethiopia could go on living off the Adwa legacy and avoiding change. He admired European efficiency and in 1924 made a tour of Europe "to see with my own eyes European civilization and the beauty of the cities of Paris, London, Brussels, Athens and Cairo, about which I have read books, first in school and later on in office."[20] En route to Europe and back, Tafari and his large entourage spent more than two weeks in Egypt (and Jerusalem), from 24 April to 9 May. His visit epitomized the pinnacle of Ethio-Egyptian friendliness.

For Ras Tafari Egypt was now also a gateway to Europe, a land of modernity as well as a historic cradle of universal civilization. He spent most his of time there touring Pharaonic sites and inspecting the Egyptian educational system, including the modern Coptic schools. His hosts, King Fu'ad and Prime Minister Zaghlul, went out of their way to give him a warm, enthusiastic welcome. Though still only an heir to the throne, Tafari was given the complete royal treatment as head of a state of the greatest importance. The educated public, too, was now ready to accept Ethiopia on terms provided by the literature examined above, which had been adopted by the liberal Egyptianism of the 1920s.

Tafari's visit was covered in much detail by the Egyptian press. Articles about Ethiopia, its oriental culture and Semitic languages, and its historic proximity to Egypt continued to appear in the leading newspapers and weeklies, even in July and August.[21] There was hardly any point in remembering the Gura calamity now. An old Egyptian ex-officer lamented this forgetfulness in the popular weekly journal *Al-Kashkul*. He wrote about the atrocities he had suffered at the hands of the Ethiopians when taken prisoner forty-eight years earlier and demanded a boycott of the representative of Ethiopia, "a barbarous land, incapable of change, which should not be accepted among the civilized nations." But his was a lone voice in the wilderness of prevailing cordiality.

For example, a series of three articles appeared on the front page of *Al-Ahram*,[22] beginning with a paragraph on the general ignorance about Ethiopia and Egypt's newly aroused curiosity. The author, "our envoy to Addis Ababa" (the name was not given), was most probably one of the Coptic Egyptian schoolmasters in Ethiopia. He had spent five years in Ethiopia and was in a good position to give solid, basic information. His

articles were full of data on Ethiopia: ethnic structure, political institutions, languages, customs, a summary of its history, the image of Tafari.
It is apparent that he wanted to enhance positive attitudes. He did his best
to emphasize how much Ethiopian culture was an extension of oriental
civilization, even including a strange story that the Ethiopian language of
Geez had originated in Gaza, "a port in Palestine with which ancient
Ethiopians traded." Ethiopians, in their color and appearance, he wrote,
were not that different from Arabs. An Arabic speaker would feel at
home there and be able to communicate, even though no Ethiopian could
speak real Arabic.

Al-Ahram's correspondent to Addis Ababa also wrote about the
Solomonian ethos and referred to it as a dimension of Ethiopia's oriental
connection. At the same time, he avoided any mention of the Christian-
Islamic dichotomy in Ethiopia's history. For example, he told his readers
about Tafari's road to power and his conflict with the declared heir of
Emperor Menelik II, his grandson Lij Iyasu (who reigned from 1913 to
1916), yet he chose to ignore any mention of Iyasu's alleged conversion
to Islam as the official reason for his 1916 deposition by Tafari's camp.
He said only that Menelik's heir was deposed "because he did not be-
have according to the country's customs." The articles contained no patronizing attitudes, even when the author surveyed the poor state of infrastructure and of modern education. He wrote that the number of
Ethiopians who had received a regular education was very small but
added immediately that by nature the Ethiopians were a very sophisticated people and "perhaps the best politicians in the world." Their best
leader, he wrote, was Tafari, portraying him as an educated person, fluent in French, even speaking some Arabic, and the great pioneer of modernization. He described Tafari as the initiator of change, standing firm
against the entrenched conservatism of the old guard. Tafari, he concluded, attached great importance to his visit to the West. In preparation
for the event Tafari had written a pamphlet, published in Amharic, encouraging the young to venture out, see Europe, and learn. It contained
practical advice as to how an Ethiopian could witness the achievements
of modernization without exposing his own ignorance.

Nearly all the dozens of articles in various newspapers were titled
"The Visit of the Heir to the Ethiopian Throne." Tafari was not yet a *najashi* of Ethiopia, and perhaps conveniently, the Egyptian press could
thus avoid writing about Islamic traditions. Even so, some of these articles reflected the traditional ambivalence. In *Al-Kashkul,* for instance, a
long letter by one reader was published,[23] reconstructing a conversation
about Tafari's visit he had overheard (probably fictitious; this was a popular literary device at the time). It began with a Muslim scholar of
Al-Azhar complaining about the excessive attention given to the

Ethiopian guest. A commander in the Egyptian navy replied that it was well deserved, since Egypt and Ethiopia were both in need of mutual understanding. An engineer then said that there was no technical feasibility to the assumption that the Ethiopians could block the Nile. A citizen added that the Ethiopians, with the help of the British, were considering invading and conquering the Sudan, to which the naval commander replied that they were not militarily capable of so doing. The Al-Azhar scholar said that they, the Ethiopians, were very devious and shrewd, and they might indeed capture the Sudan (and the Upper Nile). The engineer agreed, adding that the Ethiopians had proven their military might by defeating Egypt at Gura. But the naval commander assured him that the 1876 defeat was a result of stupid intelligence mistakes, not a true reflection of Ethiopian power.

Behind the apparent friendliness and mutual respect, there continued to loom the old, concrete issues of the Nile and the Coptic Church. Very little progress was made on these issues during the 1924 visit or the next ten years.

During Tafari's visit to Cairo in 1924, Anglo-Ethiopian interest in the Tana dam was a burning issue, but the Egyptians themselves, as mentioned earlier, had no say in it.[24] Kept in the dark about such a cardinal issue, numerous journalists discussed and repeated Egypt's old fear that Ethiopia might one day block the Nile; some articles mentioned related medieval incidents.[25] The Lake Tana project, apparently, was not discussed in Tafari's meetings with Egyptian leaders. Tafari visited a Delta barrage site, the only official tour connected with the Nile. Though Tafari was in the middle of a very difficult and frustrating dialogue with the British over the Nile, it is quite evident that he cooperated with the British in concealing the dialogue from his hosts. Tafari held his Nile cards close to his chest and ignored the Egyptians. (Thirty-five years later he would visit Cairo again. Then, in 1959, it would be his turn to protest Egypt ignoring Ethiopia as a Nile country.)

As far as Ethiopia was concerned, Ras Tafari left Egypt empty-handed in 1924. On his arrival in Cairo his main, practical goal was to advance the ancient church issue. He met with the patriarch, with members of the Coptic Holy Synod of bishops, and with their community council, and he made the demand he would repeat for the next twenty-four years: that his country be assigned an Ethiopian *abun* (following the death of Abuna Matewos) who would have the power, granted by the Egyptian patriarch, to appoint bishops. No less forcefully, he demanded the keys to the Jerusalem convent of Deir al-Sultan. But despite the general friendly atmosphere in 1924, Ras Tafari achieved nothing. The more secular wing of the Coptic community was evidently willing to compromise at least on the keys to the Jerusalem convent, but the church establishment proved less flexible. The request for an Ethiopian to replace old Abuna Matewos upon his death was flatly denied,[26] and Tafari returned, greatly frustrated, to Ethiopia to face his rivals in the conservative establishment, led by Empress Zawditu, by another prominent member of the local nobility, and by Abuna Matewos himself.

The issue of the Egyptian *abun* became a major factor in Tafari's 1925–1930 struggle for the imperial throne and absolutism.[27] The ambitious, modern-oriented prince cultivated a new generation of young intellectuals who worked to undermine the old conservative guard. One way to do this was through the new nationalist demand to Ethiopianize the church. A major platform in this context was the first Amharic weekly magazine, *Berhannena Salam,* which Tafari established on 1 January 1925. "Young Ethiopians" such as Mahtema-Worq Eshete, the editor of the weekly, spared no rhetoric in exposing Abuna Matewos as a greedy foreigner, unfaithful to Ethiopian interests.[28] Other articles began challenging the very premise of the traditional connection to the Egyptian Church. On 10 February 1927, for example, another young scholar, Afaworqi Gabra-Iyasus, informed the readers of *Berhannena Salam* that the historical-legal aspect behind the ancient tradition was questionable, arguing that the relevant article in the *Fatha Nagast,* allegedly based on the canon of the Council of Nicaea (of A.D. 325), had been forged by the compiler of the Ethiopian legal code, the Egyptian Coptic scholar Ibn al-Assal.

On 10 March 1927 Tesfahun Abebe devoted the weekly's leading article to Egyptian-Ethiopian relations. Although he titled it "On Friendship and Brotherhood" and defined relations as uniquely close and based on blood ties, he stated that the Ethiopians hated "the Coptic demand to control their church" and implied that Ethiopia might use its ability to control the Nile waters. The opening article of 14 April 1927 focused on the Deir al-Sultan issue, arguing that the Egyptian position stemmed from paternalism and deceit. Other young intellectuals went on to label the church connection "religious imperialism" and "Coptic tyranny" and demanded that Ethiopia raise the matter at the League of Nations.[29]

Tafari worked to undermine the aging Abuna Matewos by tightening imperial control over the church. In September 1926 he imposed new church regulations that officially diverted most administrative authorities to the *echage.* When Abuna Matewos died in December 1926, Tafari intensified his contacts with the Egyptian Church and government. His tactics (quite similar in principle to his game with the British over the proposed dam at Lake Tana) were to convey the anti-Coptic messages of Ethiopia's new generation, including their clear threat to cut relations altogether, but at the same time define himself as a moderate, demanding only that the new Egyptian *abun* have the authority to consecrate Ethiopian bishops. Negotiations with the Egyptians continued for nearly three years, until May 1929, when the new Abuna Qerilos VI was appointed to the Ethiopian Church.

Due to the involvement of the Egyptian government, the Coptic Church was now ready to compromise. The new Egyptian *abun* himself was not authorized to appoint bishops, but three Ethiopian monks were sent to Egypt and were consecrated as bishops by the patriarch. They were the very first Ethiopian bishops.[30] However, prior to their consecration in Cairo they were obliged to take an oath never to become involved in the election of an *abun*. The following year, early in 1930, Patriarch Yohannes paid a visit to Ethiopia,[31] consecrating the *echage* as a fourth Ethiopian bishop to work under Abuna Qerilos. When Ras Tafari was crowned by Abuna Qerilos as Haile Selassie I in November 1930, a high-ranking Egyptian delegation arrived, including the patriarch's representative, Archbishop Yusab. The latter was a member of an emerging pro-Ethiopian faction in the Egyptian Coptic Church. His alliance with the new emperor was to be of great significance.

During the five years prior to the outbreak of war with Mussolini, Haile Selassie quickened the pace of reform. As far as this study is concerned, he did his best to marginalize Abuna Qerilos's public role while he himself continued to be the initiator of change. These changes took place in at least four areas: he obtained full imperial control over the church treasury and assets (working with the *echage* and the new Ethiopian bishops); he deprived the priesthood of its judiciary powers, even in remote provinces, by declaring and implementing the 1931 Constitution; he eroded the church's monopoly in education by accelerating the revolution in general secular education; and he saw to the Amharization of Scriptures and Liturgy (a full translation of the Bible into Amharic was completed in 1934).[32] By switching the emphasis from the dead language of Geez, possessed almost exclusively by the priesthood, to the modernized, Pan-Ethiopian Amharic, he not only furthered nationalization of the church, but also tried to bridge the gap between the new generation of young intellectuals, whose emergence he had initiated, and Ethiopia's Christian legacy, of which he remained a pious devotee. As for the Egyptian Copts, Haile Selassie could only send some signals of reserved dissatisfaction during the period 1930–1935.

A modicum of disillusionment with Egyptian inflexibility can be discerned in the writings of Heruy Walda-Selassie, Haile Selassie's chief negotiator with the Egyptians, his foreign minister, and a well-known author. Heruy, Ethiopia's leading authority on church history at the time,[33] published two books following his 1923 and 1924 visits to Egypt (his two sons studied in Alexandria).[34] In both books he admired Egyptian progress (especially in education) and described relations during Tafari's early negotiations in the most cordial terms. His last prewar visit

to Cairo in 1933 also dealt with the issues of Deir al-Sultan and the
emperor's renewed demand that an Ethiopian succeed Qerilos as *abun,*
but his meetings with Patriarch Yohannes and with King Fu'ad bore no
fruit. Another of his books, published in 1934 and describing his last
tour of Egypt, reflected much less cordiality.[35]

NOTES

1. Tafla, "The Father of Rivers."
2. For a recent description of Ethiopian traditions and folklore regarding
the Nile, see Morrell and Wier, "The Blue Nile," an article based on a rafting expedition along the Ethiopian Abbai that analyzes how "the legendary river in-
spires both reverence and fear among the Ethiopians who live along its banks."
3. For Ethiopian enterprise in Jerusalem at that time, see a summary in
Erlich, *Ethiopia and the Middle East,* pp. 76–77 and nn. 28–31.
4. The following section on the Lake Tana negotiations is based primarily on
Ahmad, "Gojjam," chap. 7, and McCann, "Ethiopia, Britain, and Negotiations."
5. Tafla, "The Father of Rivers."
6. McCann, "Ethiopia, Britain, and Negotiations."
7. Ahmad, "Gojjam," p. 304.
8. Ahmad, "Lake Tana in Italian Expansionist Thinking."
9. For a fresh discussion of the Nile's centrality in Egyptian nationalism,
see Troutt Powell, "Brothers Along the Nile," and Gershoni, "Geographers and
Nationalism in Egypt."
10. Sarhank, *Haqa'iq al-akhbar fi duwal al-bihar.*
11. Rif'at, *Kitab jabr al-kasr.*
12. In his book *Egypt's Road to Jerusalem,* the Coptic intellectual and
diplomat (and a main figure in our story later) Boutros Boutros-Ghali analyzed
Egyptian involvement in the 1977–1978 Ethiopian-Somali conflict. In a chapter
titled "The Somali Syndrome," he stated that the Egyptian military had strong
ties to the legacy of Isma'il's era: "Egyptian policy favored Somalia," he wrote,
"a Muslim country whose ports had been taken by Egypt during the 'Egyptian
empire' of the Mehmet Ali dynasty, a part of the Ottoman Empire. Strong ties to
Somalia existed in the minds of many in the Egyptian military." When Boutros-
Ghali tried to explain to General 'Abd al-Ghani al-Ghamasi (then minister of defense) that because of the Nile, Egypt should not make an enemy of Ethiopia, the
general "seemed to believe that I was favoring Ethiopia because it was a Christian state. 'Do you want to defend the Coptic Church in Ethiopia?' he asked"
(pp. 62–63).
13. See Meinardus, *Christian Egypt,* pp. 28–29, 32.
14. Kirlus, *Muhadara 'an al-habasha.*
15. Tadrus, *Hadir al-habasha wa-mustaqbaluha.*
16. "Al-Habasha," *Al-Manar,* vol. 1, no. 1 (1897): 27–30.
17. Al-Qina'i, *Al-Jawahir al-hisan fi ta'rikh al-hubshan.*
18. Al-'Azm, *Rihlat al-habasha.*
19. See a more detailed analysis of this book, as well as fuller references, in
Erlich, *Ethiopia and the Middle East,* pp. 77–82.

20. Haile Selassie, *Autobiography,* p. 84. The memoirs contain a detailed description of the journey to Egypt and to Jerusalem.

21. See, for example, an article titled "Ethiopia and Its Population," *Al-Hilal,* 1 July 1924, which stated that the culture of Ethiopia was connected with Egypt and the Arabian Peninsula, that its merchants were mostly Arabs, and that its church was Egyptian. See also a two-article series in *Al-Muqtataf,* 1 July and 1 August 1924, which contains a description of Egypt's dependence on the Nile stemming from Ethiopia and brings up a related eleventh-century episode.

22. See "Wali 'ahd al-habasha" (The Ethiopian Heir to the Throne), as well as a second part to the article on an inside page, *Al-Ahram,* 3 May 1924, p. 1, and the final installment in the series in *Al-Ahram,* 4 May 1924.

23. The following passage is a summary of a letter by Zakariyya al-Maraghi, *Al-Kashkul,* 16 May 1924.

24. For British efforts to conceal their negotiations from the Egyptians, see Public Record Office (hereafter PRO) Foreign Office 371/9989, Allenby to Mac-Donald, 17 May 1924. (The British decided to talk to Tafari about the matter in London only and invited the relevant Ethiopian chiefs, Ras Hailu and Ras Nado, to return via the Sudan.)

25. For example, *Al-Muqattam,* 3 and 9 May 1924; *Al-Muqtataf,* 1 July 1924.

26. See *Al-Kashkul,* 27 August 1926.

27. See Marcus, *Haile Selassie I,* chap. 5.

28. See *Berhannena Salam,* 22 April, 13 May, and 29 July 1926.

29. *Berhannena Salam,* 26 August 1926 and 27 January, 5 February, and 21 April 1927. See also Amanu, "The Ethiopian Orthodox Church."

30. See a long opening article in *Berhannena Salam,* 15 June 1929: "On the Appointment of One Egyptian *Abun* and Five Ethiopian Bishops."

31. See description in *Berhannena Salam,* 23 January 1930.

32. See reports in PRO Foreign Office 371/22024, "The 'Great Bible' of Ethiopia."

33. Heruy's history of the church and its medieval relations with the Copts was published in Addis Ababa in 1921, titled *Wazema* (Amharic for Vigil, the day and night before church festivities). See also Amanu, "The Ethiopian Orthodox Church."

34. Walda-Selassie, *Yale' lat wayzaro Manan* (1923) and *Dastana kibir* (1924).

35. Walda-Selassie, *Ba' adame masinbat hulun lamayet.*

6

Stormy Redefinitions, 1935–1942

The year of the "Abyssinian crisis," 1935, during which Ethiopia was threatened by Mussolini, and the subsequent 1936–1941 span, when Ethiopia was occupied by the Italian Fascists, constituted a short but intensive period of change and redefinition. And for Egypt 1935–1936 was perhaps a watershed period in the history of its young parliamentary system. As totalitarian Europe began to spread its new options and ideas, an emerging generation, frustrated with the nationalistically bland and socially indifferent leadership of the liberal elite, began challenging the system. It would do so, in part, by adopting renewed Islamic concepts, as well as those of modern Pan-Arabism. The intensifying interplay between these dimensions of identity is, in itself, outside our present discussion.[1] However, this interplay also revolved around a lively debate on the Upper Nile country threatened by Mussolini. Old and new concepts of Ethiopia were forcefully readdressed and would continue to influence interpretations of the Ethiopian "other" by proponents of Egyptian nationalism, Arabism, and political Islam.

Suffering the shock of a brutal conquest for the first time since the sixteenth century, Ethiopia experienced tremendous changes. The five short years of humiliation under the rule of European Fascists would provide the country with an opportunity to reappraise its relations with Egypt. During their 1936–1941 occupation the Fascists did little about the Nile, but they deliberately made Ethiopia's religious identity a major issue. Bent on isolating Christian Ethiopia, they forced the ancient Ethiopian Church to sever its relations with Egypt and declared the church autocephalous. In 1942, however, some time after liberation, Haile Selassie decided to reestablish church ties with Egypt and resume the ancient dependence, affiliation, and bond. In his effort to rebuild

Ethiopia he would consider its special ties with Egypt an inseparable part of Ethiopia's modernization.

EGYPT AND THE 1935 "ABYSSINIAN CRISIS"

In 1935, confronted by Mussolini's threats, the Ethiopians were too overwhelmed to expect any substantial assistance from Egypt. A few Ethiopian emissaries were sent to Cairo in a vain attempt to make contact with the Sanusis in Libya, so as to spark anti-Italian riots there. Haile Selassie also tried to stem Fascist propaganda and weaken its effect on Ethiopia's Muslim community. In this he was aided by the leadership of Al-Azhar University, which in February 1935 sent two Azhari shaikhs from Cairo to Addis Ababa to open a *madrasa* in the Ethiopian capital and help rally support around the emperor. There were other manifestations of Egyptian aid during that year. In late 1935, soon after the beginning of the Italian invasion, Egypt actually sent volunteers (mostly Ethiopians residing in Egypt), led by two retired Ottoman generals, and three Red Crescent medical teams, all of whom saw action on the Harar front.[2] These were significant symbolic gestures of solidarity, the importance of which can best be appreciated in the Egyptian context.

Indeed, it is from the Egyptian perspective that the Abyssinian crisis can be described as perhaps the most revealing event in Ethiopian-Egyptian relations. For as Mussolini defied the entire system of international relations, the year 1935 became a major chapter in Egypt's history. Egypt's political public—the old guard of rival politicians and a new emerging generation of the educated *effendiyya*—long engaged in the nationalist struggle for liberation from the British, was now torn between various pressing dilemmas. An intense public debate on the nature of fascism ensued.[3] Mussolini's aggression had a double impact: in challenging the regional supremacy of the British and French, he opened new strategic options; in threatening an Eastern neighbor with violence, he revived and magnified old fears. Mussolini also introduced new forms into the political system, focusing on increased national pride and strength, and his image spurred Egypt's curiosity. The debate culminated in the year of the Abyssinian crisis and helped Egyptians realize where they really stood on democracy and parliamentarianism. Recent studies show convincingly that the overwhelming majority of opinionmakers in Egypt at that time despised fascist totalitarianism and publicly defended political openness, a topic outside our present scope.

Mussolini also represented a new and more violent form of Western imperialist aggression. Faced with this, Egypt naturally perceived Ethiopia as a negative mirror image, and Egyptian debate on this issue during

1935 was intense. But while the discussion of Mussolini and fascism was somewhat external, having to do with strategic options and the nature of politics, the debate over Ethiopia touched the very heart of Egyptian identity. In hundreds of newspaper articles, pamphlets, and books published in Egypt that year, Ethiopia was discussed in terms of its legacies during mutual regional relations, in terms of old Islamic perceptions, in terms of ancient and modern Egyptian ideas of Ethiopia, and in terms of the renewed concepts of emerging Pan-Arabism. *Al-mas'ala al-habashiyya*—the Ethiopian question—was not merely a discussion of the "other; it was also a reflection of different ideas and concepts regarding the Egyptian self-image.

Islamic Dual Perceptions

It has long been accepted that the 1930s witnessed "the return of Islam" in Egypt. Until recently this "return" was interpreted as implying the abandonment of Western ideas of tolerance and liberalism by many intellectuals. Recent studies accept the notion of this return, but they tend to highlight liberal dimensions in this renewed Islamic orientation. Examination of the Ethiopian case seems to support both observations—namely, that of liberal Islam on the one hand and that of the rather reactionary nature of a rising radical wing on the other.

Most of the Islamic-inspired expressions and actions in Egypt of 1935 were consonant with antifascist and pro-Ethiopian expressions made by Egypt's liberals. They all resorted to the medieval image of noble Ethiopia, emphasizing Islam's tolerance. Shaikh Muhammad Rashid Rida, the aging and exhausted leader of the Al-Salafiyya movement (d. December 1935), still led the field. He also inspired his followers to real action. The Young Men's Muslim Associations, guided by Rida since the 1920s, became Ethiopia's most energetic supporter. In early 1935 leaders of the organization established a Committee for the Defense of Ethiopia, later joined by other elements.[4] This committee, in which the Young Muslims remained prominent, helped to send the two Azhari shaikhs mentioned earlier to Addis Ababa and supervised the enlistment of volunteers. The committee also raised contributions for an "Ethiopian fund," which financed transportation for the three Red Crescent medical teams to the battlefield.

Needless to say, this expression of solidarity with Egypt's oppressed Christian neighbor was also clear support for an interpretation of Islam as an open and liberal religion. In 1935, however, this was not the only voice of Islam in Egypt. A more militant and less flexible Islam was on the rise, which, as it asserted itself, also dealt with the Ethiopian dimension.

The most prominent manifestation of this Islamic anti-Ethiopian stand in Egypt was the publication in November 1935 of a book called *Islam in Ethiopia*. Written by Yusuf Ahmad, a teacher and former inspector in the government's Department of Antiquities, and subsidized by the Italian legation, it was a harsh condemnation of Ethiopia and a clear call for its destruction in the name of Islam.[5] Resorting to old traditions, fomenting whatever was there of popular anti-Ethiopian racism, and using some elements of modern research, Ahmad described Ethiopia's major sins toward Islam in general and toward Ethiopia's own Muslims in particular. He provided extremely unbalanced surveys of the Islamic policies of Emperors Tewodros II (p. 46), Yohannes IV (depicted as a barbarous killer of innocent Egyptians at Gura and a cruel crusader against Ethiopia's Muslims, pp. 47–49), Menelik II (who conquered Islam in Ethiopia and destroyed its culture, pp. 49–54), and Haile Selassie (mocked by the author for finally agreeing to build a mosque in Addis Ababa, p. 77). Nearly every point made by Ahmad reflected an effort to expose Ethiopia as the worst enemy of Islam.[6]

The book's opening premise was that the initial *sahaba-najashi* story was an indication of Ethiopia's anti-Islamic nature. In his first chapter Ahmad wrote:

> Some writers talk of the *sahaba* as a reason to support Ethiopia. We want to explain that if we have some sympathy toward Ethiopia it is because Ethiopia is an Eastern country facing a Western one, but not because of anything historical. As for the honor given to the *sahaba,* it was by one man only, *najashi* Ashama. Indeed, he converted to Islam, but he had to conceal it from his people until he died. . . . As for the priests and the people, they gave the *sahaba* only troubles. They rebelled against the *najashi* because he was good to the Muslims. (Pp. 4–5)

In subsequent pages the author interpreted later Islamic sources as proving that "what the *sahaba* had met with in Ethiopia was only hatred. . . . If it had not been for the *najashi,* they would all have become Christians, died, or returned to Mecca so that the Quraysh could do with them as they pleased. . . . So what right do they have that we shall remember this story in their favor? They never respected them and only tortured them" (p. 20).

Ahmad went on to narrate an eighth-century incident in which Ethiopians killed a Muslim who fled to their country, in order to manipulate hidden racist attitudes of his 1935 readers: " And look at that savage people! How do they treat refugees who seek shelter in their country? They received them with swords, killing and expelling them" (pp.

28–29). In his conclusion the author made three claims: first, that the history of Ethiopia vis-à-vis Islam was a story of injustice; second, that the majority of the Muslims in Ethiopia were not Ethiopians—they differed essentially in language, race, and culture. He argued that they were Arabs, racially different from the barbarous Christians, and stated that their main language was Arabic, "which they have preserved since the time of their ancestors' arrival from Yemen and the Hijaz" (p. 61). And the third claim was that the majority of these Muslims lived outside historic Ethiopia and deserved complete freedom (p. 104).

In summary, Yusuf Ahmad believed that the oppressed Muslims under backward Christian Ethiopia were entitled to both Islamic and Arab liberation. He clearly implied that he looked forward to seeing such liberation promoted and achieved by Mussolini. Indeed, another book, *Italy and Her Colonies*, written by Shaikh Muhammad Num Bakr and published in Cairo in 1936, ran along the same lines, describing Mussolini as a champion and savior of Islam in Libya and wishing an equally enlightened occupation of Ethiopia.[7]

Ahmad's book was widely read. In the months following its publication newspapers such as *Al-Balagh* and *Ruz al-Yusuf* reprinted entire chapters. A very favorable review appeared in the prestigious monthly magazine *Al-Hilal*. In years to come *Islam in Ethiopia* was to become the standard text on that country for Arabic readers in the Middle East. In this capacity it went on competing with the 1908 publication *Voyage to Ethiopia* by Sadiq al-'Azm mentioned in Chapter 5, which radiated the spirit of Islamic openness and advocated recognition of Christian Ethiopia as a respected neighbor. For the Islamic radicals Ahmad's book would replace al-'Azm's. In fact, radical Islamic literature produced in Egypt today still recycles large portions of *Islam in Ethiopia*, preaching the same concept of Ethiopia's illegitimacy.

In any case, Ethiopia had been conquered by the end of May 1936, and its struggle was no longer a major focus of interest. Other issues, such as the outbreak of the Arab revolt in Palestine in April 1936, captured public attention. In the midst of all the excitement, the Society of the Muslim Brothers (distinct from the Young Men's Muslim Association) had begun gaining momentum in Cairo. It began preaching a more militant Islam, though one still much more moderate than that embraced by later radicalism. From our point of view, however, the following episode is worth mentioning. When the Arab revolt in Palestine broke out, the "general guide" of the Muslim Brothers, Shaikh Hasan al-Banna, turned to Prince 'Umar Tusun, the head of the Committee for the Defense of Ethiopia, and in the name of Islam demanded that the Ethiopian fund be transferred to help fellow Muslims struggling in Palestine. His demand was rejected. Tusun replied that the money was not only of Muslim origins. It had been donated by Egyptian Muslims, Christians, and Jews alike, and for the sake of pluralism should remain in the service of the Ethiopian cause.[8]

Egyptian Nationalism: Militancy and Liberalism

Prince Tusun's reply reflected a modern Egyptian concept of Ethiopia, a very positive dimension of pluralist Egyptian nationalism to which we shall turn shortly. In 1935 the majority of modern Egyptian nationalists detested Mussolini and identified with Ethiopia. The Committee for the Defense of Ethiopia, which supervised the activities and gestures mentioned earlier, was a coalition of moderate Muslims, modern Coptic leaders, and liberal Egyptians. However, Egyptian nationalism, a modern identity that began to emerge in the late nineteenth century, was divided in regard to Ethiopia.

On the one hand, as noted earlier, a favorable concept of Ethiopia had appeared for a variety of reasons. First was the renewed definition of Egypt as the land of the Nile, which held Ethiopia to be relevant. Second was the growing sense of equality of the Egyptian Copts, whose Ethiopian connections need no reminder. Third was the entire regional concept rooted in both the Nile Valley definition of Egypt as well as in the new, pluralist Egyptian self. Within this concept of a pluralist, diversified, yet united East, Ethiopia, considered Eastern in its religions, culture, and languages, was perceived as a fully legitimate partner. The extent of this positive image of Ethiopia, instilled partly by the authors discussed above, was internalized by the Egyptian public and perhaps exemplified by a poem written in 1932 by Ahmad Shawqi, Egypt's "prince of the poets":

> The Nile is the *najashi,* his sweetness is dark
> Golden and marble his wonder of spark,
> On *arghul* [a playing instrument] he is playing
> For us the Nile is praying
> Our lives does he give
> May forever he live.

This verse, identifying the Egyptian river with the noble, righteous Ethiopian king, became a very popular song. "Al-Nil najashi" was sung by the great singer Muhammad 'Abd al-Wahhab in the popular 1933 Egyptian film *The White Rose.* It virtually became a classic and was still popular in Arab countries at the end of the twentieth century.

On the other hand, as in the case of Islam's dichotomy and not entirely divorced from it, Egyptian nationalism had also developed a distinctly negative view of Ethiopia. It essentially stemmed from the ancient fear that Ethiopia would divert the waters of the Nile, a fear that grew with the renewed conceptual and practical centrality of the river. Interwoven with this anxiety was a sense of anger and shame in the wake of the 1876 defeat at Gura. The image of a barbarous Ethiopia ambushing an army that had been sent to spread advanced civilization in Africa, and then maltreating Egyptian prisoners, was burned into Egypt's modern collective memory. The Gura episode, Ethiopia's savage image, and—most importantly—its thwarting of Egypt's dream of unity along the Nile were themes that were recycled and retold on many occasions. Modern Egyptians of more militant bent could scarcely forgive Ethiopia.[9]

A more militant Egyptian nationalism was on the rise during the 1930s. Many members of the new generation, some established thinkers, and several movements such as Young Egypt came forward with a less pluralistic concept of Egyptian nationalism, one ready to abandon parliamentarianism in favor of military pride and authoritarian politics. Their flirtation with fascism and Mussolini is a subject of some controversy, but we shall confine ourselves to a short observation from the Ethiopian angle. In 1935 the overwhelming majority of Egyptian public opinion strongly disapproved of Mussolini's aggression. The Abyssinian question, at least for a while, exposed both the crude imperialism and the racism inherent in fascism. Thinkers such as Salama Musa,[10] youth leaders such as Fathi Radwan,[11] and others were now ready to declare their solidarity with Ethiopia. Members of Young Egypt participated in related activities. In this respect, at least during the year of "the crisis," Egypt's nationalistic-militant wing was clearly in favor of Ethiopia's survival. It was not, however, ready to go beyond this declaration and showed no real curiosity toward Ethiopia itself, its culture, or its history. After the Italian occupation of Ethiopia some Egyptian historians found the time to lament the demise of Khedive Isma'il's "civilizing mission" in the Horn of Africa during the 1870s.[12]

The mainstream of Egyptian modern nationalism, however, was quite prepared to cross this line and wholeheartedly identified with Ethiopia in 1935. Most opinionmakers attacked Mussolini in defense of political openness. At the same time, they also rediscovered Ethiopia, and for the same purpose.

The quantity of relevant literature produced in Egypt that year was enormous. The "Abyssinian question," in both its Italian and Ethiopian dimensions, was the main issue and a most stormy one. Hundreds of newspaper articles dealt with Ethiopia, as did dozens of analytical pieces and quite a number of books. Many newspapers, notably *Al-Ahram,* ran daily columns, even dispatching special correspondents to Addis Ababa. The leading opinionmakers were Muhammad 'Abdallah 'Inan,[13] 'Abdallah Husayn,[14] Ahmad Hasan al-Zayyat,[15] and, primarily, Muhammad Lutfi Jum'a. The latter, the author of the famous *The Life of the East* (1932), was a very prominent advocate of the concept of "Easternism," the idea that all Eastern peoples facing the Western challenge should enhance their cultural affinity and cooperate politically. Another of his books, *The African Lion and the Italian Tiger,*[16] depicted Ethiopia as the symbol of the entire East, its leader in the areas of bravery and survival. He went on to review Ethiopia's history, explaining in most sympathetic terms its development and victories. Like almost all of the other authors mentioned here, he wrote that he felt the need to reintroduce Ethiopia to himself and to the Egyptian public. He described Ethiopia's land, Christianity, customs, and social diversity, and he praised its leaders for their efforts at modernization. He wrote: "We are interested in Ethiopia because it represents both the East and Africa at their very best and most lofty—in terms of beauty, form, quality and dignity" (p. 9). He also referred to the old Islamic idea of Ethiopia as the land of righteousness. Published in November 1935, Jum'a's *African Lion and Italian Tiger* was the polar opposite of Yusuf Ahmad's radical Islamic and indeed racist *Islam in Ethiopia.* Both books, in trying to influence a whole new young generation storming into politics, derived from the rich, diversified reservoir of popular Ethiopian images. Paradoxically, both books were equally popular.

Needless to say, most modern Egyptians yearned for an Ethiopian victory. This time they did not ignore the 1896 Adwa victory, but rather anticipated its reoccurrence. For liberals like Jum'a such an Ethiopian victory would have enhanced liberalism and parliamentarianism in Egypt. 'Abdallah 'Inan (and many others) kept reminding the Italians of Adwa. Yet, although Jum'a predicted the African lion would defeat the Italian tiger again, a new Adwa was not to occur. Instead, the history of Egypt, its immediate politics, and its own struggle to shape its identity were forced to develop under the shadow of Mussolini's success.

Arab Nationalists and Their Ethiopian Dichotomy

The year of the Abyssinian crisis was also most significant in the history of the Arab modern identity. Mussolini's defiance of the British and the French, his militant nationalism, and fascism's emphasis on the spirit of youth were instrumental in triggering the wave of the younger generation in politics. In Egypt, Syria, Palestine, and Iraq the Abyssinian crisis was a factor in inspiring the emergence of paramilitary youth organizations, as well as in the strengthening of Pan-Arabism as the ideology of the *effendiyya*. The consequences for the history of Egypt and the entire region were far reaching, though our discussion refers only to its Egyptian dimension during the formative crisis.

Arab identity in Egypt was, at that time, an emerging element, blended primarily in the integral Egyptian nationalism of the kind mentioned above. In order to observe it in isolation, we must refer to Syrians and Iraqis residing, or influencing the debate, in Egypt. In so doing, we encounter another dichotomy reflecting an equally intense debate over Ethiopia in Syria that year.

On the one hand, again, Ethiopia found supporters. Dr. 'Abd al Rahman Shahbandar, the national Syrian Arab hero of the 1925 anti-French revolt, long exiled in Egypt, became an important figure in this history. He joined the Committee for the Defense of Ethiopia and, himself a physician, was active in organizing the Red Crescent medical aid. He published articles in the Egyptian press in which he stated that Ethiopia represented all Eastern peoples and that he was ready to die for it the way he was ready to die for Syria.[17] Another Syrian residing in Egypt, historian Amin Sa'id, published a series of pro-Ethiopian articles in the daily *Al-Muqattam,* a major platform for Egyptian liberals. He stated that the Arabs and the Ethiopians had always, even in pre-Islamic days, been part of the Orient and that all Arabs should be committed to supporting their Ethiopian sister on the basis of that Eastern bond.[18]

General Taha al-Hashimi, a sworn Pan-Arab Iraqi, one of Iraq's most important politicians, and the chief of staff of the Iraqi army at the time, answered the call of the Egyptian weekly *Al-Risala* to explain the military dimensions of the crisis, Egypt at that time having no generals of its own. He produced a series of six articles published in the last weeks of 1935, the subject of which was Ethiopia's 1896 defeat of the invading Italians at Adwa and the message of which, in terms of Arab hopes and expectations, was clear.[19]

Stronger, however, was the voice of anti-Ethiopian Arab nationalists. Bulus Mas'ad, a Lebanese Christian, a resident of Cairo, a journalist, and an author of various works on Arab history, published a book titled *Ethiopia or Abyssinia.*[20] Like Yusuf Ahmad's book, it was also subsidized by the Italian legation in Cairo, and it was equally venomous. The difference was that Mas'ad narrated Ethiopian history, depicting the country as barbarous and primitive, not in Islamic terms, but in modern progressive ones. He recycled material supplied to him by fascist propaganda machinery on Ethiopia, describing a cruel house of slavery, a land in need of a civilizing Mussolini.

Much more important was the work of Amir Shakib Arslan, a Lebanese Druze. Arslan was by far the most important figure in the context of Mussolini's influence in the entire Middle Eastern arena. He undertook to spread the word of Il Duce and to exploit the Abyssinian crisis in order to inspire the younger generations in the Middle East to revolt against the French and the British. He hoped that such an uprising would enhance Pan-Arabism, especially his brand of it—namely, Arabism with a strong element of Islamic identity and solidarity. In the dozens of articles he published in 1935, Arslan depicted Ethiopia as a historical enemy of Islam, an oppressor of its own Muslims, an enemy of the Arabic language and Arab culture. A skilled historian, he combined the negative messages of radical Islam with the modern messages of fascist propaganda.[21] Most of Arslan's work was published primarily in Syrian, Lebanese, and Palestinian papers; nevertheless, he had his share in the Egyptian press and was widely read in Egypt.

EGYPTIAN NATIONALISM AND MUSSOLINI'S CONQUEST, 1935–1941

The Italian conquest of Ethiopia and the implementation of fascist imperialism led to yet another moment of truth for Egypt's conceptualization of the Ethiopian connection. This time it focused more on church relations, reflecting a phase of Egypt's pluralist acceptance of the Copts and their Ethiopian dimension that was still valid.

Mussolini's fascist regime destroyed the Ethiopian empire and replaced it with Italian East Africa, which the occupiers restructured by separating ethnic and religious communities. The Fascists promoted Islam at a revolutionary pace and tried to reshape the church in order to detach it from Ethiopian imperial tradition. They also took revenge on the clergy for their leading role in the resistance, massacring priests and executing Bishop Petros, one of the first Ethiopians to be appointed in 1929. They took control of church infrastructure but allowed it some of the administrative and spiritual autonomy eroded by Haile Selassie.[22] In so doing, they found the Egyptian Abuna Qerilos quite cooperative; he made no real protest against the massacres or executions. His cooperation ended, however, when the Fascists decided, for obvious strategic reasons, to break the Egyptian-Ethiopian connection. In early June 1937 the Italians sent Abuna Qerilos IV to Rome, but even a fifteen-minute meeting with Mussolini could not persuade him to accept separation.[23] He then returned to Egypt on a pretext of illness while the Italians went on with their scheme. On 27 November 1937 Marshal Graziani instructed a body of seventy-two Ethiopian ecclesiastics to appoint one of the Ethiopian bishops as the new *abun;* Abuna Abraham in turn appointed six more Ethiopian bishops. Upon Abraham's death in July 1939, his Ethiopian successor, Abuna Yohannes, appointed five more Ethiopian bishops.[24]

The fact that the Italians tore the Ethiopian Church from its Coptic connection was a major issue on the Egyptian agenda. Public opinion makers from all quarters agreed that Egypt's very identity was offended. The issue of church separation ran parallel to, and was occasionally combined with, that of the Nile waters. The idea that Mussolini, the brutal, unrestrained imperialist, had obtained control over the Blue Nile aroused the deepest anxiety in Egypt. The fascist dictator was depicted as a mad, evil monster lurking behind Lake Tana, looking down the Nile, his greedy eyes fixed on Egypt.[25] Only in April 1938 did an Anglo-Italian dialogue on the Nile produce an agreement to maintain the status quo; as a result, the Egyptian government recognized Italian East Africa. Voices in late 1938 calling on Egypt to refrain from so doing prior to a resumption of the church connection faded quite quickly.

The reactions of the general public and the Copts in 1937–1938 to the church separation are, however, central to this study, for they were almost unanimous. The general public denounced the Italian action as an offense against Egypt on two fronts—first, against Egypt as the leader in the East that had special ties with Ethiopia, and second, against Egypt as the national home of the Copts. From the moment Abuna Qerilos passed through Suez on his way to see Mussolini in June 1937 until well after the appointment of Abuna Abraham, hundreds of relevant articles, all in the same spirit, appeared in the Egyptian press. Royalists, liberals, Muslims, and Arabists all wrote that Italy, in separating Ethiopia and Egypt, had humiliated the peoples of the East.[26]

The Committee for the Defense of Ethiopia of 1935 was revived and issued a public statement "in the name of all Egyptians: Muslims, Jews, Christians."[27] Many writers argued that the Fascists had not only broken the Christian bond, but had also tried to break the Islamic connection between Egypt and Ethiopia. They reminded the public that the Azhari educational mission sent in 1935 to help Haile Selassie mobilize his Muslim subjects was later expelled by the Italians. Liberals, who admitted that Ethiopia perhaps deserved religious autonomy, stated that such emancipation should be negotiated by Ethiopians and Egyptians instead of being imposed by foreign occupiers.[28]

One of Egypt's prominent journalists, the editor of the weekly *Al-Musawwar,* Fikri Abaza, wrote an open letter to Mussolini stating that severing church relations with Ethiopia undermined Egypt both culturally and spiritually.[29] Moreover, he implied that Mussolini was ready to block the Nile in Ethiopia. When the Egyptian minister to Rome was asked by Mussolini's foreign minister why the general public in Egypt was so troubled by a "Coptic matter," the former responded: "Since the days of Sa'd Zaghlul there was no longer any question of Copts and Moslems in Egypt; and that the Abyssinian church question was a national one for Egypt."[30]

By 1937 this declaration had become quite an empty slogan as various new and renewed definitions began to compete for the Egyptian soul. The Ethiopian cultural dimension was no longer as important as it was in 1935, and the general public, once it was reassured regarding the Nile waters, lost interest in the church issue. Not so for the Copts. For them erosion in Egyptian liberalism and the emergence, more forceful after 1935, of Arabist and militant Islamic trends spelled trouble.[31] The fall of "Christian Coptic" Ethiopia was another well-combined, weakening element. The rise of the Muslim Brothers, particularly after 1936, was to be the Copts' major danger, and their leader, Hasan al-Banna, as we have seen, was swift indeed to make the connection. The severing of their church relations with Ethiopia by the Italians must have intensified the Copts' growing insecurity.

The policy of the Coptic Church establishment was one of avoidance. Instead of facing the Italians and denouncing their action to the greater Christian world, the church excommunicated its Ethiopian collaborators. On 28 December 1937 a Holy Synod decree declared the new Ethiopian *abun* illegitimate, as well as his newly appointed Ethiopian bishops, and excommunicated all of their adherents.[32] From that moment until Ethiopia's liberation in 1941, the Egyptian Church avoided rendering any services to Ethiopians, even in exile.

The members of the Coptic intelligentsia proved far more loyal,[33] most of them taking the lead in denouncing the Fascists' move. They called for a prompt resumption of the Ethiopian connection, and they did so, not in the name of their community, but rather in the name of Egyptian nationalism. Indeed, the pluralist nationalism of the 1920s, though losing some ground among the general public, was maintained during the 1930s and later as the major orientation among educated Copts. In coping with the new dangers of Islamic militancy and in trying to cement Egyptian nationalism, however, various Coptic leaders began to differ in emphasis. These differences influenced their 1937–1938 responses to Ethiopian developments.

The most prominent Coptic intellectual of the time was philosopher and author Salama Musa. He was indeed the only Copt among the great *illuminaires,* prestigious enough to take the lead in spreading "Pharaonicism." During the 1930s Musa emphasized that this Egyptianist combination of ancient roots and multifaceted culture should enhance Westernization. He saw the Mediterranean and Europe as the sphere for Egypt's future and wavered between Western messages of idealistic socialism and authoritarian nationalism. In this context he even had moments of admiration for Mussolini, until the Ethiopian crisis of 1935, when, as mentioned earlier, he supported Ethiopia. Later he even admired Adolf Hitler until 1938–1939. The Eastern orientation of Egypt's long history, Musa argued, was based on anachronistic ethnicity and religiosity. He rejected Arabism as a product of the former and attached little importance to the Coptic-Ethiopian religious bond. His response to its rupture by the Fascists was mild, being more an expression of his disillusionment with imperialist Mussolini than a display of concern for the Ethio-Egyptian connection.[34]

One Copt who became more identified with this connection was Mirrit Boutros-Ghali, the leader of a group of young, modern, educated Copts who believed Egyptian identity should be viewed as originating historically from its location at the East-West juncture. In 1938 Mirrit published his major work, *The Policy of Tomorrow,* calling for humanistic socialism at home and for the enhancement in foreign relations of a strong Eastern orientation to balance Western European culture and aggression. In so doing, he echoed the writings of other Egyptian "Easternists," such as Muhammad 'Abdallah 'Inan and Muhammad Lutfi Jum'a, but Mirrit Boutros-Ghali, as a Copt, laid a greater emphasis on the Eastern-Ethiopian dimension. In the vein of Ramzi Tadrus, the first modern Coptic historian of Ethiopia, Mirrit Boutros-Ghali would spend his lifetime as both an Ethiopianist scholar and a builder of better understanding and cooperation between the two churches and societies.

In July 1937, after Abuna Qerilos was summoned to Mussolini, Mirrit suspected the Italians and feared no one would deter them from separating the churches. He presented a report to the British embassy, accusing the Coptic Church establishment of cowardice.[35] He also expressed the fear that many Copts, like his uncle, Egyptian foreign minister Wasif Boutros-Ghali, would not be moved to action following Musa's approach. He wrote:

> Ever since its foundation, some 1500 years ago by Coptic monks, the Church of Abyssinia has lived in close union with the Church of Egypt. This union is marked by a balanced system of subordination and independence: the deep respect and reverence of the Abyssinians for the supreme head of their Church, the Coptic Patriarch, and for his

representative, the Abuna of Abyssinia, is combined with their unwill-
ingness to accept other Coptic bishops or priests, and their desire that
the Abuna should become as thoroughly Abyssinian as possible, em-
bracing their causes, and feeling as they do. An instance of that spirit
expected in the Abuna is the tradition that he must always stand by the
side of the emperor in time of war. . . . The separation of the Church of
Abyssinia from that of Egypt would be a step forward for the Italians
in the subjugation of Ethiopia. . . . Although Egyptians as a whole,
Moslems and Christians alike, have been somewhat more aware in the
last years of the advantage in the relations between the Abyssinian
Church and Egypt, it is equally to be feared that, from this side also,
matters might be allowed to slide.

In the following months, as the Italian scheme materialized, the
Egyptian public was not all that indifferent. Yet no real action was taken,
and possibly the only call for retaliation was made by another leading
Copt, Makram 'Ubayd. 'Ubayd, no doubt, was the most prominent Coptic politician of the time, whose success as a major leader in the Wafd
Party reflected most vividly the integrative aspect of liberal Egyptian nationalism. For that reason he also came under frequent Islamicist fire, a
challenge to which he responded by emphasizing the common Arab
identity. Indeed, 'Ubayd's formula of highlighting the Arabist dimension
of Egyptian nationalism was a third option of the Copts, though during
the 1930s, a marginal one at best. Unlike the Christians of Syria who had
heralded the rise of modern Arab nationalism, most modern Copts, at
least during the prewar period, had failed to see Arabism's secular
legacy. They perceived Arabism to be merely a new version of Islam and
feared pan-regional unity to be a plan to absorb their new refuge, modern Egyptian nationalism, in an alien sea.

But Makram 'Ubayd was perhaps the first Coptic leader who ven-
tured to perceive Arabism as a common denominator and a safe haven in
facing resurgent Islamic militancy. It is evident, in any case, that he
never valued the Ethiopian connection for its own cultural merits, nor
was he particularly active in defending Haile Selassie in 1935. Now,
however, in 1937–1938, as acting foreign minister in the Wafdist government, he approached the British on two occasions and asked permission to retaliate against the Italian community in Egypt.[36] Nothing came
of this, as the British, busy with the Nile waters issue, did not approve.
When an agreement on the Nile was reached, both the Egyptian government and the public shelved the church matter.

These nuances in the response to the Fascists' severing of the Ethiopian connection in 1937 were the precursors of future differences among
Egyptians. It is sufficient to conclude here that, from the Ethiopian point
of view, the Coptic Church's policy was disappointing, but the reaction

of the general Egyptian public and of the Coptic intelligentsia was very encouraging. Egypt, the Ethiopians could not fail to see, appreciated the special historic connection with their country. Returning in 1941 to a liberated Ethiopia, Emperor Haile Selassie would resume his nationalization efforts based on the premise of such an Egyptianist picture.

ETHIOPIAN INTEREST IN AFFILIATION WITH EGYPT

In January 1941, as Haile Selassie was preparing his return to Ethiopia from Khartoum, Abuna Qerilos, still in Cairo, wrote to the emperor suggesting he join the campaign. The emperor sent an evasive reply and, upon crossing the border, made sure that the *echage* (the head of Ethiopia's monastic system) marched on his right. The *echage* Gabra-Giyorgis, was to remain in this position. From that moment he would run all church affairs, appoint priests, and be treated ceremonially, by the Ethiopian press as well, as though he were the titular head of the church. Ten years later, in January 1951, he would be the first Ethiopian *abun* consecrated by a Coptic partiarch.

In attempting to rebuild his base of power, Haile Selassie would relentlessly promote the centralization of Ethiopia. During this decade he did away with the power of the old provincial elite, reconstructed a new and compliant bureaucracy, and saw to the modernization of a new army and the resumption of the educational revolution, which was to create a capable, yet fully dependent, intelligentsia. During the 1940s and 1950s the emperor oversaw a truly multifaceted revolution, revolving paradoxically around his traditional autocracy. One traditional element of his formula was the role of the church. Haile Selassie needed to keep it under his complete control, and the loyal *echage* would see to it. He also wanted the church to enhance a Christianity of the type consonant with Ethiopian identity for centuries, a local traditional set of values and symbols that would facilitate his pious, nationalist blend of modernization and continuity. Moreover, after the Italian promotion of Islam both in the center and at the periphery, Haile Selassie considered the reinvigoration of Christianity essential in coping with rising internal and regional challenges. He needed Ethiopian bishops for the provinces, and he was completely willing to leave those Ethiopian bishops consecrated by the Italian-appointed Abuna Abraham and Abuna Yohannes in their posts. These bishops, as mentioned earlier, had been excommunicated by the Egyptian Coptic Holy Synod in 1938.

Yet, angry as he was with the Coptic Church for its general inflexibility and for its subsequent negligence during the occupation period,

Haile Selassie recalled Abuna Qerilos to Addis Ababa in May 1942. The latter arrived in June accompanied by an Egyptian delegation; thus, church relations and Ethiopia's continuation as a bishopric of the Coptic Church were resumed.[37]

Haile Selassie was perhaps too pious to aspire to a complete break with Alexandria and too proud to accept such an inheritance from Mussolini. But there was much more to reestablishing the connection with Egypt. It seems that during the 1940s and onward, most Ethiopians still regarded themselves as Orientals rather than Africans, connected by culture, religion, and history to the Middle East. Egypt remained central and grew in its relevance and importance in various ways. It remained essential as a source of modernization, as Egyptian schoolmasters continued to help rebuild the educational system. In fact, one of Mirrit Boutros-Ghali's young associates, Coptic intellectual Murad Kamil, arrived in Ethiopia in 1942 and (together with some other fellow Copts, notably Zahir Riyad) stayed for two years to oversee the educational reforms. By that time Murad, like Mirrit, had acquired a thorough knowledge of Geez, Amharic, and Ethiopia's history, and in years to come he would be a leader in spreading the scholarly notion of the Ethiopian-Egyptian connection in Egypt.

In reestablishing ties with the Coptic Church, Haile Selassie no doubt meant to rebuild relations with Egyptian nationalism of the kind that he had witnessed in 1924 and that seemed to prevail, in our context at least, during 1937–1938. Moreover, he surely had in mind an Egypt that, in the fateful year 1935, formed a Committee for the Defense of Ethiopia and was one of very few countries that had sent some help. Despite the Coptic Church's inflexibility, he could apparently rely on both the Coptic intelligentsia and the Egyptian government's interest in mutual understanding. The latter, as well as much of the general public, still viewed Ethiopia in modern Egyptianist terms and in the context of "Unity of the Nile Valley." These were, for the most part, friendly concepts, and Ethiopia had little to fear from Egyptianist regional ambitions at that time.

Indeed, during the 1940s Ethiopia seemed to hold most of the cards, as was demonstrated by the renewed Eritrea issue. Egypt claimed this ex-Italian colony, the Red Sea corridor to the Sudan, in 1945–1946, and it did so by turning to the United Nations and resorting to Ottoman-Egyptian legal precedents. Ethiopian diplomats, hinting at their control of the Blue Nile, successfully disputed the Egyptian claims[38] that led to the reannexation of Eritrea to Ethiopia as an autonomy in 1952, following the British evacuation. Ethiopia's acting foreign minister as of 1943 and Haile Selassie's closest adviser on foreign affairs, Aklilu Habta-Wold, had been educated in Alexandria. Aklilu—to whom we shall return in discussing the 1960s—befriended many Egyptian diplomats and considered parliamentary Egypt a close ally of Ethiopia. For all intents and purposes, the dialogue between modern Ethiopianism and modern, liberal Egyptian nationalism was at least workable, and Haile Selassie strove to reshape church relations accordingly.

When the Egyptian delegation to Addis Ababa returned home in June 1942, it brought the emperor's conditions for restoring the bond. These Ethiopian conditions were essentially similar to those presented in 1924, and they were not to change prior to the demise of the Egyptian parliamentarian regime. They were as follows: (a) the appointment by the Coptic patriarch of an Ethiopian *abun* to officially enter office after the death of the last Egyptian, Abuna Qerilos; (b) authorization for the *abun* to appoint Ethiopian bishops; (c) the formation of an Ethiopian Holy Synod of bishops; (d) the participation of Ethiopian bishops in the election process of the Coptic patriarch of Alexandria; and (e) recognition by Alexandria of the Ethiopian bishops appointed during the fascist occupation and the annulment of their excommunication. In short, the Ethiopians insisted on independence in all nationally related matters but wanted to remain affiliated with the Egyptian Church, and they therefore recognized the supreme authority of the patriarch, both spiritually and institutionally. Furthermore, they wanted to strengthen this connection by participating in the patriarch's elections themselves.[39]

NOTES

1. For a thorough discussion, see Gershoni and Jankowski, *Redefining the Egyptian Nation.*
2. See details in Erlich, *Ethiopia and the Middle East,* chap. 8.
3. See Gershoni, *Light in the Shade.*
4. Erlich, *Ethiopia and the Middle East,* chap. 8.
5. Ahmad, *Al-Islam fi al-habasha.*
6. See Erlich, *Ethiopia and the Middle East,* pp. 104–106.
7. Bakr, *Italia wa-musta'amaratuha,* pp. 61–66, 74.
8. Gershoni, *Light in the Shade,* chap. 3.
9. See note 11 in Chapter 5 above.
10. See Salama Musa, "Italy and Ethiopia," *Majallati,* 1 July 1935.
11. Fathi Radwan, second in command of the Young Egypt movement, wrote a book on Mussolini, published in Cairo in 1937, in which he did not discuss the Ethiopian dimension.
12. See Sabri, *Misr fi Ifriqia al-sharqiyya,* esp. chap. 5.
13. See 'Abdalla 'Inan, "The Conflict Between Ethiopia and Western Imperialism" (in Arabic), *Al-Risala,* 24 December 1934; "Egypt, the Waters of the Nile, and the Ethiopian Affairs," *Al-Risala,* 7 January 1935.

14. See Husayn, *Al-Mas'ala al-habashiyya.*

15. Muhammad Hasan al-Zayyat, "The Ethiopian Question: The Question of the East and of Freedom," *Al-Risala,* 5 August 1935.

16. Jum'a, *Al-Asad al-ifriqi wal-nimr al-itali.*

17. See quotation from *Al-Qabas* of 1 December 1935 in Erlich, *Ethiopia and the Middle East,* p. 113.

18. Amin Sa'id, "Arab-Ethiopian Relations: Why the East Supports Ethiopia," *Al-Muqattam,* 25 April 1935.

19. Taha al-Hashimi, "The Battle of Adwa," *Al-Risala,* 28 October 1935; 4, 11, and 18 November 1935; and 9 December 1935.

20. Mas'ad, *Ithyubia.*

21. See Erlich, *Ethiopia and the Middle East,* chap. 9.

22. For the fascist occupation and regime see Sbacchi, *Legacy of Bitterness,* and Public Record Office (hereafter PRO) Foreign Office 371/41498, "The Church of Ethiopia During the Italian Occupation," by F. Matthew, 27 October 1943.

23. The Italians carefully followed all issues related to Ethiopian-Egyptian relations at that time. The material is available at the Ministero degli Affari Esteri, Archivio Storico (hereafter ASMAE) in Rome, in two series: 1. Etiopia fondo la guerra, buste 1935–1938; and 2. Egitto, buste 1935–1938. Their almost daily reports contain long quotations from the Egyptian press. The press report on the meeting between the *abun* and Mussolini is from *La Reforme,* 21 June 1937.

24. See translation of the official Amharic declaration made in Addis Ababa on 1 December 1937 in PRO Foreign Office 371/20939. See also various reports in Foreign Office 401/ 35–38 and FO 371/41498.

25. See, for example, a cartoon on the cover of *Al-Musawwar* on 10 April 1936.

26. For example: *Akhir Sa'a,* 6 June 1937; Karim Thabit's article in *Al-Misri,* 21 June 1937; *Al-Ahram,* 20 June 1937; *Al-Muqattam,* 21 June 1937. See mainly *Al-Musawwar,* 2 July 1937, quoting Kamil Sidqi and Professor Ibrahim Takla. For a new wave of responses after the appointment of Abuna Abraham, see reports in ASMAE, Egitto 1937, quoting *Al-Ahram, Al-Balagh, Jihad, Al-Muqattam, Al-Misri,* 26 November–15 December 1937.

27. ASMAE, Egitto 1937, "Questione Chiesa Etiopica" and "Sistemazione Chiesa Copta Etiopica," 15 and 18 December 1937.

28. See *Al-Muqattam,* 15 November 1938.

29. *Al-Musawwar,* 17 December 1937.

30. PRO Foreign Office 371/20888, Lampson to Eden, 20 December 1937.

31. For general background and analysis see Carter, *The Copts in Egyptian Politics,* esp. chap. 3.

32. PRO Foreign Office 371/20888, Lampson to Eden, 28 December 1937; *Times* (London), 29 December 1937.

33. The difference between the church establishment and the modern Coptic sector in their attitudes toward Ethiopians is exemplified by the following episode. When the patriarch visited Ethiopia in 1930, he brought back to Egypt sixty Ethiopian youngsters to be educated in church schools. They were so badly maltreated that they complained to fellow Ethiopians who at the time studied in a general French school in Alexandria. One of them appealed to the Coptic foreign minister, Wasif Boutros-Ghali, who immediately bought them clothes and

hospitalized their sick. This relief was brief, for a year later the Alexandria students (headed by the future prime minister Aklilu Habta-Wold) wrote to Haile Selassie, who saw to the immediate return of the sixty youngsters to Ethiopia. See Habtewold, *Aklilu Remembers,* pp. 2–3.

34. In 1935 Salama Musa wrote extensively against Mussolini's aggression toward Ethiopia. However, in his journal, *Al-Majalla al-jadida,* of December 1937 and the first half of 1938, I could find no mention of the church rupture issue. (I did not see the publication's January and March 1938 issues.)

35. PRO Foreign Office 371/20939, Lampson to Eden, 15 July 1937, containing Mirrit's report.

36. PRO Foreign Office 401/35–38, Lampson to Eden, 3 December 1937. See also Makram 'Ubayd's conversation with the Italian minister to Cairo in ASMAE, Egitto, boxes 1937, 8 December 1937.

37. The chronology of events narrated here is based mainly on several sources: Kamil, "La dernier phase des relations historiques"; Suriyal, *Al-Istiqlal al-dhati likanisat Ithyubya;* Amanu "The Ethiopian Orthodox Church"; *Ethiopian Herald,* 1943–1951; and PRO Foreign Office 371/46086, 371/22025, 371/63129.

38. On the dispute over Eritrea compare *Al-Ahram,* 22 and 23 August 1946 and 24 and 26 September 1946 with *Ethiopian Herald,* 14 October 1946 and 9 December 1946.

39. The most detailed description of the negotiations during the 1940s is Suriyal's *Al-Istiqlal al-dhati likanisat Ithyubya;* the Ethiopian demands are presented in chap. 1.

7

From Compromise
to Disconnection, 1945–1959

The end of World War II began what may be the best period of Egyptian-Ethiopian relations ever. Haile Selassie and royal parliamentarian Egypt seemed to enjoy an era of substantial mutual trust. The emperor, pursuing his goal of church modernization centered on his absolute
authority, was more than happy to develop a dialogue with Egypt in
which he still seemed to hold the Nile waters card. And Egypt's establishment and public opinion were ready to reach a comprehensive understanding with Ethiopia.

During the 1940s Egypt was still focused on the greater Nile Valley
as its territorial and historical framework, and the issue of unity with the
Sudan was considered inseparable from national emancipation and a
British withdrawal. Population growth in Egypt had increased dependency on all-Nile planning and on Ethiopian waters. Moreover, the future
of Eritrea was placed back on the national agenda and became a subject
of international diplomacy. The ex-Italian colony, also claimed by Ethiopia, was again considered a corridor to the Sudan by Cairo, a vital asset
needed by Egypt if all-Nile Egyptian nationalism was to be realized.
Egypt's political elite and the Coptic community's modern faction were
very interested in resurrecting the ancient, Christian dimension of relations in order to promote better working relations on other issues.

By the end of the 1940s the long-awaited historical compromise was
finally achieved. Ethiopia obtained complete practical control over its
church, and the first Ethiopian *abun* was appointed by the Coptic patriarch in January 1951. The all-important affiliation with Egypt, however,
was maintained. Ethiopia, though now religiously autonomous, chose to
continue as an extension of the Coptic Church. Nothing could have better symbolized the renewed bond with Egypt, as well as Ethiopia's renewed desire to be part of a hospitable Middle East.

123

This era of warm relations was short-lived. The revolutionary regime that came to power in Egypt abruptly changed the two-dimensional premise of the ancient saga. From our perspective the Nasserist regime was comprehensively revolutionary. Its new interpretations of society, of religion, of politics, and of national identity, its new concepts of the Nile as the backbone of Egypt, of Cairo's regional relations, cannot in themselves be discussed here. However, they created an entirely different set of issues and attitudes that affected and quickly undermined the fundamentals of Ethio-Egyptian relations. By the end of the 1950s the two main supporting pillars of the Nile and the cross had fallen. With the beginning of the construction of the Aswan High Dam in 1959 and the signing of a water agreement solely with the Sudan, Nasser virtually declared Ethiopia irrelevant as a Nile country. By simultaneously terminating the church's affiliation with Egypt, Haile Selassie divorced Ethiopia from a revolutionary, alienating Arab Middle East and turned to Africa. This eye contact, broken in 1959, has yet to be reestablished.

EGYPTIAN NATIONALISM AND THE ETHIOPIAN CHURCH: THE COMPROMISE

The First Ethiopian Abun

Until the end of World War II, the Egyptian government and the public were not really involved in church negotiations, which were conducted between the Ethiopians and the Coptic Church establishment and which produced no results. The Ethiopians, on their part, launched a tough campaign. They kept Abuna Qerilos in humiliating physical conditions in Addis Ababa, barely allowing him to perform the minimal ceremonial duties. The Coptic Church, on its part, went on resisting change. In late June 1942 the Holy Synod rejected all Ethiopian demands except one: it agreed to abolish the 1938 excommunication of Ethiopian bishops appointed by Abuna Abraham but only if all of these bishops were relegated to their previous positions.[1] On 9 February 1945 the Synod officially rejected the idea of an Ethiopian *abun* and his right to consecrate bishops. The Synod would agree only in principle that, in the future, Ethiopians would be allowed to participate in the election of the patriarch; this, however, was not enough to reassure the Ethiopians.

Following the Holy Synod's rejection, there began a well-orchestrated Ethiopian campaign against the Coptic Church that would not cease until the resolution of all the issues. During the later half of the 1940s, the emperor convened various religious conferences in Addis

Ababa and published their deliberations in the Ethiopian press. These included long speeches and occasionally full-page headlines and articles about the historical damage inflicted on Ethiopia for centuries due to the unjust dependency.[2] Both young intellectuals and churchmen described the Egyptian *abuns* as ignorant of Ethiopia, loyal to the interests of a foreign country, and too accustomed to living under Islamic rule to provide Ethiopia with proper leadership in its Christian efforts against Islam. The fact that the *abuns* could not consecrate bishops, it was argued, kept the Ethiopian Church weak and stagnant. It was a major reason for its failure to change, modernize, and provide proper education and services.

No less forceful were the new arguments about the very legitimacy of the dependency itself. The fourth-century Ethiopian King Azana, it was argued, was already a Christian before he appointed and dispatched his Syrian priest Frumentius to establish the Egyptian connection. The Ethiopian kings, it followed, should have selected the *abuns;* the first one, in any case, was not an Egyptian at all. The tradition of an Egyptian *abun,* they reiterated, was based on a Coptic forgery, on decisions attributed retrospectively and falsely to the Council of Nicaea. It made no sense for some one million Copts in Egypt, who enjoyed no political sovereignty, to have sixteen archbishops, while sixteen million Christian Ethiopians under a Christian emperor should have none. Ethiopian anger peaked during a conference held on 26 November 1945, resulting in a resolution to cease negotiations, sever all relations, and begin considering the election of an Ethiopian archbishop to act as *abun.*[3]

Following the end of World War II, the Egyptian government entered the picture. Though it had significant strategic differences with Ethiopia, particularly the dispute over Eritrea, it was all for advancing a constructive diplomatic dialogue. Supported by general public opinion, expressed occasionally in the press, the government favored appeasing Ethiopia, at least in Christian Church matters. This was also the line pursued by many Coptic intellectuals led by Murad Kamil and Mirrit Boutros-Ghali, who also ensured that some of the Ethiopian complaints were recycled in the Egyptian press. For example, Murad Kamil published a series of articles (November 1945–February 1946) in *Al-Katib al-Misri,* the prestigious journal of Egyptian intellectuals (edited by Taha Husayn), summarizing his two years' work in Ethiopia. In one article, explaining and identifying with the Ethiopian stand on the *abun* issue, he translated verses by the Ethiopian poet Kidane Walda-Kifle:

The Copts are happy, what do they have to worry about?
They do not do anything, but their glory is just words.
In our country they enjoy great titles for their bishops.

But in their country they are not free like other religious people.
We also cannot talk openly of freedom and liberty
For the Syrians and the Armenians elect patriarchs for themselves
While they do not have a king as we have.
Nowhere in the world is there another race but the Ethiopians,
Who do not even elect a bishop from among their own.[4]

This coalition of pro-Ethiopian factors was spearheaded by a faction in the church establishment led by Archbishop Yusab. When Patriarch Makarios died in September 1945, Yusab's candidacy was strongly supported by Haile Selassie. Although the Ethiopians had no official say in the elections, they sent a strong delegation to Cairo in the spring of 1946, headed by the *echage* and governmental ministers. Under the auspices of the Coptic Community Council (and probably with the help of the government), they threw their weight on the side of Yusab's camp, and on 10 May 1946 the latter was elected as the next patriarch of Alexandria.

There was, of course, a very strong conservative camp in the church establishment and the Holy Synod, aided by dignitaries and some intellectuals and allegedly led by the secretary of the Community Council, Dr. Ibrahim al-Minyawi.[5] This camp was also enthusiastically supported by Abuna Qerilos, who on 11 May 1945 returned once more to Egypt and began an intensive defense of the traditional institution of the Egyptian *abun*. The Ethiopian connection and bishopric, he argued, comprised a pillar of the Egyptian Coptic Church, a spiritual as well as political asset. These conservatives had their day in February 1945, but a year later, when the issue became a more public matter, they began to lose ground. On 31 January 1946 the Holy Synod finally made its first revolutionary change. Having hosted an Ethiopian delegation, it decided that, in principle, an Ethiopian would replace Abuna Qerilos upon his death. The Synod rejected the request that the *abun* be authorized to consecrate bishops and that an Ethiopian Holy Synod be established. It also reiterated the Egyptian demand that the Ethiopian bishops, because of their nomination during the fascist occupation, be demoted in rank.

Under the authoritative orchestration of Haile Selassie, the Ethiopians refused to compromise. During early February 1946 Egyptian prime minister Mahmud Fahmi al-Nuqrashi (who had served as Egyptian consul in Ethiopia) found time to intervene in the negotiations, though they came at the height of the Anglo-Egyptian crisis, as well as during bloody student riots. On the very eve of his resignation he helped reach a new decision, according to which Abuna Qerilos would not return to Ethiopia and an Ethiopian replacement would be authorized to function immediately as

Ethiopia's acting head of church, to be appointed *abun* upon Qerilos's death. In addition, the authority to appoint bishops would be reconsidered shortly.[6]

The Ethiopians refused to compromise.[7] As noted above, they had sent a delegation that was actually involved in the May 1946 election of the new patriarch, Yusab II. The latter, their firm supporter, immediately formed a committee that met with the new Ethiopian ministerial delegation and recommended consecrating five additional Ethiopian bishops in Egypt but only on the condition that they agree, in writing, never to elect an Ethiopian *abun*. Five Ethiopian monks were sent to Cairo in June, and a fierce argument broke out over the demanded signature. Egypt's new prime minister, Isma'il Sidqi, apparently much more interested in the culminating Ethiopian-Egyptian diplomatic dispute over Eritrea, was ready to compromise.[8] He intervened twice, hosting the Ethiopian delegation in a government meeting, though to no avail. In July 1946 the emperor ordered the return of the monks and the intensification of a public opinion campaign against the Coptic Church (including a denouncement of Abuna Qerilos as a collaborator with the Italians during the occupation).[9] Again, some of the Ethiopian arguments were recycled by their Egyptian supporters in the Egyptian press. The Coptic conservatives were blamed for stubbornly preventing Ethiopian development and for dismissing the general Egyptian interest.

During the next two years other delegations shuttled between the two capitals. On 24 July 1947 Patriarch Yusab managed to pass a new resolution in the Holy Synod to the effect that the five Ethiopian monks would be consecrated as archbishops and would themselves be authorized to appoint bishops, all in exchange for a written commitment.[10] Again, the emperor rejected the idea, and a new wave of controversy swept the Coptic community. Finally, on 25 July 1948 Yusab II consecrated the five Ethiopians; one of them, Gabra-Giyorgis, *the echage,* was given the title and name Abuna Baselyos. Abuna Qerilos died in Cairo in October 1950, and on 14 January 1951, during a very friendly ceremony, Yusab II consecrated Baselyos in Cairo as the first Ethiopian *abun*.[11]

For Haile Selassie's Ethiopia this was a major achievement. The emperor could now continue promoting his blend of traditionalism and modernization with a revitalized, nationalized church under his complete control. The church went on to lose its autonomous role in education and justice, but it was nevertheless strengthened as a political and cultural branch of the imperial regime. Together with its new bishops—each of Ethiopia's provinces (including Eritrea in 1952) became a bishopric—it served the emperor's drive to spread an Amharic-Christian ethos of national unity during the 1950s and 1960s. An Ethiopian bishop was now appointed to Jerusalem. Of particular significance was the role of the church and its new bishops in Eritrea. After years of debate in the UN, the ex-Italian colony was reannexed to Ethiopia as an autonomous province. During the remainder of the 1950s Haile Selassie successfully used his revitalized church to undermine Eritrea's constitutional autonomy and win over the province's Christian elite to the cause of Ethiopian centralization.

Egyptian Recognition of Ethiopian-Eritrean Federation

Parliamentarian Egypt lost its cause in Eritrea. The Egyptian diplomatic campaign to regain Eritrea began just as World War II ended and ran parallel to the Ethio-Egyptian Church issue. Literature produced in Cairo praised Egyptian administration there during the 1870s.[12] In London, Paris, and then the United Nations, the Egyptians, led by the Coptic diplomat Wasif Boutros-Ghali, clashed with Ethiopian diplomats over the legacies of the Isma'il-Yohannes period. They argued that the Italians had captured Massawa in 1885 from the Egyptian garrison and had promised to preserve it under Egyptian sovereignty. Now that the Italians had left Massawa, they said, the Arab-populated town should be restored to Egypt. The Ethiopians, led by acting foreign minister Aklilu Habta-Wold, countered by referring to Egypt's Eritrean defeat in Gura in 1876, to Ras Alula's government in Asmara, and to the June 1884 Hewett Treaty under which Egypt renounced Massawa.

When bilateral contacts between the two missions failed, Egypt decided to claim all of Eritrea on 17 November 1947. However, it gradually became clear that it stood no chance in the UN of regaining Eritrea. Moreover, the Ethiopians exerted more pressure by again airing the issue of the Nile. In December 1949 Aklilu met with King Farouk and the Egyptian government in Cairo. He refused to tell them anything about Ethiopian plans regarding Lake Tana (the British and the Egyptians had renewed their interest in the Lake Tana dam idea),[13] but he showed no ambivalence in connecting Egypt's stand on Eritrea with the fact that his country was in a position to interfere with the Blue Nile.[14] In 1950, just after Haile Selassie declared that Ethiopia had the right to use the river's waters, the Egyptians abandoned their claim. In December 1950, in defiance of the other Arab delegations, Egypt joined the majority in the UN and voted for an Eritrean federation with Ethiopia.[15]

Despite its diplomatic defeat over Eritrea, Egyptian relations with Ethiopia, as reflected by the church compromise, remained workable, if not friendly. The Egyptian Church was to remain the spiritual mother of Ethiopia's religious establishment, and Ethiopian *abuns* were to continue to be appointed and consecrated by an Egyptian patriarch. Further, as Ethiopians were to be involved in the election processes of future patriarchs, the bond of spiritual, religious affiliation seemed even to be strengthened. The new arrangement, made possible by the involvement of the Egyptian government and public, added a very positive dimension to relations of the utmost nationalist importance. Still focused on the Nile as the source of the country's life and identity, the Egyptian public attached growing importance to the Ethiopian connection. Indeed, during the period that began with the 1948 arrangement and lasted until the mid-1950s, Ethiopian-Egyptian relations were those of mutual cooperation and understanding.[16]

PAN-ARABISM AND ETHIOPIA, 1955–1959

The 1948 compromise regarding the nature of the church connection reflected a workable accommodation between modern Ethiopian nationalism and Egyptian nationalism. The traditional Christian-Ethiopian identity had been organically linked to the Middle East, to Egypt, and to Jerusalem, and the new formula was designed to transform, yet retain, that linkage. Modern Egyptian nationalism, a rather pluralistic concept of both the region and Egyptian society, proved ready to redefine this connection. Basing Egypt's identity on the Nile Valley and perceiving their fellow Copts to be equal partners, the leaders of territorial-parliamentarian Egyptian nationalism cherished the special ties with Ethiopia.

But this new arrangement did not last long. This time the major change occurred in Egypt, where the revolutionary regime, which came to power in July 1952, gradually initiated fundamental changes that quickly led to a final, historic break between the two countries and cultures. By 1959, the year in which church relations were finally severed, the Nasserist regime had already been at work changing the very definition of the country's identity. It strove to emphasize its Arab dimension at the expense of territorial-Egyptian aspects, and the leadership of the new United Arab Republic (UAR), established in 1958, did its best to marginalize the historical concept of Egypt's uniqueness.

Nasser's departure from the terminology of Egyptian nationalism and his embrace of a Pan-Arab identity stemmed from a variety of deep-rooted social, cultural, and ideological reasons that are too complicated to be discussed here. These were combined with a new set of strategic priorities. The "Middle Eastern option" that had been closed in the later years of Muhammad 'Ali's reign now seemed to be reopened in regard to Egypt. Particularly after the 1956 Suez War and Egypt's political victory,

Cairo's leading role in an "Arab circle" took precedence over what Nasser defined as its "African" and "Islamic" circles. The Nile Valley, in practice and in ideology, ceased to be the main national theater, and Egypt's long-desired unity with Sudan was shelved. In 1954 the new regime had given in to British insistence on a separate Sudan, and the latter was given independence in January 1956.

The Nasserist Challenge: Eritrea, Somalia, and Ethiopian Society

The comprehensive transformation of the Nasserist revolution had a direct impact on both the conceptualization of Ethiopia and all pertaining concrete issues. One such meaningful change concerned Eritrea. Where the legalistic international diplomacy of parliamentarian Egypt had failed to win Eritrea in the 1940s, the new regime turned to ethnic subversion. In 1955 Cairo began working for the instigation of an "Arab" revolution in the now-autonomous Ethiopian province. Hundreds of young Muslims from western Eritrea, mostly of the Banu 'Amir clans, were invited to study and enjoy special benefits in the old Riwaq al-Jabartiyya corner of Al-Azhar. Although they were not native Arabic speakers (Muslims of western Eritrea spoke the Tigre language), they absorbed the spirit of Arab revolution in Cairo and adopted a modern Arab identity. There they also learned how to set up a modern guerrilla "liberation front" from the widely admired Pan-Arab Algerian FLN. By 1959 they had been trained in Egypt and were ready to establish the Eritrean Liberation Front (ELF).[17] They returned to the Sudanese town of Kassala, the headquarters of the Sudanese Al-Mirghaniyya movement, which, as mentioned earlier, had ensured the Islamization of the Banu 'Amir in the 1820s. Indeed, the ELF, integrally connected with the pro-Egyptian Mirghaniyya, was supposed to be a key to a future Nasserist victory in the entire Nile basin. More concretely, the ELF launched an open anti-Ethiopian revolt in Eritrea in 1961, manufacturing and transmitting an Arab-Eritrean identity. "The Arabism of the Eritrean People" remained one slogan of the rich revolutionary repertoire of Nasserism to its end.[18]

In order to promote Eritrea's liberation from Ethiopia, Nasser was also ready to help local Christian Tigreans who resisted reunification with Haile Selassie's "Amhara" absolutism. Their prominent leader (later the father figure of Christian-Tigrean Eritreanism), the protestant Walda-Ab Walda-Mariam, was invited in 1955 to broadcast daily anti-Ethiopian messages on Radio Cairo to the Eritreans. The Nasserist regime remained the main pillar of support for the Eritrean separatist movement until 1963. The Nasserist-instilled myth of Eritrea's Arabism, adopted and advanced by Eritrean Muslims, was to survive until the 1980s.

No less significant was the issue of Nasserist influence on the Somali nationalists. Beginning in the mid-1950s Nasserist policy, literature, and agents worked to enhance the anti-Ethiopian dimension of emerging Somali nationalism and render it revolutionary and Arab. The Somalis, following their own ethnic identity (they joined the Arab League in 1974) and encouraged by such potential Arab backing, began claiming around one-third of Ethiopia's territory. When the Somalis united and received their independence in July 1960, they continued to present a serious, ongoing challenge to the integrity of Haile Selassie's empire.

A third issue was the antimonarchical revolutionary zeal that radiated and spread from Cairo to Egypt's various "circles." Nasserism presented itself as a progressive, popular, and anti-imperialist movement. It worked actively to undermine Arab monarchies by exposing them as both reactionary and collaborating with Western domination. Ethiopia, monarchical and allied with Israel and the West, was often scorched by the same fire, portrayed as backward and anachronistic. The regional momentum of Pan-Arab revolution reached its peak in 1958 with the formation of the UAR, the fall of the Hashemite monarchy in Iraq, and what seemed to be a near escape, due to direct U.S. and British interference, of the Hashemites in Jordan and the Christians in Lebanon. Nasser himself, however, remained very cautious about his direct relations with Haile Selassie. In his various speeches he had only praise for Ethiopia's historic friendliness with Islam and for its heroic historical struggle against Western imperialism. In 1957 he even raised the idea of a tripartite regional treaty with Ethiopia and Sudan. He continued to court Haile Selassie and for three years repeatedly invited him to Cairo. Haile Selassie would finally pay the visit in 1959 but merely to finalize a disconnection.

The Aswan High Dam: Ignoring Ethiopia

In our context the more meaningful change introduced by the Nasserist regime was its Nile policy and the decision to construct the Aswan High Dam. In October 1951 the old Egyptian government, together with the British, had made yet another attempt to negotiate the Lake Tana dam idea with the Ethiopians.[19] However, barely two months after coming to power in September 1952, the young officers took their most important step ever. By adopting a plan, already circulated and rejected by the experts of the old regime, to erect a high dam in Aswan,[20] they set in motion a variety of processes that, combined, were to determine much of Egypt's domestic and foreign affairs. The centrality of the High Dam concept, the questions related to its financing and construction, and its impact on the history of Egypt's strategy, politics, economy, society, and culture are reflected in nearly every study of the Nasserist and post-Nasserist periods. The concept, primarily the notion that the lake to be created behind the dam would be controlled by Cairo, enabled the new regime to abandon the "Unity of the Nile Valley" concept and sign the 1953 evacuation agreement with the British. The complicated story of financing the ambitious project led to a crisis with the West, the opening of Egypt to the USSR, the nationalization of the Suez Canal, and the 1956 war with Britain, France, and Israel—a chain of events that ended in a political victory and the culmination of regional Nasserist prestige as the leader of a victorious revolutionary Pan-Arabism.

In 1958 Egypt's triumph in the "Arab circle" seemed to be completed by the formation of the UAR. The November 1959 signing of the water agreement with Sudan and recognition of its entitlement to a share in "historic rights" of the Nile seemed to have finalized Egypt's divorce from the old concept of Nile unity. All of this, along with the role of the High Dam in influencing Nasserist relations with the major powers, is in itself beyond the confines of this discussion. Here we can only refer briefly to the introduction to this book and to the absence today of an all-Nile water control system. According to a recent analysis by the leading historians of Nile hydropolitics, Robert Collins, Rushdi Sa'id, and John Waterbury, the Aswan High Dam, finally completed in 1971, "is the wrong dam in the wrong place." It provided a local, short-term, one-sided political solution where hydrological irreversible shortcomings, exposed more forcefully after the Ethiopian droughts of the mid-1980s, are becoming more and more painfully visible.[21]

More in line with the Egyptian-Ethiopian aspect would be a mention of the internal Arab-Egyptian dimension of the High Dam as a monumental metaphor symbolizing the new spirit of revolution and victory. As recently analyzed by Yoram Meital, the initial, daring plan, its execution in defiance of the old colonial powers, and the dominating presence of the monumental structure reflected both the regime's ability to recruit popular support as well as the authentic, enthusiastic response. Egypt becoming its own master, taking its destiny into its own hands, challenging both foes and nature, producing electricity and harnessing the river—this all became the focus of vast, varied creativity in all avenues of cultural expression from the mid-1950s onward.[22] Perhaps this was the cardinal point behind the idea of the Aswan High Dam: a demonstration of independence, a victory for the newly emerging Arab superstate. "The War of Arab Destiny" (according to one popular slogan) was conducted against the old dependency, not only on the West, but also on the Nile's upstream countries. Seen against the backdrop of the history narrated above, the dam turned the wheels of revolution in the other direction. Lake Nasser was to become the main source of the Nile, not Lake Tana. Ethiopia's threat to interfere with the Nile—from the time of twelfth-century Lalibela and fifteenth-century Zar'a Ya'qob to Aklilu Habta-Wold in 1949, Haile Selassie in the 1950s, and Mangistu Haile Mariam in the 1980s—lost its sting the moment the High Dam was born. If the great singer Muhammad 'Abd al-Wahhab had popularized the poem "Al-Nil najashi" in 1933, as mentioned in Chapter 6, the identification of the river with the Ethiopian king was no longer valid in the 1950s. True to the new spirit of the time, 'Abd al-Wahhab composed the lyrics for an equally popular poem sung by Umm Kulthum, "Tahwil al-Nil" (The Transformation of the Nile):

> Who, who would have believed
> That the river which has run for millions of years,
> Its direction left and right
> We would change at our own will,
> And even install adjustments in it.[23]

Haile Selassie's Response: Turning to Africa

Once Nasser felt assured of the future consummation of the High Dam idea in late 1956, he made it a point to ignore Ethiopia as a Nile country. The days of Ethiopian negotiations with the British over a Tana dam and the Nile system, keeping the Egyptians in the dark, were over. From 1956 Nasser dealt with the Sudanese directly, discussing water distribution and doing his best to bluntly ignore Ethiopia as a Nile country. Haile Selassie responded by airing old threats, trying to play the Sudanese against Nasser, calling for pan-regional conferences, and inviting the Americans to give their advice on new Abbai and all-Nile projects (in August 1957).[24] The final U.S. report (mentioned in Chapter 1 herein) was submitted in 1964, but to no avail. The Ethiopians, who from medieval times believed the claim in the *Ta'amra Maryam* that they were the masters of the Nile, could only watch from a distance. On 8 November 1959 Nasser signed an agreement with Sudanese president Ibrahim 'Abbud in which they divided the "historic rights" over the Nile between them. The 1959 agreement, still valid today, was tantamount to declaring Ethiopia irrelevant.

Haile Selassie's response to Nasserist policy in the 1950s did not ameliorate matters. On the face of things he reciprocated with pleasant words to Nasser's verbal courting, but he grew increasingly suspicious. The Nasserist brand of antimonarchical revolution, Egypt's acquired control over the Nile coupled with its concomitant dismissal of Ethiopia, and Nasser's intended Arabization of the Muslims of the Horn of Africa and Ethiopia all combined to revive Ethiopia's old anxieties, siege spirit, and pride. Haile Selassie's reaction was to counter, disconnect, and dictate a new game.

His first attempt at counteraction was to try to play the Sudanese against the Egyptian Aswan idea. The Ethiopian ambassador to Khartoum, Meles Andom, was put in charge of dealing with Nasser. In December 1956 he described his recent conversation with Nasser to the British ambassador to Ethiopia. The latter reported:

> Nasser had . . . asked whether a military alliance between Egypt, the Sudan and Ethiopia would not be in their common interest. "We drink of the same water," he said. My Ethiopian colleague had replied bluntly, to the following effect: "You claim to be an Arab and to lead the Arab world but you interfere with the affairs of your Arab neighbors and have tried to cause trouble for the governments of Iraq, Libya, Lebanon and Sudan. We Ethiopians are not Arabs. We are Africans and we are black. We do not belong to your world although like you we drink the water of the Nile. You have tried to interfere in our affairs also and make trouble for His Majesty. . . . Secondly, you may have military objectives. We do not know exactly what they may be but we have no confidence in the strength of your armed forces, and we are strongly against the Communists who arm you. For these reasons your proposal is unacceptable and we are not prepared to discuss it even."[25]

This statement, that Ethiopia and Arab Egypt belonged to two different worlds, reflected a new mood in Addis Ababa. Still, Haile Selassie was willing to mix threats with promises and to play the old Nile card in an attempt to force Nasser to enter into a Nile dialogue. In his Crown Speech of 12 November 1957, Haile Selassie stated:

> It is of paramount importance to Ethiopia, and a problem of the first order, that the waters of the Nile be made to serve the life and needs both of our beloved people now living and those who will follow us in centuries to come. However generously Ethiopia may be prepared to share this tremendous God-given wealth of hers with friendly neighboring countries for the lives and welfare of their people, it is Ethiopia's primary and sacred duty to develop her water resources in the interest of her own rapidly expanding population and economy.[26]

As U.S. planners were surveying the Abbai area, the Ethiopian government made it clear that it had taken all measures to utilize the waters should an agreement between Egypt and Sudan not take into account Ethiopia's needs or should Ethiopia be excluded from participation in any further talks.[27]

As mentioned earlier, however, Ethiopia's intensive campaign and threats to force Nasser into a Nile dialogue bore no fruit. In his Crown

Speech the following year, on 12 November 1958, the emperor seemed to have despaired of his ability to communicate with Nasser over the river. It was, remember, a year of victories for revolutionary Arabism in the Middle East as well as among Muslim Eritreans and Somalis. The Israeli consul general in Ethiopia analyzed the situation thusly:

> The speech was a declaration on foreign policy of historic importance. . . . Ethiopia is now doing its utmost to count itself among the African peoples that have obtained independence and that will break their isolation. . . . As remembered, Ethiopia was until lately hesitant to participate in African affairs and claimed, for historical reasons, that it was a Middle Eastern not an African country. We have no doubt that Ethiopia would have continued along that line if not for the Nasserist threat. This threat grew to an extent that it forced Ethiopia to look for allies not only to the north but also to the south and west. Relying on Africa will be the most natural result of the Arab and Islamic pressure.[28]

Haile Selassie, as we shall see below, would indeed score major victories in the new sphere of Pan-African diplomacy. By 1963 he would lead the African camp, which advocated sanctioning territorial integrity, to victory, and Addis Ababa would be declared the headquarters of the Organization of African Unity. Building thus on the centrality of Ethiopia in African awareness, he also forced Nasser to adopt this premise of intra-African relations and restrain his pro-Eritrean secessionist policy. Moreover, as Haile Selassie began building his African option in 1958, he also began constructing his anti-Nasserist Middle Eastern option: his relations with Israel.

A few days prior to his Crown Speech in 1958, Haile Selassie received the following message from David Ben-Gurion, the Israeli prime minister:

> There is a growing danger that the military junta in Egypt will double its efforts to subvert its neighbors and undermine their independence. . . . Moreover, the initial help pledged by the USSR to Egypt to build the Aswan High Dam constitutes another source of danger to Egypt's African neighbors. Unfortunately, there is little awareness in the world that the Nile is not exclusively an Egyptian river, but that rather it is above all an Ethiopian and Sudanese river. I have instructed all our representatives abroad to mention this geographical fact in their communications with governments and public opinion makers. . . . It is my hope that Ethiopia will gain strength and will forcefully stem the hostile and subversive policy of its northern neighbor.[29]

Israeli-Ethiopian relations had begun to gain momentum in 1957 when the Mossad (Israel's secret intelligence agency) sent its highest-ranking team to coordinate intelligence efforts. In 1958 these relations became a cornerstone in a new Israeli strategy aimed at building an alliance among non-Arab Turkey, Iran, Ethiopia, and Israel. Ben-Gurion envisioned this "periphery alliance" not only as an anti-Nasserist asset, but also as an Israeli contribution to U.S. policy, a way to open the gates of Washington, D.C., and get American support. This was the beginning of a multifaceted, complicated Ethiopian-Israeli saga that was of great mutual benefit until 1973. It was already, however, very meaningful in 1958–1959. The emperor was happy to send Israeli water experts to tour the Abbai area and made sure the Egyptians monitored their actions. (The Israelis, on their part, did their best to convey an Ethiopian Nile threat to Nasser. In their internal discussions, however, they found no way to use this card apart from its psychological effect.) No less significant was the intelligence aspect. Israeli agents and counterespionage equipment were sent to Ethiopia. They monitored much of the Nasserist activity in Ethiopia and among its Muslims.[30] The evidence piled on Haile Selassie's desk was conclusive: Nasser was working to spread the word of Arab revolution in Ethiopia. It was high time to sever all ties.

THE DISCONNECTION

The Nasserist-Copt Collision and Ethiopia

The Nasserist revolutionary effort also created an entirely new environment for the Copts. Their fears that Arabism, like political Islam, would deprive them of their place in modern society, won through their embrace of Egyptian nationalism, had grown during the 1940s. Most historians agree that the Nasserist regime ended the Coptic golden age. The regime, with its policy of destroying the parliamentarian period's legacy applicable to the society as a whole, worked to put an end to the institutionalized autonomy of the Copts. One landmark action, Nasser's abolition of the community's religious courts on 21 September 1955, was taken simultaneously with the regime's growing intervention in the Copts' deepening internal crisis.[31] The crisis revolved around Patriarch Yusab II and dragged the Ethiopian Church connection back into the center of Ethio-Egyptian relations.

The first stages of the 1955–1959 Ethio-Egyptian Church developments grew out of the internal Egyptian crisis of the Nasserist-Copt collision. The Coptic community was undoubtedly ill prepared to cope with the challenge of the new regime; the crises of the 1940s were among the reasons for their internal disunity. They had missed their opportunity to regroup as the new regime and the Muslim Brothers fought each other during 1952–1954. Patriarch Yusab II failed to provide proper leadership and was himself accused of corruption. His closest personal aide, Malik Jirjis, was said to have systematically arranged church nominations in return for bribes. A militant group of young radicals called the "Coptic Nation," formed to counter radical Islam, kidnapped the patriarch on 25 July 1954. The group itself was dispersed by the police, but Yusab, apparently failing to improve his image, was finally forced by the Holy Synod to abdicate on 20 September 1955 and take refuge in a monastery in Upper Egypt. A body of three archbishops was established to head the church until his death.

At this moment of intense crisis the Ethiopians reentered the picture. Patriarch Yusab had been a close ally of Haile Selassie, and in any case, the Ethiopian establishment was no longer willing to accept the issue of the patriarch solely as an internal Egyptian matter. Following a wave of protests in the press, the new Ethiopian Holy Synod of bishops issued an announcement on 3 October 1955 that the Ethiopians still recognized Yusab as the patriarch. A patriarch could not be legally forced to resign, they said. Ethiopian emissaries, churchmen, and state officials were sent to Egypt to intervene. They led the way in regrouping the pro-Yusab camp within the Coptic Church establishment, a camp that was opposed by a coalition of most of the Community Council and other members of the clergy. As the dispute heated up, Yusab's opponents argued that the Ethiopians were working behind the deposed patriarch to later inherit the patriarchate themselves.

The escalating crisis culminated in the summer of 1956. On 19–20 June 1956 a joint Holy Synod of Egyptians and Ethiopians met in Yusab's monastery and agreed that if the patriarch fired his corrupt aide, the Synod would allow him to return to his position in the patriarchal palace in Cairo. However, when Yusab returned to the capital three days later, government troops prevented his entry to the palace. The government announced that the common Holy Synod was invalid, and the Ethiopian bishops returned home. Patriarch Yusab II died on 14 November 1956, at the height of the Suez War. Nasser, who emerged victorious from the Suez crisis, was about to accelerate the general transformations he envisioned for his country, including the further weakening of Coptic institutions. He would ensure that no new Coptic patriarch was elected during the next two and one-half years.

A locum tenens was appointed to oversee the election process of a new patriarch, but this election committee soon became the focus of the Copt community's deepening crisis. One major issue, though not the only one, was Ethiopia's demand for an equal number of voting delegates. A new demand, aired for the most part verbally, was that Ethiopians be among the candidates. In November 1957 the Ethiopians, embittered (as evidenced in Haile Selassie's Crown Speech of that month) by Nasser's Nile-Aswan policy, threatened to boycott the process and secede altogether. Meanwhile, the Cairo government, intensifying its sociopolitical and cultural centralization, obtained control over the election process through new regulations. It allowed its resumption only upon completion of changes in January 1958.

The last effort to bridge the gap was made in May–July 1958. A four-member Ethiopian delegation, headed by Dajazmach Asrate Kassa, arrived in Cairo and held fourteen meetings with the election committee, finally reaching an agreement on 21 July. Each side would have eighteen voting delegates, and the next Coptic patriarch would be an Egyptian. But this compromise was soon rejected by both sides. The Coptic public was horrified by what was now perceived as an Ethiopian threat to conquer the patriarchate by sheer numbers and political backing, with the possible transfer of the See of Saint Mark to Addis Ababa. Given the situation, most Copts, members of the clergy, the intelligentsia, and others naturally tended to rely on their own government, resulting in their growing dependency on the Nasserist regime.

The End of the Church Connection

The Ethiopian government, for its part, was already determined to break off relations. The revised Constitution of 1955 had further institutionalized imperial control over the church. It defined the emperor as "Defender of the Faith" and "Head of the Ethiopian Orthodox Church" and gave him the right to legislate in all matters concerning the church, other than those purely spiritual and monastic in nature. It also gave him control over the appointment of all bishops, including the *abun* himself. Now, with the deepening crisis of the Coptic Church in Egypt, Haile Selassie was convinced it was falling under Nasser's control. He believed that most of the Egyptian schoolmasters or monks arriving in Ethiopia were no longer religious functionaries but Nasserist agents. The Ethiopian Church establishment was reportedly anxious to launch its own foreign enterprises, such as opening branches in other newly liberated African states and rebuilding relations with other Orthodox churches in the Middle East. In short, by 1958 the nature and policy of the new regime in Cairo had convinced Haile Selassie that it was time for Ethiopia to have its own patriarch.

The appointment of Dajazmach Asrate Kassa to lead the talks in Cairo was a step in this direction. The Ethiopian court was already witness to a long-standing argument among the emperor's close advisers regarding Ethiopia's Middle Eastern strategy. Asrate, a prominent member of the nobility, was well on his way to becoming one of the closest of Haile Selassie's inner circle of advisers, most influential in shaping his domestic and foreign policies during the 1960s. Promoted to rank of *ras,* he would later become the governor of Eritrea (1964–1970), president of the Senate, and leader of the stronger clique competing for the responsibility to crown Haile Selassie's successor. Though he maintained good ties with Egypt, Asrate was the chief Ethiopian architect of the Israeli connection beginning in the mid-1950s. From 1959 onward he worked to build the Ethiopian-Israeli alliance, which was meant to thwart what he perceived as a growing Arab threat to Ethiopia's state and culture. His trip to Cairo in May 1958 at Haile Selassie's initiative was to prepare for separation from Egypt. Asrate's reports to Addis Ababa were clear: Nasser himself had little interest in the religious aspect, and the Coptic Church had become a branch of the Nasserist government. The compromise he seemed to be about to reach with the Coptic Church establishment (in July 1958) was mutually undesirable.

On 25 December 1958 the locum tenens wrote to Haile Selassie but failed to invite Ethiopian delegates. The emperor took his time and responded in February 1959. He stated that if the July 1958 agreement was not honored, Ethiopia would take no part in the elections and would secede. Following Nasser's instructions, no further invitation was sent to Addis Ababa, and on 18–20 April 1959 the elections took place. The new patriarch-elect hastened to invite the emperor to the consecration ceremony, but no Ethiopian official or churchman was present on 10 May 1959. Patriarch Cyril VI, a strong-minded person of proven integrity, immediately declared that he considered the resolution of the Ethiopian crisis to be a top priority. In early June he sent a delegation to Addis Ababa, the members of which spared no effort, through official meetings and radio interviews, to try to save whatever was possible of the ancient connection. They even went as far as to imply that Egypt had erred in the past.[32] When Dajazmach Asrate Kassa left for Cairo on 11 June, heading an Ethiopian team to prepare for Haile Selassie's scheduled visit, an agreement had already been reached: Ethiopia would have her own patriarch, while some form of affiliation and spiritual superiority of the Egyptian patriarch would be maintained.[33]

There were only two relevant issues left to resolve. As the Ethiopians had accepted the custom that the Egyptian patriarch would continue to consecrate his Ethiopian counterpart and that his name would continue to be mentioned in Ethiopian prayers, it was agreed to distinguish between titles. The Ethiopian patriarch, it was decided, would be called "patriarch gathlik,"—namely, Catholicus (like the Armenian patriarch).[34]

The Egyptian would retain the title of patriarch and pope. The other issue was the new Ethiopian patriarch's right to ordain bishops outside of Ethiopia. The idea was fiercely resisted by the Egyptian Copts. Only a last-minute order from Nasser to agree to Haile Selassie's demand paved the way for the imperial visit in late June 1959. On 28 June 1959, in the presence of Haile Selassie and Egyptian government officials in the main Coptic Church of Cairo, Patriarch Cyril VI appointed the Ethiopian *abun* as a metropolitan and head of an autocephalous church.

The break in the ancient church relations was final. On 8 November that year Nasser signed his water agreement with the Sudanese, practically declaring Ethiopia irrelevant to the Nile. In combination it was a mutual declaration of historical divorce.

Nasser wanted to break the special Christian ties because he was not appreciative of the ancient religious connection. He regarded its traditional diplomacy as obsolete, and Egyptian public opinion makers acted accordingly. For example, Fikri Abaza, the editor of *Al-Musawwar,* who in 1937, still a guardian of Egyptian pluralism, had declared that breaking the historic church bond meant undermining Egypt both spiritually and culturally, now stated nothing of the kind. He devoted much of the 3 July 1959 issue to Haile Selassie's visit and depicted his meeting with Nasser as an event of global symbolism. He dismissed the church issue in a few lines, praising the act of separation as though it were a cordial agreement between two anticolonial freedom fighters to remove a minor obstacle.

Nasser also sought to weaken the Copts at home. In this he would be very successful. However, as mentioned earlier in Chapter 1, his belief that building the Aswan High Dam would emancipate Egypt for good from the Nile connection with Ethiopia would prove less successful. In any case, by departing from the Egyptianist Nile identity, Nasser made the Middle Eastern "Arab circle" his definite priority. In the "African" Nile and Red Sea basins, in Eritrea, in Somalia, and among Ethiopia's Muslims, he was content merely to prepare the initial infrastructure for a future Arab revolutionary option. Meanwhile, it suited him to "leave the Abyssinians alone," and as of 1963 his dialogue with Haile Selassie would be conducted mainly through the Organization of African Unity. The fact that this African-Nile "circle" was now rendered secondary was reflected in Egyptian literature on Ethiopia, to be analyzed in Chapter 9.

Haile Selassie wanted to sever ties because the ancient but renewed bond of identity with Egypt had become too dangerous. Cairo had ceased to be the capital of Egypt and had become the center of the United Arab Republic. By attempting an Arabization of the Horn's Muslims, Nasser, perhaps unconsciously, followed in the exact same footsteps of Ahmad Gragn and Mussolini. The only two historical figures who managed to destroy Ethiopia had also worked for the politicization

of its Islamic communities, trying to unite them against Christian political hegemony. One of their main methods was the introduction of the
Arabic language as a common bridge for the Islamic ethnic-linguistic diversity. The fact that Ethiopia's Muslims failed to unite because of the
local weakness of Arabic had been observed also by promoters of anti-
Ethiopian, radical Islam, such as Shakib Arslan and Yusuf Ahmad. For
the Ethiopians it made little difference that the Nasserist campaign was
not aimed at restoring a Muslim *najashi*. In the eyes of Ethiopian leadership Nasser's actions were equally, perhaps even more, threatening.
The effort to turn the Muslims of Ethiopia and the Horn of Africa into
modern, revolutionary Arabs was viewed by Addis Ababa as the ultimate
danger. Though couched in modern terms and occasionally sweetened by
appeasing gestures and speeches, Nasserism reactivated Ethiopia's
"Ahmad Gragn trauma." If the Middle East was to become a United
Arab Republic, it would influence the Muslims of the Horn in much the
same way as the sixteenth-century Ottoman Islamic reunification of the
Middle East had led to the destruction of Christian Ethiopia. It was time
for redefinition. In 1958–1959 Haile Selassie opted to turn to the new,
more promising world of Africa. In the Middle East, having severed sixteen centuries of intimate affiliation with Cairo, he would continue to act
as haunted by the Ahmad Gragn trauma.

NOTES

1. Suriyal, *Al-Istiqlal al-dhati likanisat Ithyubya,* chap. 2.
2. PRO Foreign Office 371/46086, "The Ethiopian Church," 21 August
1945.
3. See *Ethiopian Herald,* 1 September, 20 November, and 3 December
1945, and especially a series of long articles titled "Relations Between Ethiopian
and Coptic Churches," *Ethiopian Herald,* 1, 8, 15, and 22 July 1946.
4. The series from *Al-Katib al-Misri* was published in a separate pamphlet:
Kamil, *'Amani fi al-habasha.* In Cairo in 1949 Murad Kamil published a fuller
account of his stay in Ethiopia: *Fi bilad al-najashi,* in which he reiterated his
pro-Ethiopian stand and quoted the same poem. See also his French translation
in his "La Dernier phase des relations historiques."
5. See *Ethiopian Herald,* 22 July 1946.
6. Suriyal, *Al-Istiqlal al-dhati likanisat Ithyubya,* chap. 4.
7. *Ethiopian Herald,* 8 April and 20 May 1946.
8. *Ethiopian Herald,* 22 July 1946.
9. *Ethiopian Herald,* 29 July 1946.
10. See PRO Foreign Office 371/63129, Baker to Bevin, 4 October 1947,
containing text of decisions as reported in *Al-Misri,* 5 September 1947.
11. Details in Suriyal, *Al-Istiqlal al-dhati likanisat Ithyubya,* chaps. 5 and 6.
12. See analysis of this aspect in Murad Kamil's 1949 book *Fi bilad al-najashi,* in Erlich, *Ethiopia and the Middle East,* p. 142.

13. See PRO Foreign Office 371/96805, "Tana Project," in British Embassy, Addis Ababa, to African Department, 14 March 1952.

14. See Habtewold, *Aklilu Remembers,* pp. 35, 43, 52 (and see discussion of this book in Chapter 8 below).

15. See Harraz, *Al-'Umam al-muttahida,* pp. 6–12. See also Erlich, *Ethiopia and the Middle East,* pp. 128–129.

16. Just before the fall of the royal-parliamentarian regime in Egypt, the League for Strengthening Friendship with Ethiopia was established in Cairo; see *Al-Ahram,* 16 June 1952.

17. For new documentary evidence on the establishment of the ELF in Cairo under the auspices of Nasser, see Fadab, *Harakat tahrir iritriya;* for 1958–1959, see mainly pp. 42–76. See also Erlich, *Ethiopia and the Middle East,* pp. 130–133. For more information on Eritrean students in Egypt (there were 2,682 between 1960 and 1985, 1,413 of them subsidized by the Egyptian government), see Salim, *Al-Tabadul al-tulabi bayna,* pp. 141–142.

18. See Erlich, *Ethiopia and the Middle East,* pp. 151–164.

19. PRO Foreign Office 371/96805, "Tana Project," British Embassy to Foreign Office, 18 March 1952.

20. See Collins, "In Search of the Nile Waters."

21. Ibid.

22. Meital, "The Aswan High Dam."

23. Quoted from Meital (his translation), ibid.

24. On the activities of the U.S. Bureau of Reclamation, its seven years of studying the Blue Nile, and the report it produced, see Collins, "In Search of the Nile Waters."

25. From Erlich, *Ethiopia and the Middle East,* p. 133.

26. Sudanese Press Agency, Local News Bulletin, 14 November 1957.

27. Sudanese Press Agency, 26 December 1957.

28. Quoted in Erlich, *Ethiopia and the Middle East,* p. 136.

29. Ben-Gurion, *Rosh hamemshala harishon,* pp. 418–419.

30. Israeli journalist Ronen Bergman (for *Ha'aretz*) is currently engaged in writing an extensive book (in Hebrew) on the security ties between Israel and African countries. He has conducted an extensive archival study and interviewed some ninety relevant figures from the Israeli Army Intelligence, the Mossad, the Ministry of Defense, and academic experts. His first draft chapter deals with Israeli-Ethiopian relations until the early 1960s and contains many details about Israeli anti-Nasserist activities in Ethiopia. I thank him for allowing me to read it. For background and further references see Erlich, *Ethiopia and the Middle East,* pp. 165–178.

31. On the Copts under Nasser and their crisis as discussed here, see, inter alia: Wakin, *A Lonely Minority,* chaps. 10 and 11; Shafiq, *Al-Aqbat bayna al-harman,* pp. 77–88; Suriyal, *Al-Istiqlal al-dhati likanisat Ithyubya,* chap. 7 and conclusion; and Philipp, "Copts and Other Minorities."

32. See PRO FO 371/138108, Embassy to Lloyd, 13 June 1959, analysis and documents.

33. For details on the church negotiations during the said period, and for a relevant summary of the coverage in the Egyptian press, see U.S. National Archives, RG 59, Egypt Internal Affairs 1955–1959, C-0027, "Ethiopian Coptic Church Affairs." For Ethiopian views and reports see also *Ethiopian Herald,* 11

August 1956, 14–15 January, 23 April, 8 May, 9, 12, 19, 26, and 29 June 1959 ("First Ethiopian Patriarch Crowned in High Ceremony").

34. See "Translation of Protocol on the Relations Between the Church of Egypt and the Church of Ethiopia," in PRO Foreign Office 371/138108. More on the agreement and Egyptian interpretations in *Al-Musawwar,* 3 July 1959; *Akhir Sa'a,* 1 July 1959; and *Ruz al-Yusuf,* 22 June 1959.

8

Ethiopian Concepts of Egypt, 1959–1991

The dramatic double break of 1959 marked a significant turning point in the history of Ethiopian-Egyptian relations. It seemed to have ended old "oriental" connections and heralded the transfer of this ancient dialogue to the African sphere. However, it did not affect the mutual relevance of the ties between Egypt and Ethiopia. Although Egypt declared Ethiopia irrelevant to the Nile, and although Ethiopia declared Egypt irrelevant to its Christian culture, the two states remained deeply interconnected. By 1987, as discussed in the introduction, the Nile connection would be forcefully resumed when the Egyptians' illusion that the Aswan High Dam and Lake Nasser were their source of life was shattered, along with the false belief that the land of the Blue Nile could be ignored. This chapter addresses Ethiopian conceptions of Egypt over this long period, whereas Chapter 9 addresses Egyptian views of Ethiopia over the same span of time. The period of 1959–1991 would produce yet another cycle of Islamic-Arab-Egyptian attitudes and dichotomies in Egypt, which would be modified once more before the emergence of the Nile's present crisis.

Egypt itself, needless to say, underwent a series of profound changes during the said period. They were highlighted in September 1970 by the sudden death of Nasser and the ensuing move from his revolutionary Arabism back to Egyptian nationalism. The historical changes instituted by his successor, Anwar al-Sadat, not only revived some of Egypt's liberalism but also activated the return of Islamic radicalism, both trends influencing a renewed discussion of Ethiopia.

The change in Egypt from Nasser to Sadat ran nearly parallel to a no less fundamental change in Ethiopia. The fall of Haile Selassie in 1974 and the rise of Mangistu Haile Mariam to power (1974–1991) was equally influential in transforming Ethiopian concepts of Egypt. The nature of

Haile Selassie's regime of the 1960s and its collapse in 1974, it will be argued in this chapter, had much to do with the nature of these complicated interrelations. Moreover, Mangistu's revolutionary regime would renew Ethiopian threats regarding the Nile and would recycle traditional Ethiopian concepts of Egypt, giving them a further twist. Only in 1987 would a more constructive dialogue be resumed.

The Nile itself was hardly an international issue during the 1960s and the early 1970s, and Ethiopia under Haile Selassie seemed to have accepted, painfully, the loss of its leverage against Egypt. Church relations were also rendered marginal following the 1959 separation, and they have remained so to this day. Church-related issues continued to resurface on the Ethio-Egyptian agenda, but very seldom did they reside at the top.

In 1960–1961 the internal Christian Coptic Ethiopian dispute over Deir al-Sultan in Jerusalem reached a climax. After some deliberation the Jordanians forced the Copts to hand the keys to the monastery over to the Ethiopians (12 February 1961), but in the wake of Egyptian pressure and Nasser's interference, they reversed their decision (25 March 1961).[1] In 1970 the Israelis, having conquered east Jerusalem, handed the keys back to the Ethiopians,[2] and during the same year, upon the death of Abuna Baselyos, the Ethiopians abolished the last remnant of Ethio-Egyptian affiliation, the consecration ceremony of their patriarch by the Coptic patriarch.

Relations between the two churches went from bad to worse. When a new regime in Ethiopia deposed and replaced the Ethiopian patriarch in 1976, the Egyptian Coptic Holy Synod protested and boycotted the ceremonies.[3] Literature produced by both churches began either minimizing the historical importance or emphasizing the bad aspects of their now-defunct historical bond.[4] After Egypt made peace with Israel the Egyptians demanded the return of the Deir al-Sultan keys. The Ethiopians, on their part, launched their relentless Jerusalem campaign, both parties exerting pressure on Israel. In March 1971 the Israeli Supreme Court ruled that the keys should be returned to the Egyptians, but it also left the final decision with the Israeli government, which never reversed its 1970 decision. So although the Deir al-Sultan issue continued to mar Ethiopian-Egyptian-Israeli relations, it became rather a sideshow that cannot be narrated in detail here.[5] In the general context of Ethio-Egyptian relations, matters of interchurch rivalry have become of secondary importance.

HAILE SELASSIE AND THE
AFRICANIZATION OF RELATIONS

The fall of the two main pillars of the ancient oriental bond, the Nile and the cross, coincided with the beginning of an "African" dialogue between

Ethiopia and Egypt. Throughout the 1960s Haile Selassie and Nasser co-operated in the rising continent's new diplomatic sphere. Based on multilateral recognition of territorial integrity, and centered on Addis Ababa, the field of Pan-African diplomacy seemed at the time far more convenient for Ethiopia. But the Africanization of Ethiopian-Egyptian relations (which also suited Nasser) was to prove illusory. Beyond this new African facade old Egyptian-Ethiopian "oriental" issues and dynamism continued to operate. As far as this study is concerned, they played a central role in shaping the history of Haile Selassie's imperial Ethiopia and in determining its dramatic collapse.

Nasser as Gragn: The Arabization of Islam in the Horn of Africa

Although the Nile and the church were sidelined, other old, bilateral issues made Egypt of this period centrally relevant to Ethiopia. One of these was Eritrea. In 1961 the Eritrean Liberation Front, established in Cairo, began an open revolt in the still-autonomous federated province. Dominated by Eritrean Muslims and aided by Egyptian agents, the ELF declared its war to be a part of the Pan-Arab revolution and went on producing vast literature to this effect.[6] Official Cairo refrained from open, verbal endorsement of Eritrea's Arabism, but the Egyptians encouraged the Eritrean Muslims to promote the idea. In August 1964, to quote just one example, Ibrahim Sultan, a prominent ELF leader, stated in Cairo: "We the Eritreans are Arabs no less than the Palestinians. We fight the Jews of Africa as personified by the emperor and his government—the offspring of Solomon, the Lion of Judah, just as the Palestinians fight the Jews of Palestine."[7]

In September 1962, following a revolution in nearby Yemen, the Egyptian army landed there and for the next five years launched a war against the local "royalists" in the name of revolutionary Arabism. Egypt's strategic return to the Red Sea theater caused Haile Selassie to annex Eritrea to Ethiopia in November 1962 and annul the remainder of its autonomous features. All of Ethiopia's policymakers, as we shall see, were convinced that Nasser's goal was the Arabization of Ethiopia's Muslims and that although his first relevant priority was Yemen, he was, in the meantime, preparing his Eritrean-Arab, as well as his Somali-Arab, options. Nasser's verbal assurances and his expulsion of the ELF from Cairo in 1963 (the ELF training camp near Alexandria was closed in 1964) did not assuage the Ethiopians' deep-rooted suspicions. The war in Eritrea was depicted as even more "revolutionary Arab" in 1969 when the Eritrean People's Liberation Front (EPLF), rival of the ELF, was established in a Palestine Liberation Organization camp in Jordan. Its titular leader, 'Uthman Salih Sabbe, was the chief ideologue of Eritrea's Arabism.[8]

Arab-Egyptian involvement in the history of the struggle over Eritrea during Haile Selassie's rule cannot be summarized here.[9] Nor can
we afford a discussion of Nasserist involvement in encouraging the Somalis, independent as of July 1960, to claim the Ogaden area, which
covered nearly one-third of Ethiopia. In September 1960 Haile Selassie
was quoted as saying that "the Somalis would have never dreamt of such
an idea without being incited by Nasser."[10] Literature produced in Egypt
aimed at reviving the national Somali memory of Harar as Somalia's ancient capital of Islam and Ahmad Gragn.[11]

No less significant was the impact of the Nasserist revolution on the
Muslims of Addis Ababa and central Ethiopia. On the one hand, they
themselves began producing militant underground Islamic-Arab literature in the vein of Yusuf Ahmad and Shakib Arslan, claiming that Muslims were the majority in Ethiopia and that its Christian establishment
had deprived them of their basic rights throughout history.[12] On the other
hand, they evidently began sensing the onset of change. When Nasser
landed at the Addis Ababa airport for the inauguration of the Organization of African Unity (OAU) in May 1963, hundreds of thousands of
Muslims gathered to greet him. "The thunderous cry of Nasser! Nasser!"
wrote an Ethiopian minister at the time, "still rings in the ears of many
of the Ethiopian police and military."[13]

The so-called Ahmad Gragn trauma—the fear of Arabization, politicization, and unification of Islam in Ethiopia and the Horn, inspired by
an actively interested Middle East and leading toward the destruction of
Ethiopia as a Christian state—was arguably the single most important element shaping Haile Selassie's policy, both internal and external, of the
1960s. Moreover, the old Islamic-Arab threat was now strengthened by
a new phenomenon of revolutionary ideas among the middle class and
young officers. Mentioned earlier was the effect the 1958 wave of antimonarchical Pan-Arab eruptions and changes had on Haile Selassie. He
and his elite were especially shocked and panicked by the bloody end of
the Hashamite family in Iraq in July that year. Also of lasting impact was
the brutal mutilation of Nuri al-Sa'id's body in the streets of Bahgdad, a
sophisticated and moderate Arab leader Haile Selassie had come to respect.[14]

In December 1960 the emperor and his elite barely escaped a similar fate. A coup masterminded by the commander of the Imperial Body-
guard and his revolutionary, intellectual brother was carried out while
the emperor was abroad and led to the massacre of many leading figures.
It was quelled only due to mistakes made by the mutineers, sheer luck,
Israeli intelligence, and the resolve of Ras Asrate Kassa. Though it was
never established that an Arab-Egyptian hand was behind the abortive

December 1960 coup, many Ethiopians believed Nasser was more than merely its source of inspiration.[15] Throughout the 1960s Nasser would be much on the mind of many Ethiopian students, young intellectuals, and young officers. They feared him for being an aggressive Arab, but they also considered him to be the model for a new type of leadership, more answerable to the needs of the masses, more in line with their new ideas of representative politics.[16]

For reasons that shall soon be discussed, the official Addis Ababa line chose to embrace Nasser and even Nasserist terminology. In public speeches the emperor and his ministers heaped compliments on the Egyptian president. In his June 1959 visit to Cairo (which resulted in the final break of church relations), Haile Selassie praised his host as one of the world's great leaders. He would visit Cairo again in 1963, 1966 (when he made a highly symbolic visit to the Aswan High Dam), and 1969, contributing his share to an image of personal intimacy between an aging father figure and his favorite son.[17] In public interviews Haile Selassie told journalists he admired Nasser,[18] and upon the latter's death Haile Selassie described him as "an outstanding leader and a great friend."[19]

Perhaps even more significant was the fact that the Ethiopian authorities themselves now seemed ready to please the Arab world by referring to Ethiopia's Muslims, or at least some of them, as "Arabs." In October 1966 the "president of the Arab community in Ethiopia" sent telegrams to Nasser and other Arab leaders assuring them that "the Arabs in Ethiopia live in peace with their fellow Ethiopians and are among the most prosperous segments of the population."[20] The Ethiopian press was encouraged to broadcast the notion of Arab-Ethiopian friendliness. A journalist for the *Ethiopian Herald,* for example, described Haile Selassie's October 1966 visit to Arab countries, which culminated in a meeting with Nasser, as follows: "Ethiopia's relations with Arab countries go back for centuries. But owing to certain misunderstandings, fears and suspicions, the contact between the Arab world and Ethiopia has fared badly from time to time. During his visit His Imperial Majesty carried the message of goodwill, harmony and fraternity. As a result, prejudices have been removed, misrepresentations rectified and fears and suspicion dispelled."[21] And the *Ethiopian Herald*'s editorial lamenting Nasser's death in September 1970 went accordingly:

> Nasser was one man who did not need to die before he was praised. He was a leader who became a legendary figure in his own time. In the last 14 years of his highly regarded leadership Nasser has probably done more for Egypt than his predecessors had done in 1400 years. It was to the common man that he dedicated his service. His great leadership did not hinge on having Arabs hate Israel, but mainly on uniting the Arabs,

and even more so in carrying reforms in Egypt to benefit the mass of his people. While his ancestors built the pyramids for the dead, he built the Aswan dam for the living. . . . In him, Ethiopia loses a great friend.[22]

To state that the man who united the Arabs and built the Aswan Dam was Ethiopia's great friend and to refer to Ethiopia's Muslims as "Arabs" were perhaps brilliant exercises in the Ethiopian verbal art of hidden meanings. For what was barely hidden throughout the 1960s, persisting until the fateful year of 1974, was a clear consensus among all members of Ethiopia's imperial elite. Nasser, Nasserism, and revolutionary Arabism (as distinct from Egypt and Egyptian nationalism), as well as the potential Arabization of Ethiopia's Muslims, embodied all that they feared and hated. In private Haile Selassie would confide: "The Arabs were always our enemies. Till lately they were weak and powerless. The Europeans, unfortunately, inflated their strength and will regret it. Meanwhile we Ethiopians have to be considerate of their power, especially as we have such a big Muslim minority in Ethiopia. . . . Colonel Nasser is trying to stir up the large Muslim minority with the aim of dismembering this Christian country."[23] He would also state: "Frustrated with his Arab unity dream Nasser is looking in all directions trying to create problems and difficulties anywhere he can."[24]

Indeed, the Israeli archives are filled with similar statements made throughout that period by practically all leading personalities. Of special importance here are the words of Haile Selassie's prime minister from 1961 to 1974, Aklilu Habta-Wold, a major figure in the following analysis. In March 1963 Aklilu Habta-Wold told Shimon Peres: "I know the Arabs. We cannot trust them. They incite against us everywhere. What did the Americans find in Nasser? Why did they not allow you to finish him off in the 1956 war? We have a common enemy and a common danger, we have to cooperate."[25] In March 1968 he told the director general of the Israeli Foreign Ministry: "Ethiopia is a Christian island in a Muslim sea, and the Muslims make no distinction between religious and political goals. Their aim is to destroy Ethiopia."[26] In May 1972 he told a very high Israeli official: "Ethiopia is weak, poor, war-torn, and at any given moment she can be exposed to the Arabs' collective hatred of her."[27]

Nasserism in Ethiopians' Eyes

For many in the Ethiopian imperial elite, revolutionary Arabism had not only snatched the Nile by building the Aswan Dam and threatened to unite Ethiopia's Muslims against their hegemony. It had also created a new kind of Egyptian. One prominent member of Haile Selassie's establishment published his detailed memoirs in 1995. Emmanuel Abraham, like all leading diplomats stationed in various capitals, was asked by the emperor to follow Egyptian affairs as well. When explaining to Haile Selassie what he thought of the new generation of revolutionaries in Cairo, he said:

> We Christians believe and know in some measure that our Christian faith is superior to any other, and that it is able to raise the human person to a very high level both materially and spiritually. As a result when we see someone of another faith at fault, we are at times prone to fall into the temptation of thinking, if not actually saying, "What is to be expected from a person following such a faith!" Without assuming the attitude of the Pharisee and trying to raise the so called Christian peoples to a higher plane than the Egyptian people, it seems to me that the modern people of Egypt, and especially that section which has had a smattering of modern education and which in consequence has assumed the leadership of the common people, have abandoned the faith of their forefathers and have not fully grasped modern ideals and knowledge. They are like a man who goes out on a boat without oars.[28]

He later elaborated: "Colonel Abdel Nasser and his colleagues, after having declared that they were determined to afford welfare and chance in life to the poor common people of Egypt . . . abandoned their declared policy and, posing as leaders and champions of the Arab peoples and the whole of Africa, interfered right and left in the private affairs of other nations, inflicting wounds on great and small alike, like biting dogs."[29]

Bereket Habte Selassie, an Ethiopian minister in the 1960s (and later a leading ideologue of Eritrean nationalism) published his analysis of the Horn affairs, *Conflict and Intervention in the Horn of Africa,* in 1980. He dealt with Nasserist Egypt in a chapter titled "Neighbors and Meddlers." He blamed Nasser for reviving Khedive Isma'il's imperial and territorial ambitions in the Red Sea, "cloaking it in an ideology of pan-Islam and pan-Arab socialism, augmented by pan-Africanism."[30]

Perhaps the most blunt expression of what members of the Ethiopian elite felt in facing the Nasserist Arab world of the 1960s was made by Ahadu Sabore, a journalist, ambassador, and finally a minister in Haile Selassie's last government of 1974. In prison, after the collapse of imperial Ethiopia, he wrote:

> The Arabs were our enemies who for a long time had never let up in wounding and bleeding us by looking for opportunities to attack us and injure us. Leaders like Gamal Abd al-Nasser and King Faysal [of Saudi Arabia] were the utmost faithless knaves who made sweet words and promises, whose breaths stank, whose pledges were completely untrustworthy, who used prevarication as major political method and

instrument and who, while they turned their face five times a day toward Mecca and prostrated themselves in worship to Allah, were only
plotting this swindling action of theirs.[31]

The challenge presented by Nasserism to Ethiopia in the 1960s was
a pivotal factor in its history. It was a decade that witnessed an impres-
sive culmination of the ancient Ethiopian state and its imperial system.
With the reannexation of Eritrea, the state of Ethiopia reached the historical peak of its territorial size. Political and cultural unification, combined with new elements of modernization in education, the military,
communications, and the like, seemed to bring the ancient political
ideals of imperial benevolent authoritarianism to their highest state of ef-
fectiveness. International prestige, with Addis Ababa acting as the capital of awakening Africa, helped solidify a sense of successful continuity
among members of the elite.

Nevertheless, this was also a decade of growing anxiety for the elite.
It saw the rise of new forces at home and their growing expectations.
The 1960s in Ethiopia witnessed the accumulating challenges of a rapidly expanding, new generation of educated youth, as well as the revival
of provincial, regional, and religious forces. The Nasserist threat, radiating both sociopolitical revolutionary Arabism and the politicization of
Islamic and provincial communities, was very relevant to all these internal challenges. Indeed, Haile Selassie's response to the threat of Arabism had a direct impact on the way he dealt with affairs at home. In the
final analysis, "the Ahmad Gragn trauma" had much to do with the
regime's failure to accept the new internal forces, a failure that was to
lead to a tragic end and brutal consequences.

Aklilu's Strategy: Meeting in Africa

In spite of the authoritarianism centered on one of the world's most experienced politicians, Haile Selassie's government knew no institutionalized planning. According to the best-informed sources, even the Eritrea
problem was never really discussed or seriously analyzed by the higher
echelon of the imperial establishment.[32] The emperor himself, aging and
overworked, tended more and more simply to ignore difficult issues,
concentrating instead on areas yielding immediate reward and prestige.
Decisions, when made, were made by Haile Selassie alone and were primarily the result of his listening to his closest advisers and politicians,
individually and separately.

As such, Ethiopian politics of the 1960s was, for the most part, a rivalry among quite a small number of leading figures for proximity to the

imperial ear. None of the leading members of the imperial establishment was ready to challenge the absolute authority of the emperor, but they all bided their time, waiting for the new order to be formed after his death, all maneuvering for the position of the future strongman behind Haile Selassie's successor as they opted for different contenders among his descendants. They were also all aware of the various threats and challenges mentioned above, so they shared a deep anxiety for the very survival of their system. But they differed in advice as to the general strategy to be adopted, and their differences arose no less from their rivalries and jealousies than from varying viewpoints. The emperor himself, in line with a long tradition, also made his decisions and changed course in accordance with his interest in playing his men off against one another.

As the scope of the present discussion does not allow going into details here, we shall confine ourselves to portraying the two main protagonists in the current action and the options they represented. One set of options for Ethiopia consisted of downplaying the Middle East, building an African strategy, placating Nasser, and neutralizing him in Africa while at home solidifying the centralization of power and culture. The other set of options entailed confronting Nasserism through an Israeli–Middle Eastern strategy while on the domestic front opening up the government to some of the provincial-regional forces, particularly the Tigrean Eritreans, and, to a lesser extent, to the new educated generation. The tension between these two contending sets of options was a major factor in the events leading to Haile Selassie's fall in 1974.

The man who, more than any other, worked to promote the first combination was Prime Minister Aklilu Habta-Wold (1961–1974). Born to a family of priests in Shoa, Aklilu was one of three brothers who entered politics and owed their careers to Haile Selassie. Before his execution, together with almost all other prominent figures of Haile Selassie's regime in November 1974, Aklilu wrote a long report on his life, published in Sweden in 1994 under the title *Aklilu Remembers: Historical Recollections from a Prison Cell*.[33] The memoir reveals a very strong sense of personal dependency on the emperor and unconcealed animosity toward "the nobility." One dimension of Aklilu's work was to strengthen and institutionalize centralized imperial absolutism. He was a great proponent of the 1955 Constitution and the later legislation of the 1960s, which prevented the introduction of any sort of modern political organization. Aklilu was equally opposed to any compromise with provincial factors, and he urged Haile Selassie not to grant even limited powers of self-administration to the various districts. In 1967, for example, the Ethiopian Parliament rejected the idea of such self-administration on the grounds that it would encourage separatist tendencies.[34]

Indeed, Aklilu was behind Haile Selassie's fateful policy that, militarily and inflexibly, sought to quell the Eritrean revolt, a point to which we shall return.

Aklilu was also Haile Selassie's chief adviser on foreign affairs and had been the acting foreign minister since 1943. In Aklilu's vision of global affairs Egypt had a special prominent place, a result of the most formative stages in his life. Born, as mentioned earlier, to a family of priests, he was one of those youngsters handpicked and promoted by Ras Tafari (the future Haile Selassie). Tafari, in his 1924 visit to Egypt, much impressed by Egypt's new liberal education, arranged to send his young protégés to the Nile Valley country. Aklilu was sent to Alexandria in 1925, where he attended the French Lycée for six years. According to his own memoirs, he became the leader of some thirty young Ethiopian students in Alexandria (including the two sons of Heruy Walda-Selassie who studied at Victoria College). Confident in their role as Tafari's men and the future leaders of Ethiopia, Aklilu's flock of protégés also assumed responsibility for the younger Ethiopian students educated by the Coptic Church. Aklilu undertook to improve their lot and got in touch with Egypt's leading politicians, particularly the Coptic foreign minister, Wasif Boutros-Ghali. For a while young Aklilu managed to conduct a successful campaign, on which he reported to Tafari.[35] This was, remember, the heyday of Egyptian liberalism and the peak of Ethio-Egyptian friendliness.

Aklilu's six years in Egypt were to have a lasting impact. Fluent in both French and Arabic, he made quite a number of Egyptian friends.[36] Some members of that circle of Alexandria students were to become his future associates and aides in the Foreign Ministry. Together with many graduates of the American University of Beirut, they constituted an Arab-oriented old guard in the ministry during the 1960s.[37]

According to his memoirs, Aklilu's major achievement in life was the diplomatic struggle over Eritrea in the late 1940s.[38] Already in charge of foreign affairs, Aklilu spent much time in the UN, masterfully conducting a campaign against the Egyptian claim to Eritrea. He resorted to his expertise in international law and his knowledge of the Yohannes-Isma'il period to win the case. He also combined threats regarding the Nile with quotations from the Prophet about the *najashi* and Islam to skillfully outmaneuver the Egyptians. Not only did they give up their claim to Eritrea, they were also the only Islamic country finally to vote for federating Eritrea with Ethiopia. In the process Aklilu developed special relations with Egypt's representative to the UN, Dr. Mahmud Fawzi, who would be a major factor in Egypt's international diplomacy in the 1960s as well. Closing his deal with the Egyptians, Aklilu also managed to persuade Haile Selassie to pay a price. On 29 November 1947 Ethiopia abstained in the vote on the partition of Palestine and the establishment of a Jewish state. A short time later it joined all the Arab missions in voting against the admission of Israel to the UN.[39]

It is apparent that Aklilu had a thorough understanding of the change from the parliamentarian Egypt he knew (and the one with which Haile Selassie was anxious to remain connected) to the revolutionary Arabism of Nasser. He was not really "taken with Nasser," as one British diplomat said,[40] but was fully aware of the threat to Ethiopia from "the Arabs." In fact, one of his closest associates, and Aklilu's foreign minister during most of the 1960s, Katama Yifru, said in 1974: "The ex–prime minister was one who from the start was frightened every time the Arab name was mentioned, and he believed they could hurt us in various ways, i.e., by stirring up the Muslims of Ethiopia against us, by helping the Eritrean secessionists with arms and money, and also by supporting our neighbor and antagonist Somalia."[41] However, it is equally apparent that Aklilu was confident that, through sophisticated diplomacy, he could still revive at least some of the old cooperative Egypt he knew.[42] Moreover, it seems he thought that even without the lost card of the Nile, he could play a winning game against Nasser. Indeed, for quite some time he was proven right.

Aklilu was Haile Selassie's chief adviser and architect of the grand move to Africa. The significance of this tremendous change can be better appreciated in light of the long history narrated in the previous chapters.[43] As Ethiopia severed its connections with the Egyptian Church in 1959, breaking a major, ancient "oriental" bond, it was already in the process of creating ties with the rising spirit of Africanism. Here again we cannot go into detail, nor even mention the various backgrounds and processes that led to the establishment of the OAU in 1963. When Haile Selassie first began discussing Ethiopia's African identity in 1958, a Pan-African arena of competing conceptual trends was already in action. The emancipated continent was centered primarily on West African leadership and ideas, and already Nasserist and Algerian revolutionary Arabism was playing a significant role in a new circle of African diplomacy.

Haile Selassie and Aklilu entered the picture intent on stemming Pan-African ideas of revolutionary unity led by an "Accra bloc," which was connected with what Aklilu defined as an "Arab bloc" and which, in January 1961, together formed a "Casablanca bloc."[44] Aklilu, appointed prime minister in March 1961, was instrumental in organizing the more moderate "Monrovia bloc" in May that year, which stood for Pan-African solidarity and cooperation but also for retaining the territorial integrity and full sovereignty of the different states.

In 1962 Aklilu managed to shift the center of Pan-African activity to Addis Ababa, where he himself oversaw the preparation of the first draft of the OAU's charter. By Aklilu's own account in his memoirs, "I began

to lobby various foreign ministers, such as Dr. Fawzi, the Egyptian Foreign Affairs Minister, and urged them to prepare the draft for a signing
immediately before the closure of the meeting of the Heads of States" (p.
76). Aklilu's old friend Dr. Fawzi, instructed by Nasser to recognize
Ethiopia's leadership in Africa, endorsed the draft, even though Egypt's
demand that Israel's illegitimacy be mentioned in the OAU's charter was
rejected.[45] Nasser himself (whose pragmatic dimension will be analyzed
in Chapter 9) attended the signing ceremony in Addis Ababa in May
1963 and embraced Haile Selassie as the two of them led a symbolic
march. In August 1964 Cairo hosted the second meeting of the OAU,
and there it was decided that Addis Ababa would be the organization's
permanent headquarters.[46]

Although most groups and peoples of historical central and northern
Ethiopia never really identified themselves as blacks,[47] Ethiopia has always, in many ways, been no less African than oriental. The short process
of reemphasizing Ethiopia's "African-ness" was therefore intense, effective, and multidimensional. The diplomatic road from marginal partnership in a dangerous Middle East to distinguished seniority in a continent
of rising expectations was swift and clear. In no time Addis Ababa became the capital of African diplomacy, with most African states establishing double missions, one accredited to Ethiopia, the other to the OAU.
In their wake UN officials and other Pan-African international bodies established themselves in the Ethiopian capital during the 1960s.

All of this was accompanied by intense parallel changes in equally
significant spheres, such as academic scholarship. During the 1950s the
field of Ethiopian studies was still led by historians, sociologists, lin-
guists, and scholars of religions and cultures, all "orientalists" in their
training and approach. Their writings, as reflected, for example, at the
First International Conference of Ethiopian Studies held in Rome in
April 1959, were very compatible with the historical centrality of
Ethiopian issues linking Ethiopia with the Middle East.[48] In the 1960s,
however, a new generation of Africanists was happy to adopt Ethiopia,
while a new generation of Ethiopianists had good reason to begin studying Ethiopia as an African state and culture. Indeed, the new "Africanist" approach, in line with the timely revolutionary development of the
social sciences, rendered more justice to Ethiopia's ethnic and cultural
diversity and put Ethiopian studies at the forefront of a new global
scholarly endeavor to study non-Western societies in a more balanced
manner. The Africanization of Ethiopian studies was also spearheaded
by the new Haile Selassie I University, opened in Addis Ababa in 1961.
During the 1960s Ethiopia's African-ness became the main feature of its
self-awareness, image, and identity.

The establishment of OAU headquarters in Addis Ababa was a major achievement as well as a great diplomatic victory. More to our point, it rendered the Ethiopian-Egyptian dialogue "African" rather than "Middle Eastern."[49] In accordance with the principles of the OAU, it successfully forced Nasser to avoid subversion, at least verbally. Much to the emperor's relief, Aklilu's strategy seemed successful. In 1964 Ethiopia's Foreign Ministry was reorganized, and Egypt was included in a new "Division of North Africa" in the "Africa and the Middle East Department." The Middle East Division has dealt with most other Arab countries and Israel ever since, but Egypt has remained "North African" in official Ethiopian eyes to this very day (in 1994 a new Africa Directorate General was established, containing Egypt in the North Africa Division).[50]

The Africanization of Ethiopian-Egyptian relations enabled the two parties to conveniently ignore their old "Middle Eastern" differences and build a dialogue of diplomatic politeness. Ethiopia's leadership in diplomatic Africa was also a field Haile Selassie was all too happy to enter. His personal role as the elder statesman of the continent undergoing emancipation was perhaps his final victory in a life filled with struggle and anxiety. It proved, however, a mixed blessing, for during the 1960s, especially after the December 1960 coup at home was foiled, the aging monarch spent much less time worrying about Ethiopia's internal challenges.

Asrate's Middle Eastern Option

Aklilu's chief rival throughout the period under discussion was Asrate Kassa. A leading member of the nobility of Shoa, Ethiopia's central province, Asrate was the son of Haile Selassie's closest ally, and he himself remained loyal to the emperor to the end. He has already been mentioned as the chief negotiator with Nasser during the 1959 break of church relations and as the man who saved Haile Selassie by quelling the December 1960 coup. As the more prominent among a loose group of "nobles," he offered options different than Aklilu's during the 1960s. One was to halt the pretense that Nasser was a good "African" neighbor, a topic to which we shall soon return. The other had to do with the nature of imperial centralization and domestic affairs.

Asrate had this to say to an Israeli diplomat in July 1963:

> Ethiopia is undergoing a crisis and faces a revolution that may topple the regime. The widespread popular belief is that the system should be changed promptly, either peacefully or through violence. The urge for change, which until recently motivated only some intellectuals, is now a matter for the masses. The people are disgusted with the government, the administration, and its corruption. They are willing to take part and

influence matters either through a new modern constitutional life or the old traditional ways. Whatever there is in Ethiopia of economic development is concentrated in the capital, while the provinces are left behind and ignored. The general comprehensive unrest could erupt at any time. The imperial establishment is tired and washed out, incapable of action despite the fact that all are aware of the need for quick and drastic reforms. There are three foci of unrest. One is the army, where the rank and file hate the officers. The junior officers, lieutenants, and some captains, are complete revolutionaries, and the intermediate officers are immersed in jealousies and rivalries. The second focus is the young intelligentsia. They can eventually help the young officers but cannot themselves initiate a change. The third is the common peoples of the various provinces. They want to restore decentralization and they are capable of challenging the government. Indeed, some decentralization of government should be introduced promptly and as a first step toward deeper reforms. . . . The emperor is fully aware of the situation and knows he should begin to delegate power to the people and their representatives. But after forty years of absolute power, and with all his achievements, he has difficulties drawing the conclusions. . . . The prime minister is hated by the people, the army, and the intelligentsia. His power stems from the emperor only, he is a courtier with no ideological spine.[51]

In 1964 Dajazmach Asrate Kassa (promoted to *ras* in 1966) was appointed the emperor's "representative" and governor of Eritrea. He held this post for more than six years, during which he did his best to turn the province into his power base in the context of his rivalry with the prime minister. But his efforts to solidify his own administrative autonomy went far beyond fighting for local budgets or refusing to transfer revenues from the ports of Massawa and Assab. Asrate believed the rebellion in Eritrea was essentially Islamic secessionism incited by Nasserist Arabism, and in that field he continued to find much evidence of ongoing Egyptian subversion. He believed that Islamic-Arab Eritreanism went against the interests of the local Christian Tigreans. The latter, by far the stronger community in highland Eritrea, had indeed supported reunification with Ethiopia in the 1940s and remained loyal to Haile Selassie during the 1952–1962 federation period.

In 1964 Asrate, assuming leadership of the local government, had regretted much of the absolutist centralization and the outright cancellation of all local political or administrative organizations imposed by Addis Ababa on Eritrea. Though he never really challenged the newly imposed Amharization of culture and education (teaching in Tigrinya, Arabic, and Tigre was now prohibited by the central government), Asrate began working for reimplementation of local Christian Tigrean autonomy under his personal authority. By 1966 virtually all local functionaries, the governors of the nine subprovinces, his chief administrators, judges, advisers, and members of the local royal court he built with all due pomp and circumstance in his Asmara palace were local Tigrinya-speaking Eritreans.

Additionally, opposing the intervention of the central army as far as possible, Asrate built local Eritrean police forces, an intelligence apparatus, and a special battalion-size "Commando 101" unit (trained by his Israeli advisers), wearing local provincial Eritrean uniforms. They were all composed of Tigrinya-speaking Christian Eritreans. Securing much local Christian loyalty, Asrate even tried to reach some understanding with those Christian Eritreans who joined the revolt. Yet he also cooperated closely with Ras Mangasha Seyum, his next-door neighbor, governor of the Tigre province, and great-grandson of Yohannes IV. The two aristocrats (their families were connected through marriage) had much in common in trying to promote decentralization and some political openness.[52]

The six years of Asrate's government in Eritrea were marked by a struggle between himself and Aklilu over the way to quell the rebellion. Whenever the central army intervened with its customary brutality, more Christians identified with the revolt. In October 1970 a chain of successful guerrilla operations enabled Aklilu finally to persuade Haile Selassie to terminate Asrate's appointment and declare martial law in Eritrea. Asrate's Tigrean policy in Eritrea collapsed as the central army was given a free hand to solve the problem in its own way. Asrate himself returned to Addis Ababa and assumed the chairmanship of the Crown Council, losing more and more ground in his competition with Aklilu. His loss to Aklilu, judging retroactively, ruined Ethiopia's chances of retaining Eritrea. It also ruined any chance that the imperial regime would open up politics to the young forces in both the center and at the periphery.

Asrate's efforts in Eritrea and the north to build an alliance with the local Tigreans should be evaluated from a much longer perspective. In the long run Ethiopia was to lose Eritrea not because of Islamic secessionism, but merely because the Tigrean Eritreans would despair of Ethiopian centralism, first under Haile Selassie, then more forcefully and brutally under Mangistu Haile Mariam. Furthermore, the struggle over Eritrea was in large part the struggle over the nature of Ethiopia's political system. While the imperial center of Addis Ababa went on ignoring the need to modernize politics, the northern Tigreans' efforts to decentralize the system constituted perhaps the country's best chance for some degree of openness.

During the 1960s Tigrean Eritreans still represented the constitutional parliamentarianism of their defunct autonomy. Tigreans in general, as in the days of Yohannes, represented a decentralized system and cultural diversification. Many of them integrated into Haile Selassie's regime but resented its political closure. A prominent example of this trend was the Tigrean Eritrean Lieutenant General Aman Andom, a lifetime friend of Asrate, who became the Ethiopian army's chief of staff and a hero in the clashes with the Somalis of the early 1960s. In 1965 Aman deviated from Haile Selassie's instructions and was transferred to the meaningless Senate. He remained, however, in close touch with the university's students, young army officers, and other intellectuals who yearned for a change.[53] He also remained in very close contact with his brother, Meles Andom, the Ethiopian ambassador to Cairo[54] and, as we have seen, a sworn opponent of Nasser. Aman, like Asrate Kassa, saw clearly the connection between the Eritrean issue and the modernization of Ethiopia's politics. Like Asrate, and perhaps more so, he and his brother in Cairo opposed avoiding the Nasserist threat, restricting internal politics, and escaping to African diplomacy.

The fact that those who preferred not to ignore the internal challenges were those who preferred not to ignore the Arab revolutionary threat was not coincidental. Ras Asrate was no party to the new and seemingly rewarding Pan-African diplomatic enterprise, nor would he consider Nasserist Egypt as a friendly African neighbor. He preferred facing what he saw as the facts by allying closely and openly with Israel.

It is beyond the realm of our discussion here to deal with Ethiopian-Israeli relations in and of themselves,[55] but their main premise was the common Nasserist threat, and their development and outcome are quite relevant to the essence of our story. Earlier, I mentioned David Ben-Gurion's motives for attempting to build an Ethiopian-Israeli alliance. After 1959 this became a prime strategic target for Israel, and the Jewish state made every effort to reach this goal. Early in the 1960s, prior to Ethiopia's agreement to establish full diplomatic relations in May 1962, Israeli investment in Ethiopia in terms of quality manpower, sharing know-how, training, building, managing, teaching, and so forth, was already far greater than any other Israeli diplomatic foreign output. Of special interest, of course, was the common strategic cause, and during the 1960s most of Israel's top military and security leaders toured Ethiopia.

In March 1963, for example, Shimon Peres, then Ben-Gurion's deputy as minister of defense, and Yitzhak Rabin, then deputy chief of staff, spent a whole week together in the country. At that time Peres was in the middle of negotiations with the French on a secret missile deal crucial to the then-culminating Dimona nuclear enterprise. Yet the two of them went to meet secretly with Haile Selassie, Aklilu, ministers, and generals and have a firsthand look at the Blue Nile, "where the life of Egypt begins," as Peres put it. Back in Israel, Peres wrote a forty-page top secret report on Ethiopia and Israeli interests that contained this long excerpt:

> Ethiopia's intelligentsia is far larger than that in other African countries, but its poverty is African. The land is ethnically diversified, but most groups are under the hegemony of one, the Amharas. The country, however, is in a transitory stage. On the one hand, it is immersed in expectations and tensions, but on the other hand, it is equipped with strong tradition and much patience. . . . The people have fought bravely throughout history and won their independence but they have won little welfare and meager progress. A new generation, vocal yet capable, is yearning to assume leadership, but it faces an old guard that is articulate, experienced, and stubborn. It is possible the emperor may be assassinated. It is possible his heir may be deposed. It is possible a constitutional monarchy will emerge. It is possible that the young army officers will ally themselves with the university students. It is equally possible that these revolutionary officers will ally themselves with the proletariat of the countryside. Nasser is quite popular in wide circles, but only as a model for revolutionary change. Egypt is widely seen as the enemy, but what happens in Egypt's domestic affairs—not what it does in foreign strategy—is something they consider worth following. This prerevolutionary atmosphere does not change the basic facts: Ethiopia is a large and important country, it is neither Arab nor Muslim. Christians are the majority and they are filled with a deep historical sense in whose heart Israel features squarely. Ethiopia is situated south of Egypt and holds the key to Egypt's very future, for it controls the Blue Nile. Ethiopia has an army, a proud military tradition, and it respects Israel and would gradually like to become allied with us. Israel should work intensively and carefully. Ethiopia is a vital element in our effort to break the Arab hostility around us with power, connections, and resourcefulness. . . . It is our goal to reach an alliance with Ethiopia—cultural, economic, and military. We must spare no effort and resources in working toward this aim.[56]

Ras Asrate was the chief architect of Ethiopia's relations with Israel. For him and for many others, including Haile Selassie, the issue went far beyond strategic practicalities. Israel, in many ways, resembled the long-yearned-for non-Islamic ally who, like the Portuguese in the days of Ahmad Gragn, could help stem Arabization. For many Ethiopians, especially members of the Christian elite, the old biblical Ethiopian-Christian dimension, combined with the traditional Ethiopian Zionist-Solomonian ethos, made the Israeli connection a matter of identity.[57] Indeed, Ethiopia's trust in Israel seemed also to have originated in the deep Ethiopian-Christian belief that the Ethiopians, the "true children of Israel," shared a common destiny with Israel. When Israel defeated the Arabs in the June 1967 war, Nasser's humiliation was popularly celebrated in Addis Ababa as a

historical Ethiopian victory. Israeli experts were invited to participate at
the most intimate junctures and in the most crucial and delicate spheres.
Of special importance were the activities of the Israeli Mossad and the
Israeli army's military mission. The former was much involved in Asrate's policy in Eritrea. The latter was deeply involved in the Ethiopian
army's intelligence, security services, staff school, planning, and training of most of the elite battalions. (Even the small special security unit
formed in 1963 to protect Nasser during the OAU's first gathering in
Addis Ababa was trained by an Israeli.)[58] The intimate involvement of
the Israelis in the Ethiopian army peaked during 1968–1971, when General Avraham Orli served as military attaché. He also became a close
confidant of both Aman Andom and Asrate Kassa.

The Collapse

As mentioned earlier, Aklilu was for downplaying the Israeli connection
from the very beginning. Although he cherished Israeli aid, he wanted it
all under the table. Afraid to annoy the Arabs, he managed to delay
Ethiopian recognition of Israel until 1962. He then continued to persuade
Haile Selassie not to open an embassy in Israel[59] and to meet Israelis
(such as Peres and Rabin) in secret. Israeli experts were asked to conceal
their activities and never to wear Israeli army uniforms, not even at official banquets. In 1969 Israel offered a full open alliance but was rejected. When, in early 1970, the Israelis enabled the Ethiopians to finally
recover the keys to the gates of Deir al-Sultan, the Ethiopian press celebrated the historical event in tremendous headlines. But Israel was not
mentioned, and the public was told that the ancient Jerusalem monastery
had been recovered due to a Jordanian decision dating from 1961.[60]

By that time Arab African states, led by Egypt, had begun using the
African arena to threaten Ethiopia. Arguing that Israel had occupied
African territory in 1967, they managed to put Israel on the OAU's
agenda. In 1971 an African delegation went to the Middle East and met
with an Israeli refusal to consider the Sinai Peninsula an African territory. Aklilu, who had just defeated Asrate over Eritrea, persuaded Haile
Selassie to take the lead in an anti-Israeli OAU campaign. To Israeli officials Aklilu explained that Ethiopia needed a strong Israel to curtail the
Arabs but that Ethiopia itself was too weak and had to pretend it sided
with them.[61]

In 1973 the Somalis obtained new MiG 21 jet fighters from Moscow
while the Americans refused to rearm Ethiopia. The Egyptians and the
Libyans threatened to move OAU headquarters from Addis Ababa, and in
May 1973 Haile Selassie went to Cairo to plead for Egyptian assistance

in blunting the Libyan diplomatic offensive.[62] As Sadat promised Aklilu he would restrain the Somalis, and as King Faisal of Saudi Arabia promised to compensate Ethiopia with $200 million, Haile Selassie, following the leaders of other African states, broke off diplomatic relations with Israel on 23 October 1973 during the Yom Kippur War, when Arab armies still seemed victorious.

Cutting the second bond that tied it to the East did not help Ethiopia. African diplomacy wanted little to do with Ethiopia's accumulating problems. They were aggravated following the quick, abrupt expulsion of the Israelis. One major problem was the regime's inability to cope with, or even merely to follow, the ever-intensifying crisis in the army and the growing unrest among the junior and intermediate officers. Since Israeli trainers and experts had been a major linking element between the imperial establishment and this revolutionary-minded layer in most army units for years, their sudden absence created a critical vacuum.[63] Moreover, severing relations with Israel, a decision made by Haile Selassie on Aklilu's recommendation, created a profound shock for many in the elite. It was strongly suggested by those close to the emperor that even the aging monarch himself could not recuperate from this act of betrayal and self-uprooting.[64] After traveling to Saudi Arabia in January 1974 just to discover that King Faisal was not really serious about financial compensation, Haile Selassie barely showed his face to his closest advisers. Indeed, it is difficult to understand the nature of the developments of 1974—the spontaneous, smooth organization of the young junior officers' revolutionary council by June of that year, the virtual paralysis of the imperial elite, the victory of the less qualified among the mutineers over the better educated—without taking all of the above into account.[65]

More to our point, the basic, fundamental, long-range reason for the collapse of the imperial order and the nature of the 1974 revolution was the old regime's failure throughout the 1960s to open up internal politics and face up to its real socioeconomic challenges. This fateful closure had much to do with the nature of the Nasserist Pan-Arab and the Nasserist social revolutionary threats, as well as with the victory in Ethiopia during the early 1970s of those who, out of traumatic fear, offered evasive solutions.

MANGISTU RECLAIMS THE NILE

By the mid-1970s both Egypt and Ethiopia had changed character and roles. After the 1973 war with Israel, Sadat's new orientation on the United States, combined with his historic return to the values and structures of

Egyptian nationalism at home, became more visible. Under his leadership Egypt sidelined the ideology and regional politics of revolutionary Arabism. The Suez Canal was reopened in 1975, and in 1977 Sadat initiated a reconciliation process with Israel that yielded the 1978 Camp David Accords and the 1979 Israeli-Egyptian Peace Treaty. In the next chapter we shall discuss the implications of these fundamental changes on Egyptian concepts of Ethiopia. Part of the internal liberalization, for example, was reflected in Coptic politicians and scholars retaking the lead in influencing regional Egyptian policy and Egyptian understanding of Ethiopia. If Haile Selassie's regime had survived to the late 1970s, one may speculate, a new chapter of mutual trust could perhaps have begun.

But Ethiopia was now heading in exactly the opposite direction. By the end of 1974 the old imperial regime had been wiped out. In June the young officers' revolutionary council, the Derg, became the only effective body in the country. Facing a self-paralyzed establishment, the Derg imprisoned members of the elite one by one. In July, the ignorant, young officers invited their long-admired idol, the retired General Aman Andom, to head their body. On 12 September they deposed Haile Selassie and had him arrested. While Aman, envisioning a pluralist new republic, tried to build a compromise with the Eritreans, Major Mangistu Haile Mariam gained power over the least-educated members of the Derg. On 23 November 1974 they executed, without trial, fifty-eight members of the old elite, including both Aklilu and Asrate. They also killed Aman Andom in a gunfight the same night. In August 1975 a group of them, headed by Mangistu, strangled the isolated, aged Haile Selassie in his bed. The man who, with all due reservations, was undoubtedly the most important leader in Ethiopian modern history was quickly and secretly buried in the yard just beneath Mangistu's toilet.

It would take Major Mangistu the next two years to liquidate all other contenders and defeat their ideas.[66] His bloody path to power reflected the new political culture he was about to impose. His regime claimed to broaden the political game and, in time, did introduce bodies such as peasant associations, urban committees, and finally (in 1984) a one-party system. But the resulting outcome was little more than the brutalization of the old system. Until his end in 1991 Ethiopian politics remained for Mangistu a sphere of primordial relations with himself as an absolute, merciless, sole ruler striving for complete centralization of state and power.

Sadat as Isma'il and Hitler

Uprooting everything reminiscent of the imperial past, the new regime borrowed its terminology and symbols from Marxism-Leninism. It tried

also to retain its African identity, but the new Ethiopia had lost its spe- ◄—
cial standing in the continent. For Mangistu, in any case, the main external sphere of affiliation for his new Ethiopia was the USSR and the
Communist bloc.[67] The Middle East, a world Haile Selassie had worked
to avoid, was now to be depicted as the main enemy. In Mangistu's eyes
most Arab countries were considered "reactionary" and "imperialist"
(and Israel fared no better). But it was Sadat's Egypt that became the
embodiment of evil, the force behind what was perceived to be a new
Arab-Islamic jihad against Ethiopia. Unlike Haile Selassie's pretended
view of Nasser, however, Mangistu did not try to portray Sadat as a good
African neighbor. As long as the latter, no less a blunt politician, was
alive, Mangistu fought Western-oriented Egypt, resorting to verbal aggression and threats. It was also in this context that he deviated from
Haile Selassie's policy of indirect diplomatic hints regarding the Nile
and began openly and forcefully challenging Egypt by reclaiming
Ethiopian rights over the river.

Like many dictators in pursuit of internal centralization, Mangistu
needed an external historical enemy. In 1975–1977 he was still struggling for power, facing many rivals within and outside of the Derg. After
his murder of Aman Andom Ethiopia began losing most of the territory
of Eritrea to the separatists. In Somalia President Siad Barre was building a strong Soviet-equipped army, especially after his 1974 treaty with
Moscow, far superior to the now politicized and weakened Ethiopian
forces. Siad continued to declare that he was about to liberate all the
Somali-populated areas in Ethiopia, a territory covering nearly one-third
of the country.

Eliminating internal opposition amid a murderous "red terror" campaign that lasted until 1978, Mangistu worked to convince the Soviets to
abandon the Somalis and adopt revolutionary Ethiopia. He was also
making good, systematic use of the old fear of an Islamic-Arab plot to
erase Ethiopia. Beginning in 1975 he made endless speeches calling on
Ethiopians to prepare for an Arab holy war aimed at their destruction. He
accused "reactionary Arabs" of supporting the Eritreans, as well as his
opponents at home. In working to unite the country behind him,
Mangistu was also helped by the fact that the Red Sea was again a main
focus of Egyptian and Arab interest.

After the reopening of the Suez Canal in 1975, the shipment of oil
from the Persian Gulf to the West was resumed; this time, however, the
Soviets were entrenched along this vital route. They had built positions
in South Yemen and Somalia, and Mangistu was doing his best to win
their hearts. To curtail the Soviets, the Egyptians, with encouragement
from the United States, began to work closely with Sudan and Saudi
Arabia, as well as with the ELF in Eritrea in 1976. Claiming that the Red

Sea had always been "an Arab lake," they coordinated naval and military activities. Their goal was not the perpetuation of Nasser's revolutionary Pan-Arabism of the 1960s; Egypt had little interest now in spreading revolutionary ideas.[68] Cairo had long ceased promoting the "Arabization" of Ethiopia's Muslims. In Ethiopia, however, this anti-Soviet Arab-Islamic concentration of effort and the Egyptian slogan "Arabism of the Red Sea" both helped Mangistu. By awakening long-entrenched anxieties and evoking the collective memory of Ahmad Gragn, he could rally popular support behind his toughness. In early 1977 Mangistu managed to convince Moscow to send arms not only to Siad Barre, but to him as well. In April he began building a new, huge, Soviet-equipped army. On 23 July 1977 the Somalis, sensing this to be their last chance, invaded the Ogaden. Their initial success was the greatest threat to Ethiopia since the time of Mussolini. It also enabled Mangistu to consolidate his hold on the country.

The 1977–1978 Ogaden War has to be mentioned here because of its Egyptian and Christian-Islamic dimensions. By September 1977 the invading Somalis had captured almost all the disputed territory with the exception of two towns, notably Harar. They laid siege to Ahmad Gragn's medieval capital of Islam and the strategic key to heartland Ethiopia. Only a very concentrated Ethiopian effort, the help of an elite Cuban division, and active Soviet involvement (in August the Somalis expelled their Russian advisers) checked the Somali attack. After months of siege the Soviets' decision to opt for Mangistu rather than the Somalis tipped the scales. In March 1978 the new Cuban-backed Ethiopian army pushed the Somalis back to their border. The Ethiopians avoided penetrating Somalia only because their new priority was in Eritrea. By late 1978 Mangistu's new army had managed to recapture most of Eritrea's urban centers.

The significance of the Ogaden War should be understood in the light of the history narrated in the earlier chapters. The idea that an Islamic-Arab Middle East might join in supporting the Muslims in the Horn of Africa and help them destroy their Christian state had been on the minds of Ethiopians ever since the sixteenth century. Mangistu and his tame press did complain that a sister socialist country had helped the Somalis, but they mostly led their public to believe it was the Egyptians. Prior to the July 1977 invasion, while some 3,000 Soviet experts were still preparing the Somali army, Mangistu had blamed Sadat for "fuelling the invasion plans against our country."[69] But it was only in January 1978, after the Somalis had broken off relations with the Soviets and after their military momentum had been completely lost, that Sadat ("whose hostility towards Mangistu was matched only by Mangistu's hostility towards him")[70] openly came to their rescue. He first tried to coordinate a common Arab League–OAU action to prevent an Ethiopian counterinvasion of Somalia. He then called upon the Americans to help the retreating Somalis. In early February he admitted he had sent some arms to Siad Barre. He also criticized Mangistu as a corrupt, pro-Soviet dictator and "threatened him with military intervention if he dared touch the waters of the Nile."[71]

Sadat's action, mostly verbal, enabled Mangistu to portray the Egyptian as Ethiopia's worst enemy. In January 1978 the Ethiopian press began an anti-Egyptian campaign of unprecedented harshness, which lasted until the death of Sadat in October 1981. Dozens of editorials and articles condemned Egypt's "anti-Ethiopian crusade" and its " Islamic holy war." Sadat was accused of contemplating the conquest of Ethiopia and striving for control of the Ethiopian Nile and Lake Tana.[72] Depicted as a collaborator with American imperialism, Sadat was also contrasted with Nasser. In the eyes of Mangistu the late Nasser had been a source of revolutionary inspiration to Africa and the third world, a historic figure like Mahatma Gandhi or Mao Tse-tung. Sadat, however, was a petty-minded reactionary who had "already reversed the progressive gains of the Nasser Era, and is in the process of auctioning the only remaining gains."[73]

A significant theme in the Ethiopian press campaign referred to Sadat as Egypt's "khedive." This, remember, was the title of the nineteenth-century Egyptian ruler Isma'il, who sought to control the entire Nile basin and was humiliated by the Ethiopians in the 1876 battle of Gura. Indeed, after Sadat's call to rescue the Somalis, Mangistu revived the old medieval Nile threat: "If Sadat wants to protect the Nile basin because water is life to his people," ran one of many articles in the Ethiopian press, "he must know that the Nile has one of its sources in the Ethiopia he wants to destroy. It is from here that comes the dark blue alluvial soil so dear to the Egyptian fellahin. Furthermore, Ethiopia has a head of state who cares for the lives of his people. Those dying in the Ogaden are Ethiopian nationals—human beings like the ones for whom Sadat wants the Nile waters."[74] On 13 May 1978 a spokesperson for the Ethiopian government made no bones about it: "No one in his right senses can question Ethiopia's inalienable and self-evident right to use her natural resources for the benefit of her struggling masses. . . . Revolutionary Ethiopia would like to make it emphatically clear that she is at full liberty and within her rights to utilize her natural resources for the advancement of her people. . . . [However,] she does not believe in the exclusive exploitation of her water resources against the well-being of the masses in the neighboring countries."[75]

Perhaps the publication most reflective of the new set of attitudes toward Sadat's Egypt was a book issued in late 1979. *Egypt's Imperial*

Aspirations over Lake Tana and the Blue Nile was authored by Wondim-neh Tilahun of Addis Ababa University and distributed throughout the country, widely read, and often quoted by officials and academics. Considered the most comprehensive expression of Mangistu's Nile thinking, it was later translated by the Egyptians into Arabic. Wondimneh's first chapter repeated the accusation that Sadat was behind the Somali invasion and that his goal was the conquest of the Blue Nile. The second chapter, titled "New Headlines for Old: Historical Background," was devoted to equating Sadat with Khedive Isma'il and his 1875–1876 Ethiopian adventure. Isma'il, in turn, was equated by Wondimneh with Adolf Hitler (p. 15), and his attempt to conquer the Blue Nile was analyzed as part of an American plot. (Isma'il, as discussed in Chapter 4, employed U.S. mercenaries, who led his army in Gura.) Over a century later Sadat, Wondimneh stated, was again plotting with the Americans to convert the Red Sea into an Arab lake and seek the "Unity of the Nile Valley" by occupying Ethiopia (pp. 15–23).

The main argument of the book was presented in its third chapter, "The Nile System and the Risks to Ethiopia of Unutilized Water Resources" (pp. 25–29). After briefly mentioning a few cases in point, the author asserted: "The great danger of unutilized rivers to Ethiopia is that it creates an insane desire on the part of her neighbors to see to it that she will never attain the capacity to utilize these rivers" (p. 30). Most of the book's remaining eight chapters are devoted to early-twentieth-century British and Italian designs to control Ethiopia's waters and the Blue Nile. As long as Ethiopia failed to develop Lake Tana and the Blue Nile itself, it followed, the Egyptians would be tempted to capture them or to interfere in Ethiopia's affairs, creating internal unrest to prevent Ethiopia from developing its Nile resources. However, "Ethiopia is rapidly moving towards its goal of establishing a science-based society with all that this implies regarding the quality of the relations of that society with nature" (p. 26). "With the realization of this aspiration, Lake Tana and the Blue Nile will cease to be the fifth-columns of nature planted in the heart of Ethiopia, beckoning and tempting Egyptian aggressors to disturb its peace and security" (p. 30). How would Ethiopia achieve this goal? The Soviets, "the people who built the Aswan dam for the Egyptian fellahin, they will assist the Ethiopian masses in the same way as they assisted the Egyptian masses nearly a generation ago" (pp. 29–30).

The anti-Egyptian campaign reached one of its peaks following the Egyptian-Israeli Camp David Accords. Sadat's declaration that he would make the recovered deserts of Sinai bloom with Nile waters, and perhaps even sell some to Israel, angered the Ethiopians. They now added a dose of a new Soviet-styled anti-Zionism to their old frustration regarding

Egypt's one-sided usage of the Nile waters and claimed it was yet one more piece of evidence of the imperialist plot they faced. Sadat responded by blaming the Soviets for inciting the Ethiopians to cause trouble over the Nile.[76]

Evicted from Egypt less than two years after the inauguration of the Aswan High Dam, the Soviets must have been quite bitter over the issue. They might have had some hand in encouraging Mangistu to threaten Sadat with the Nile card, but the Ethiopians, as we have seen, have never really needed a reminder about the river. They hardly needed the Soviets to connect what they considered a Somali Islamic-Arab invasion with the idea of interfering with the Nile; it had been their traditional countermeasure from medieval times. However, Mangistu did need the Soviets to develop related projects and was surely hopeful that Moscow would be interested. But nothing emerged from an Ethiopian-Soviet dialogue regarding the Nile. It is hardly conceivable that the Soviets were politically inclined toward, or were financially capable of, being involved in such an enterprise. In any case, Mangistu was to spend the rest of his years caught up in fratricidal wars and famines, not in constructing dams and irrigating land.

The assassination of Sadat on 6 October 1981 marked the beginning of some relaxation of tension, at least at the diplomatic level. Less than two months earlier Ethiopian-Egyptian hostility had seemed to reach yet another climax. In August Mangistu signed a tripartite pact with two of Sadat's enemies: 'Ali Nasser of South Yemen, and Muammar Qaddafi of Libya. (The latter was said to have persistently encouraged Mangistu to begin interfering with the Nile.) But the new Egyptian leader, President Hosni Mubarak, was quick to change the tune. Although he never departed from Sadat's combination of Egyptian nationalism and Western orientation, he did depart from his predecessor's air of paternalism and defiance. Mubarak proved much more attentive to Boutros Boutros-Ghali's ideas about the importance of Africa to Egypt's identity and strategy and the centrality of Ethiopia. Egypt's Horn of Africa and Nile policy will be discussed in the next chapter. The so-called Boutros-Ghali thesis represented the calming and stabilization of the entire region and the work toward all-Nile cooperation. Though the Egyptians continued to ignore Ethiopia's claim to a share in the Nile's waters, their new approach of appeasement enabled the renewal of some dialogue.

Ethiopian Academics and Egypt

After Sadat's assassination the mutual, deep-rooted suspicion remained, but the overt hostility was shelved. On 8 February 1982 a modest

Ethiopian-Egyptian commercial agreement was signed, and in July, when Ethiopian forces were reported to have patrolled inside Somalia, Cairo confined its reaction to an expression of "anxiety and regret."[77] On 24 August 1982 Boutros-Ghali's efforts to build an all-Nile consultation framework bore the first fruit. Representatives of the nine riparian countries, including Ethiopia, met in Khartoum and discussed the possibility of setting up a technical body to draw up plans for joint Nile ventures. The Ethiopians refused to join officially and agreed to participate as observers only,[78] but at least it was a beginning.

The Ethiopian press had stopped attacking Egypt, and in 1983 the Egyptian ambassador to Addis Ababa was invited to deliver a series of public lectures. Ambassador Samir Ahmad titled his series "Egypt and Africa: On the Road to Cooperation," in which he summarized the essence of the Egyptian promise. Egypt, he said, was the product of the Nile, and its dependency on the river was total. It was the Nile that taught the Egyptians cooperation, science, and solidarity, and it was therefore the obligation of Egypt to transfer this knowledge to the riparian African nations.[79] In other words, Egypt was ready to help in various fields but not to share its (and, as of 1959, Sudan's) "historic rights" over the waters.

Boutros-Ghali's relentless diplomatic efforts had a calming effect. In 1984 he traveled to Ethiopia twice to see Mangistu, and in November Egyptian Foreign Minister 'Ismat 'Abd al-Majid declared, in Addis Ababa, that relations were good and that Egypt respected Ethiopia's territorial integrity.[80] The old pro-Ethiopian scholar Mirrit Boutros-Ghali paid a visit in November, and Ethiopian academics Alame Eshete and Negussay Ayele were invited in early 1985 to Egypt to lecture on the Nile and mutual relations. In July 1985 Mubarak came to Ethiopia and met with Mangistu. As Mubarak made no mention of Ethiopian water rights, he failed to persuade his host to officially join an all-Nile consultation body. The two leaders, however, seemed to share a rather relaxed atmosphere. Mangistu, on his part, reiterated the Ethiopian position as stated in May 1978—namely, that whatever Ethiopia would do regarding the Nile would not be against Egypt and would be in accordance with international law.[81]

But Mangistu's Ethiopia was in no position to develop the Blue Nile. By the time Mangistu met with Mubarak, the comprehensive failure of his dictatorial centralization was cruelly apparent. Unable truly to compromise with the country's diversity, Mangistu sought to crush decentralizing tendencies in much the same way he had done to his opposition in the center. After reconquering most of Eritrea in 1978, he proved incapable of any dialogue with the separatists. He continued to depict the two rival Eritrean organizations, the ELF and the EPLF, as mere bandits and stooges of "Arab reactionaries" (the Ethiopian press was told to refer to the groups by their Arabic names).[82] Ignoring reality, he began losing not only to the Eritrean Christian Marxist EPLF (which began defeating the ELF in 1982), but also to various other provincial resistance movements, notably the Tigrean People's Liberation Front (TPLF).

By the mid-1980s the whole of northern Ethiopia had long become an active war zone. Moreover, the ceaseless war and the government's intentional neglect of the rebellious north worsened the growing effect of three years of drought, which had began in the summer of 1984. The whole of northern Ethiopia was now exposed to horrible famine and death, and the entire world was shocked by the magnitude of the disaster. Though Mother Nature had her hand in the Ethiopian drought of 1984–1987, its terrible consequences were no less the result of internal wars and politics.

The cruel paradox that the land of the Blue Nile was dying of thirst had to be addressed. Part of the blame, with the help of the regime, was placed on the river itself. According to Ethiopian historian Bairu Tafla, the popular image of the Nile was now changed from a natural phenomenon of awesome presence, admired as a national symbol, to that of a criminal thief. Analyzing relevant works of Ethiopian poets, especially Mulatu Ayyalnah's "Tekur Abbai" (The Black Abbai) of 1985 and Gabre-Yohannes Hailu's "Innatkin Belulgn" (Insult Him on My Behalf) of 1989, Tafla concluded: "The lamentation of the new generation is understandable: drought and famine have taken their toll on the Ethiopian population in recent years while the Abbai waters thundered unused down the precipice as always. The contradiction made many Ethiopians restless. . . . [In these poems] the Abbai is visualized as a full-fledged person and is told his crimes straight to his face in plain words."[83]

As orchestrated by the regime, the great Ethiopian famine was also placed at Egypt's doorstep. The argument made earlier in 1979 by Wondimneh Tilahun—that it had been foreign interests, mostly Egypt's, that had prevented Ethiopia from developing the Blue Nile throughout history—was now put forcefully. I shall briefly relate only the relevant academic dimension of the argument.

Throughout the 1970s Mangistu was trying to turn the national university into a branch of his totalitarian regime. Established in 1961, the Haile Selassie I University (HSIU) had been, from the start, a direct extension of the imperial system, but under the monarchy it had enjoyed some air of freedom. Faculty and students were unable to organize politically, but they did pursue traditional and modern means of expressing ideas and protest. The Addis Ababa campus of that time was also a

fertile meeting ground between a privileged student sector and a quite
cosmopolitan academic staff. American, European, Israeli, and other
professors, including some leading figures in the rapidly developing international community of Africanist scholars, spent years at HSIU, also
contributing to the Africanization of the Ethiopian self-image. A good
number of graduates were sent to Western universities and returned to
assume positions of academic leadership.

After Mangistu came to power the newly renamed Addis Ababa
University was among the first institutions to be targeted. Students were
exiled to the remote countryside, and many faculty members spent years
in jail. Still some air of defiance did remain about the Addis Ababa campus, and the university during the entire Derg period retained a remark-
able degree of independence in many respects. The regime's direct control, however, was efficiently applied. When Mangistu's anti-Arab and
anti-Egyptian campaign began, the university staff responded to the call.
A committee of professors was formed to reconstruct the history of
Ethiopian-Sudanese relations, and a new literature on the Somalis, emphasizing their inherent aggression, was published. Wondimneh Tilahun's
1979 book, discussed above, was the cornerstone of regime-encouraged,
renewed academic focus on Egypt.

In January 1985, as mentioned above, Professor Aleme Eshete of the
History Department was invited to Cairo by Boutros-Ghali to participate
in a conference on the Horn of Africa. He made good use of the renewed
dialogue to present a paper titled: "Egypt and the Conflict in the Horn of
Africa, 1941–1974."[84] Analyzing the interplay between the various dimensions of Egyptian foreign policy, he summarized the Ethiopian position for his hosts:

> Pan-Islamism and pan-Arabism have long been a pillar of Egyptian pol-
> itics in the Horn. . . . Egypt has often posed as the protecting power of
> Ethiopian Muslims crying over what she calls the "persecution" or "op-
> pression" of Muslims in Ethiopia, and [worked] to incite the same to re-
> bellion. In political terms one may interpret this to mean that Egypt
> considered the Ethiopian Muslims to be a last-resort reserve army to
> safeguard her interests, mainly with regard to the Nile. . . . Egypt's in-
> volvement in the conflicts in the Horn, in Eritrea and in Somalia, is tied
> to the Nile issue, and is used as a measure for weakening Ethiopia mil-
> itarily and economically, so that Ethiopia may have her hands tied, and
> may not have the strength to utilize the waters of the Nile, with which
> Egypt enhances her own development and production.

Ending his paper by stating that Haile Selassie had broken off
relations with Israel in 1973 as an appeasement gift to Egypt, Eshete
concluded:

Egypto-Ethiopian, and in general Arab-Ethiopian relations, improved momentarily. But the Horn of Africa had not yet seen peace. The Ethiopian revolution broke out in 1974. Abandoned by the U.S. and having broken with Israel, there was no power to save the decaying imperial regime, as it had been during the 1960 coup. With the outbreak of the Ethiopian revolution the entire political picture gradually changed. Egypt and the Arab world, embroiled in class and big power politics, now united to ignite the conflict in the Horn so that it could explode louder than ever! *Plus ça change plus c'est la même chose!*

Attesting to the new, guided, hostile curiosity about Egypt are undergraduate papers written during these years. Beginning in the early 1960s, students of the humanities and social sciences were required to submit a final work based on extensive research. Most students spent their entire fourth year preparing papers almost the equivalent, in size and often in quality, of a master's dissertation in Western universities. All of these papers, including works containing rare findings of oral traditions and old texts, are kept in the library of the university's Institute of Ethiopian Studies. A survey of the catalog reveals a dramatic rise in the number of papers, beginning in 1983, devoted to Egypt and its relations with Ethiopia.

For example, in June 1983 Erqu Tesfaye submitted his thesis, "Egypt Combats Socialism," which used Marxist terminology to compare the periods of Nasser and Sadat. Analyzing Nasser's "Arab socialism" as incorrectly based on nonmaterialistic concepts of idealistic nationalism, he nevertheless praised Nasser's achievements in social justice and the anti-imperialist struggle. Sadat, however, betrayed the Soviets and sold his country to capitalist and imperialist interests. No wonder, he concluded, that Sadat, facing social unrest at home, was considered a traitor by progressive Arabs and worked relentlessly to undermine the Marxist-socialist revolution in Ethiopia.

In May 1984, to take another example, Abebe Amanu submitted his "Egypt's Policy on the Nile." In 119 pages he provided a rich survey of the Nile's modern history, all interpreted in the spirit of his introductory text:

> Egyptian rulers have followed a definitive policy on the Nile since Egypt herself emerged as a modern state. Muhammad Ali formulated a policy designed to incorporate the entire Nile basin into an Egyptian Empire, and this policy has been pursued consistently by almost all Egyptian rulers since then, though the means they employed varied from one another. . . . The Egyptian rulers followed the monopolistic policy over the usage of the Nile waters claiming "natural and historical rights" over the river's waters. . . . [E]ven today, they prefer war to cooperation. During Sadat's rule, Egypt attacked Ethiopia through the

press and the mass media, thinking that Ethiopia was going to use the Nile's waters for domestic development purposes. The Egyptian support of the secessionist movements created by colonial powers in northern Ethiopia is one of the means used to weaken Ethiopia and make her submissive to Egypt's policy, and in the meantime create the "Greater State of the Nile Valley" of which Egypt had dreamed for a century.

At least ten more such works were written up to 1988: "Egypt's Policy in the Horn of Africa Since 1952" (Abd al-Rahim Ali, 1984); "Egyptian-Sudanese Relations on the Question of Revolution with Particular Reference to Ethiopia" (Mahetami Marawi, 1985); "Great Powers' Intervention in Egypt: The USA and the USSR, 1952–1975" (Wandyerad Gadlu, 1986); "The Nile Factor in Ethio-Egyptian Relations" (Mulugeta Worku, 1987); "The Nile Water Question and Ethiopia's Relations with Riparian States" (Abebe Worku, 1987); "Red Sea Politics and Its Implications on Ethiopia" (Alamayyahu Telahun, 1988); "Egyptian Influence on Sudanese Politics" (Kahsay Tasfay, 1988); and so on.[85] In essence they all revolved around the same themes: Egypt had always wanted to destabilize Ethiopia so that it would not be able to attend to the Nile; the Egyptians used Islam, Pan-Arabism, imperialism, and "reaction" to undermine Ethiopia's revolution.

Practically all of these papers were written for the political science and international relations faculty, the dean of which, Professor Negussay Ayele, became a political adviser to Mangistu and perhaps his closest confidant on Nile policy. In August 1986, during the Ninth International Congress of Ethiopian Studies held in Moscow, he presented a paper that probably reflected Mangistu's ideas; for example, "With hundreds of thousands of human beings falling like flies from famine in one country, it can not be expected to just watch its billions of cubic meters of water disappear every year so that the populations in other riparian states are not affected by famine. Likewise, if a riparian state downstream, which enjoyed the continued flow of water from an upstream riparian, watches this disaster and does not consider it to be its own problem, then that downstream state has no moral right to demand anything from the upstream state."[86] He concluded his paper by stating that earlier in February 1985 he had been invited to Cairo to deliver a public lecture on the issue. He elaborated on the international dimensions of hydropolitics and the main guidelines of international law with regard to the utilization of international rivers. He emphasized to an Egyptian audience two relevant principles: equity in sharing water resources and the need to arrive at bilateral or multilateral agreements on the distribution of those shares. He was then asked to relate these abstract principles to the

Blue Nile and be more specific. His hosts demanded to know what he thought was Ethiopia's and what was international as per the Nile. The response was that what was within Ethiopia's sovereign territory was Ethiopia's and that what was agreed on internationally would be recognized as international.

A Belated Rapprochement

In late 1986 the chaos in Ethiopia climaxed. Yet Mangistu continued to blame external enemies and local "stooges," and he further intensified his revolution. Exploiting the famine and the control he obtained by distributing foreign aid, Mangistu coerced a population transfer from the rebellious north to the south. Simultaneously, beginning in early 1986, a new "villagization campaign" was imposed on regions under government control. Millions of peasants in central Ethiopia and the south were forced to abandon their traditional habitats and assemble in new, hastily planned villages. Cadres of the Workers Party of Ethiopia were instructed to see to the rapid collectivization of agriculture and society. A referendum in January 1987 affirmed the proclamation of a new Constitution providing for more communist institutions and structures. On 12 September 1987, amid festivities inspired by North Korea, Ethiopia was proclaimed a "Peoples' Republic." Radicalization reached the point where the Ethiopian press was instructed to avoid any mention of the new spirit of early liberalization in the USSR. The renewal of some rain in the summer of that year encouraged Mangistu to plan a final military showdown against the Tigreans and the Eritreans.

Mangistu's policy was now considered too crude for the new leadership in the Kremlin. He had long been led to understand that the Soviets would not risk a total conflict by helping him interfere with the Nile. He was now told that the USSR could hardly afford to go on financing his endless internal wars. In March 1987 Mangistu returned frustrated from Moscow. Though the Soviets did continue to help him militarily, Mangistu was ready to look for new external options. Since he could expect nothing from the West, he turned now back to the Middle East.

Ethiopia's renewed relations with Israel during the last years of Mangistu's reign can only be mentioned here. Mangistu's assumption that, as in the past, Israel would come running to resume a bond with the land of the Blue Nile proved illusory. Having made peace with Egypt and being firmly allied with the United States, Israel had only one remaining interest: Ethiopia's Jewish community. It was in the context of its effort to bring the Beta Israel community to Israel that an ill-advised Israeli Mossad and Ministry of Defense provided some military aid to

Mangistu. It was surely not enough to save him from his approaching downfall.

No less significant was Mangistu's rapprochement with Egypt. In April 1987, just as he returned frustrated from Moscow, he paid his first visit to Cairo. Egypt, as mentioned in Chapter 1, was experiencing a time of great distress. After three years of drought in Ethiopia, with the water level in Lake Nasser at a most alarming level, Egypt was dreading an approaching catastrophe. In March 1987 a highly publicized Egyptian diplomatic-academic symposium on the Nile problem ended with a near consensus that an all-regional cooperative measure was vitally needed.[87] Mubarak hurried to extend an invitation to Mangistu, and the Ethiopian was happy to respond. Having convinced himself that "the Arabs" had been behind the Eritreans and the Tigreans, he valued the opportunity to embrace Mubarak. His April 1987 visit to Cairo, barely eight months after Professor Negussay Ayele had threatened Egypt in Moscow, turned into a demonstration of mutual cordiality. Mubarak reciprocated somewhat later. He arrived in Addis Ababa on 12 September 1987, the day Ethiopia was proclaimed a "Peoples' Republic," and attended the ceremonies, showering compliments on his hosts. Mangistu traveled to Cairo again in November 1990 and this time laid a wreath on the tomb of Anwar al-Sadat.[88]

This Ethiopian-Egyptian saga reached a historic moment of truth in the year 1987. From the Ethiopian point of view it seemed to bring to an end some four decades of avoidance and self-deception. Haile Selassie tried to avoid coping with Nasserist Egypt and sought refuge in African diplomacy. Mangistu created an image of a monstrous Sadat and a demonic Egypt. However, an old, ancient reality was now reasserting itself. Indeed, Ethiopian-Egyptian interdependence called for a much more sober conceptualization.

In September 1987 a correspondent of the *Ethiopian Herald* traveled to Egypt. He made it a point to visit the Aswan Dam and two irrigation projects initiated by Sadat in 1978. His description of Egypt was enthusiastic, and he spared no words in stressing the necessity to cooperate for the benefit of both nations. Reflective, hopefully, of a new period were his following words:

> People who have stayed long in this country say that the Egyptians are friendly and kind to foreigners. Easy to talk to, interested to ask you questions and willing to answer your inquiries. However, no matter how long you stay there, you will easily notice that the attitudes and approaches of Egyptians towards Ethiopians are particularly more friendly and brotherly. When an Egyptian, in his own land, asks you

where you come from, you reply that you are from Ethiopia and then you will immediately notice the quick change in his facial expression—a broad smile followed by the word "El-Nil" meaning the Nile. From such spontaneous and friendly gestures one will soon come to understand that the River Nile from which the peoples of the two countries have drunk since time immemorial, is a symbol of the continuity of friendship and brotherhood.[89]

NOTES

1. In May 1960 King Hussein of Jordan paid a visit to Ethiopia. This was a period of great tension between the king and Nasser, and Haile Selassie talked him into transferring the keys to Deir al-Sultan to the Ethiopian monks. However, by March 1961 Jordanian-Egyptian relations had improved, and the king formed a committee that quickly decided to restore the status quo. See *Ethiopian Herald*, 14–17 May 1960, 19 and 21 March 1961, and 23 April 1961. For the Egyptian side see Suriyal, *Mushkilat dir al-sultan bil-quds*, pp. 93–107.

2. See details in Erlich, *Ethiopia and the Middle East*, pp. 168–170.

3. *Ethiopian Herald*, 24 August 1976.

4. See, for example, Shanuda, *Ta'rikh al-aqbat*. The author practically ignored the Ethiopian connection. On the Ethiopian side see a publication of the Ethiopian Orthodox Church, *The Church of Ethiopia* (containing chapters written by Sergew Hable Selassie and Taddesse Tamrat). See also Church of Ethiopia, *The Church of Ethiopia Past and Present*, Addis Ababa, 1997; and Teklahaymanot, "The Egyptian Metropolitans" and *The Ethiopian Church*.

5. The Department of Christian Communities in the Israeli Ministry of Religious Affairs has dozens of files containing relevant Ethiopian and Egyptian correspondence. Both Ethiopians and Egyptians published numerous articles on the subject. For example: Begashaw, "A Note on the Ethiopian Der es-Sultan"; Suriyal, *Mushkilat dir al-sultan bil-quds*.

6. For a detailed discussion see the section "The Terminology and Literature of Eritrea's Arabism" in Erlich, *Ethiopia and the Middle East,* pp. 157–164.

7. "Statement of the Eritrean People: An Appeal to the Second Arab Summit Conference," Cairo, 31 August 1964, as quoted in Kendie, "Internal and External Dimensions," pp. 324–325.

8. For the internal development of the Eritrean movement and the ELF-EPLF rivalry during the said period, see Erlich, *The Struggle over Eritrea,* pp. 21–33.

9. See ibid., pp. 55–70.

10. Quoted in Erlich, *Ethiopia and the Middle East,* p. 134.

11. For example: Yahya, *Al-'Alaqat al-Misriyya al-Sumaliyya,* pp. 7–23; Barawi, *Al-Sumal al-kabir,* pp. 20–23.

12. See a discussion of the book *The Wounded Islam in Ethiopia* by Abu Ahmad al-Ithyubi, in Ahmed, "Historiography of Islam."

13. Habte Selassie, *Conflict and Intervention,* p. 155.

14. Abraham, *Reminiscences of My Life,* pp. 158–162.

15. Eshete, "Egypt and the Conflict in the Horn."

16. Israeli State Archives (Ginzach haMedinah; hereafter IGM), Ethiopia 1963, "The Internal Situation After the OAU Meeting," an assessment of the situation at Haile Selassie I University by the Israeli Dr. Zvi Yavetz, Dean of Humanities, 17 June 1963.

17. See *Ethiopian Herald,* 30 June 1959; 5 and 6 November 1963; 18, 19, and 20 October 1966; and 18 June 1969. An episode reflecting these relations was narrated by Nasser's closest adviser, Muhammad Hasanayn Haykal. In June 1969 during his visit to Cairo, Haile Selassie offered his mediation in the Arab-Israeli conflict. In his talks with Nasser "the emperor was sympathetic, saying that he too had once lost his country, and that when he was in exile the Italians offered him $3 million and four palaces if he would abdicate. He was also directly involved in the Arab-Israeli dispute because he had documents which proved that at one time President Truman had offered the Israelis as a homeland parts of Ethiopia. Nasser put the same proposition to him: 'You are going to see Abba Eban in Ethiopia in a few days,' he said, 'get me a map of what they think the final frontiers of Israel should be.' Again no more was heard" (in Heikal, *The Road to Ramadan,* p. 60).

18. He said this to a group of Israeli journalists on 29 May 1963; see *Lamerhav* and *Ma'ariv,* 30 May 1963.

19. Quoted in *Ethiopian Herald*, 30 September 1970.

20. See "Arab Community Head Refutes Religious Oppression in Ethiopia," *Ethiopian Herald,* 13 October 1966. The *Ethiopian Herald*'s editorial of 14 October repeated the same message, explaining it referred to "the more than 100,000 Arabs living in Ethiopia in peace and prosperity, free to worship in their own faith and with all rights and privileges possessed by every Ethiopian citizen."

21. "HIM Spreads Harmony, Goodwill," *Ethiopian Herald,* 19 October 1966.

22. "The Man That Was," *Ethiopian Herald,* 30 September 1970.

23. From Erlich, *Ethiopia and the Middle East,* p. 134.

24. IGM, Ethiopia 1962, Ambassador Divon to Africa Department, "Conversation with Haile Selassie," 23 March 1962.

25. IGM, Ethiopia 1963, Shimon Peres to Foreign Ministry, "A Report on the Ministry of Defense's Mission to Ethiopia" (in Hebrew), 4 April 1963.

26. IGM, Ethiopia 1968, Deputy Director General Bitan to Africa Department, "Protocol of Conversation with the Emperor and the Prime Minister," 4 March 1968.

27. IGM, Ethiopia 1972, Shimoni to Foreign Minister, "Political Report: Meetings in Ethiopia, 12–19 May 1972," 19 May 1972.

28. Abraham, *Reminiscences of My Life,* p. 95.

29. Ibid., p. 139.

30. Habte Selassie, *Conflict and Intervention,* p. 155.

31. Ahadu Sabore was minister of information in 1974. While in jail following the revolution he wrote his Amharic diary "Years of Darkness and Trial," which was smuggled out of prison. The diary was translated by Thomas Kane and is yet to be published. I am indebted to Dr. Kane for allowing me to read relevant passages. I have included a larger section in *Ethiopia and the Middle East,* pp. 176–177.

32. See Erlich, *The Struggle over Eritrea,* pp. 34–42.

33. Habtewold, *Aklilu Remembers.*

34. See Schwab, *Decision-Making in Ethiopia,* p. 53.

35. Habtewold, *Aklilu Remembers,* pp. 2–3.

36. See al-Huss, *Ithyubya fi 'ahd Hayla Silasi al-awwal,* pp. 62–63.

37. IGM, Ethiopia 1962, "A Conversation with Vice-Minister Getachaw Makesha," by Arye Levine, Middle Eastern Department, Israeli Foreign Ministry, 27 May 1962.

38. Habtewold, *Aklilu Remembers,* pp. 37–56.

39. Kendie, "Internal and External Dimensions," p. 289.

40. PRO Foreign Office 371/125355, "Ethiopia: Annual Report, 1956."

41. Quoted in Sabore, "Years of Darkness and Trial" (see n. 31 above).

42. In 1956 Ethiopia's prime minister, Makonnen Endalkatchew, thought that Nasser was an "unsophisticated theater actor and a shallow thinker rather than a statesman" and that if Israel had not been strong, the Arabs would have been all over Ethiopia (IGM, Ethiopia 1956, Pilpul to Africa Department, 16 May 1956). However, his foreign minister, Aklilu, after Nasser nationalized the Suez Canal and created an international crisis, led a diplomatic effort of mediation in September 1956, showering Nasser with praise and indirectly putting much of the blame on the Western powers. See *Ethiopian Herald,* 22 and 29 September 1956.

43. For a detailed analysis see also Hess, *Ethiopia,* chap. 16, esp. pp. 234–239.

44. Habtewold, *Aklilu Remembers,* pp. 74–78.

45. Kendie, "Internal and External Dimensions," p. 295.

46. Habtewold, *Aklilu Remembers,* p. 76.

47. See Kaplan, "Can the Ethiopian Change His Skin?"

48. See Pankhurst, "The First International Conference."

49. See, for example, the editorial in the *Ethiopian Herald,* "Emperor's Visit to the UAR," 5 November 1963, and comments on Haile Selassie's meeting with Nasser: "Hence, the meeting is highly significant. The topics of discussion are mostly African in nature and will therefore open means and ways to settling many African problems."

50. This information is from an interview with the director general of planning in the Ethiopian Ministry of Foreign Affairs, Fantahon Haila-Michael, in March 1999.

51. IGM, Ethiopia 1963, Bar-On to Africa Department, 15 July 1963.

52. The section above is taken from Erlich, *The Struggle over Eritrea,* pp. 34–42; see this work for more details.

53. IGM, Ethiopia 1963, "The Internal Situation," by Zvi Yavetz, 17 June 1963.

54. From a report on the Israeli ambassador's conversation with Aman and Meles Andom, in IGM, Ethiopia 1963, Levine to Israeli Embassy in Washington, 9 June 1963. Though Nasser personally asked Haile Selassie during the 1963 inauguration of the OAU to replace Meles Andom, the emperor decided to keep him there (IGM, Ethiopia 1963, "Egyptian Activities in Africa and Ethiopia," by A. Levine, 15 July 1963). Meles remained in Cairo as Ethiopia's ambassador until the 1974 revolution and continued to warn Nasser not to meddle in Ethiopian affairs.

55. For more details see Erlich, *Ethiopia and the Middle East,* chap. 13; the following section is partly derived from that chapter.

56. IGM, Ethiopia 1963, Peres to Foreign Ministry, "A Report," 4 April 1963.

57. Interview with Ras Asrate's son, Lij Asfa-Wossen Asserate, Koln, 1998.

58. IGM, Ethiopia 1963, Peres to Foreign Ministry, "A Report," 4 April 1963.

59. The Ethiopian consul in Jerusalem, since 1953, was the prominent historian Takla-Tsadiq Makuriya. During his stay in Jerusalem he wrote extensively on Ethiopian history, emphasizing the sixteenth-century conquest of Ahmad Gragn as a central event in Ethiopian history. (In *Ya'ityopia tarik* he covered 360 years but devoted nearly one-third of the volume to Gragn's conquest. Later in 1974 he published an entire volume on Gragn in Addis Ababa, *YaGragn Ahmad Warara*.) Takla-Tsadiq, perhaps because of his perception of Gragn, was very close to Aklilu and kept warning his superiors in the Foreign Ministry never to irritate the Arabs nor to upgrade or overexpose relations with Israel. He also reported directly to Haile Selassie and was said to be highly regarded by the emperor. See IGM, Ethiopia 1964, Embassy in Addis Ababa to Africa Department, 23 July 1964. (It was perhaps part of Haile Selassie's game to keep a pro-Arab representative in Israel, just as he kept the pro-Israeli Meles Andom in Cairo.)

60. "Ethiopian Church Recovers Passageway to Monastery," *Ethiopian Herald,* 29 April 1970; on the Jordanian decision of 1961 see a long piece in the *Ethiopian Herald,* 21 March 1961. According to the memoirs of the Israeli ambassador to Ethiopia from 1971 to 1973, Hanan Aynor, in 1969 Abba Eban and Haile Selassie agreed verbally that in return for the keys to the monastery Ethiopia would upgrade its consulate in Jerusalem to an embassy. The Ethiopian promise was never fulfilled (from Hanan Aynor, "Africa in Crisis, Part II: Haile Selassie's Ethiopia," a manuscript completed just before the death of Aynor in 1993).

61. IGM, Ethiopia 1972, Shimoni to Foreign Minister, "Political Report," 19 May 1972.

62. Aynor memoirs (see n. 60 above); Kendie, "Internal and External Dimensions," pp. 299–300.

63. Israeli archives and press contain much evidence on close ties between Israeli trainers and young Ethiopian officers, especially in the Holetta Military Academy, the paratroopers battalion, and the Third Division's tanks battalion. Since the army's upper echelon was mostly indifferent and indulging in corruption, the Israelis in the field had to take care of actual training and the daily supply of the soldiers' basic necessities. Their sudden departure in late October 1973 contributed directly to an already-escalating crisis. Most of the leading revolutionaries of 1974 indeed came from those units.

64. From interviews with Dajazmach Zewde Gabre-Selassie (Addis Ababa, 1999) and Lij Asfa-Wossen Asserate (Koln, 1998). Lij Asfa-Wossen, Ras Asrate's son, has kindly shown me parts of his father's diaries. On 28 October 1973 Ras Asrate met with Haile Selassie in Geneva. Much to his frustration, he failed to persuade the emperor at least to ask the Israeli experts to stay in Ethiopia. He reached the conclusion that Haile Selassie was completely detached from reality and was no longer capable of making any proper assessments or decisions.

65. Hanan Aynor concluded in his memoirs ("Africa in Crisis"):

Possibly I will be accused of committing an error of emphasis regarding the impact the severing of relations with Israel had on the Ethiopian revolution. In that case I find myself in good company. The *New York Times* and *Le Monde,* following the Ethiopian revolution in detail through their Addis Ababa–based correspondents, both came to similar conclusions.

Over the years I tried to clear this point with my Ethiopian acquaintances who played important roles in the initial stages of the revolution. All agree, in their own distinctive ways, that the break of relations and especially the sudden disappearance of Israeli military teams added considerably to the rebellious ferment in the armed forces.

Emperor Haile Selassie I has inspired and guided Ethiopia for over half a century. He was the respected first spokesman of independent Africa. As he was fond of explaining his time-consuming caution and often ambivalent policies, 'One can make history only if one avoids being thrown into its traps.' During his lifetime, he avoided many traps, but fell into history's last one, dying alone—in solitary confinement—refusing food and medical care. On 28 August 1975 the Derg announced his death.

66. For a detailed description of the events in Ethiopia of 1974–1978, including Mangistu's road to power and the war in Eritrea, see Erlich, *The Struggle over Eritrea,* chaps. 4–9.

67. See analysis in Henze, "The Strategic Long View." For a general analysis of the Soviets in the Horn of Africa, see Henze's *Horn of Africa,* pp. 65–89.

68. See the chapter "Arabization of the Red Sea, 1975–1977" in Erlich, *The Struggle over Eritrea.* For resumption of Egyptian aid to the Arab-oriented Eritrean ELF in the mid-1970s, see also al-Sultan, *Al-Bahr al-ahmar wal-sira',* p. 204.

69. See *Times* (London), 2 May 1977.

70. Boutros-Ghali, *Egypt's Road to Jerusalem,* p. 321.

71. Ibid., p. 327.

72. See, for example, the *Ethiopian Herald's* editorial of 11 February 1978, "An Anti-Ethiopian Crusade." More in this spirit in *Ethiopian Herald,* 25, 26, and 31 January 1978; 3, 10, 12, and 18 February 1978.

73. See a cartoon in *Ethiopian Herald,* 16 February 1978.

74. See "Anwar El Sadat Africa's Gendarme," the first in a series of articles by J. P. Makuol, *Ethiopian Herald,* 16 February 1978; see also 18 and 24 February issues of the *Herald.*

75. *Ethiopian Herald,* 14 May 1978.

76. See *New York Times,* 6 June 1980; also *Al-Ahram,* 27 May 1980.

77. Middle East News Agency (MENA) from Cairo, 14 July 1982, in FBIS 15 July 1982.

78. *Egyptian Gazette,* 25 August 1982.

79. Samir Ahmed, "Egypt and Africa: On the Road to Cooperation," Egyptian Embassy, Addis Ababa, 1983, Institute of Ethiopian Studies (IES) Library, Addis Ababa University.

80. MENA, in FBIS, 29 February and 13 November 1984.

81. *Ethiopian Herald,* 20 July 1985.

82. The ELF was referred to as the Jabha (Arabic for "front") and the EPLF as the Sha'biyya (namely, the "people's [front]").

83. Tafla, "The Father of Rivers."

84. Eshete, "Egypt and the Conflict in the Horn."

85. All these works are available at the IES Library, Addis Ababa University.

86. Ayele, "The Blue Nile and Hydropolitics."

87. *Al-Musawwar,* 20 March 1987.

88. *Ethiopian Herald,* 10 April and 12 September 1987, and 1 November 1990.

89. Tekle Tesfa-Lidet, "Egypt: A Reporter's Impression," *Ethiopian Herald,* 11 September 1987.

9

Egyptian Concepts of Ethiopia, 1959–1991

An examination of Egyptian attitudes toward the Blue Nile country during the period already covered from the Ethiopian angle will be less dramatic. Sheltered behind the idea (and, from 1971 onward, the reality) of the Aswan High Dam, Egypt now seemed to be far less vulnerable.[1] Revolutions, wars, and general instability in the Horn of Africa further reduced the ancient fear that Ethiopia would actually interfere with the flow of the river. The double break of 1959—the severing of church affiliation and Nasser's declaration that Ethiopia was irrelevant to the issue of Nile water rights—seemed to have changed the very fundamentals of our history. Haile Selassie's new policy of distancing Ethiopia from the Arab Middle East and finding shelter in a new world of African diplomacy was welcomed by Cairo. During the period under discussion Egyptian-Ethiopian relations underwent Africanization by both parties. The sixteen-centuries-old Christian-Islamic and intra-Christian "oriental" dialogues were sidelined. Cairo, like Addis Ababa, became more comfortable with a new common "African" environment.

Retrospectively, however, "Africanization" proved to be merely another development in an ancient continuity. It enabled the Nasserist regime to pursue its new revolutionary agenda but also, much in line with previous regimes, resort to pragmatism and realpolitik. Ethiopian-Egyptian relations, in whatever guise, could not really depart from their unique history. Ethiopia's multifaceted connection to the Middle East remained intact throughout, and in 1987–1988, amid an acute water crisis, Ethiopia's relevance to the Nile was painfully reemphasized. Revolutionary transformation in Egypt, as in Ethiopia, did not really change old mutual dilemmas and ancient conceptual dichotomies. Both "African" and "oriental" Ethiopia remained a major issue on Egypt's agenda.

183

NASSER AND ETHIOPIA:
THE ARAB REVOLUTION AND THE NILE'S CONTINUITY

Previous chapters discussed the crisis in Ethiopian-Egyptian "oriental" relations. In 1959 the two main pillars of the Nile and the church seemed to
have collapsed. In coping with the third mutual element, Egyptian historic
patronage over the Horn of Africa's Muslims, Haile Selassie sought shelter in the new Africa. The 1963 establishment of the Organization of
African Unity, based on sanctioning boundaries and headquartered in
Addis Ababa, was his major achievement. It also became a mixed blessing
for the Ethiopian imperial regime. Haile Selassie's commitment to African
diplomacy would force him, ten years later, to cut his last link to the Middle East by disastrously depriving himself of the Israeli connection.

Africanization of relations was also Nasser's goal. The new revolutionary regime that came to power in July 1952 was ready to transform
nearly every dimension of Egyptian life, including its very identity.
Adopting the High Dam idea, it was quick to divorce the nationalist goal
and slogan "Unity of the Nile Valley." Egypt, recognizing the Sudan as
a separate entity, was no longer to be defined by the old river and its
basin.[2] A new terminology reflecting, or heralding, the new trends was
provided in 1954 when Nasser published his endorsed pamphlet "The
Philosophy of the Revolution." Although the Nile was mentioned as the
country's source of life, the river was to be tamed, mastered, and controlled by the revolution and its dam. Identity was to be determined neither by water necessities nor by borders bequeathed by colonialism.
Egypt was to be redefined by wider spaces, by the spheres of its ideals
and inherent potentialities. These spaces, in Nasser words, formed three
"circles" around Egypt's centrality: Arab, African, and Islamic.

Under Nasser's leadership the "Arab circle" was soon to become the
core of Egypt's new self-definition. The entire Middle East and its Pan-
Arab revolution quickly replaced the concept of "Egypt." After the 1958
unification with Syria the country was renamed the United Arab Republic. In June 1959, when Haile Selassie arrived in Cairo to disconnect
Ethiopia from this revolutionary new Arab dimension of Egypt, Nasser's
identity revolution had reached its culmination. For example, the local
press, which for the occasion reviewed the long history of Ethiopian-
Egyptian relations, did its best to avoid the very word "Egypt." (*Al-
Ahram* discussed the ancient relations between Ethiopia and "the Copts
of the United Arab Republic.")[3] In previous chapters we covered the implications of the Nasserist revolution on the issues of Eritrea, Ethiopia's
Muslims, and the Somalis. As far as the Ethiopians were concerned, the
threat of Arabization was now Cairo's essential message.

For Nasser, however, Ethiopia was part of his "African circle," particularly after the "oriental" disconnection of 1959. He was happy to develop an "African" dialogue with Haile Selassie, and there they shared a common interest. But they had a different Africa in mind. Nasser's African circle was no less a revolutionary sphere than his Arab circle. Nasser's Africa was to be a major theater for his anticolonial, anti-Western, anti-Israeli visions, as well as a continent united in the spirit of popular uprisings and revolutionary republics. Nasser tried to promote the Accra bloc, the more radical Pan-African wing organized in December 1958. Haile Selassie and Aklilu Habta-Wold allied with the rival Monrovia bloc, which gradually won in shaping the OAU to follow their rather more conservative spirit.[4]

In 1954, the same year "The Philosophy of the Revolution" was published, the Egyptian Foreign Ministry established its African Department. Ethiopian affairs were now its domain, and for the first time Ethiopia was considered part of the whole black continent. Indeed, much of the literature produced in Egypt during the Nasserist period dealt with Ethiopia in the Pan-African context. This new context, we saw, enabled the UAR, in the Ethiopian context at least, to pursue also a very pragmatic diplomacy. Moreover, the following discussion of the relevant literature produced in Nasserist Egypt will reveal a great deal of intellectual openness. The Nasserist discussion of Ethiopia, beyond its new terminology, rather recycled the old dichotomies and dilemmas.

Anti-Ethiopian Nasserists

The African perspective created a new wave of positive images of Ethiopia (which we shall soon address) but also recycled the old negative views. Silhouetted against the rest of the awakening continent, Ethiopia was depicted as reactionary and backward, as well as a collaborator with imperialist outsiders. Instead of helping Islam to enhance Pan-African affinity, Ethiopia continued to oppress Muslims. Of special gravity was Ethiopia's oppression of Islam in Eritrea, an area of direct Egyptian interest and, in the eyes of many Pan-Arab ideologues, a direct extension of the all-Arab revolution.

Perhaps the most revealing source of this anti-Ethiopian dimension in Nasser's Africanism is Muhammad Muhammad Fa'iq's book *Nasser and the African Revolution*.[5] The author, a prominent Egyptian diplomat, was arguably Nasser's closest confidant and adviser on African affairs. As Nasser's personal envoy to various African forums, movements, and leaders, Fa'iq accompanied the Egyptian president whenever he toured in Africa and often served as the head of the Egyptian delegation to the

OAU. During Nasser's last two years (1968–1970) he served as minister of information.[6] In May 1971, when Sadat purged the leading figures behind what he called Nasser's "centers of power," Fa'iq was sentenced to ten years in prison. It was there that he wrote his analysis of Nasser's African policy, published in Beirut in 1980 upon his release. His book, we may assume, reflects many of Nasser's concepts and ideas.

Fa'iq's introduction discusses Nasser's general Pan-African role and analyzes his achievements:

> It will not be an exaggeration to state that the July revolution in Egypt influenced Africa and changed it much the same way the French Revolution had changed and influenced Europe. The French Revolution introduced the principles of freedom, fraternity, and equality and planted them deeply among the peoples of Europe. It also did away with feudalism and the privileges and titles of the nobility. The Egyptian revolution worked to the same effect. It gave the African peoples the power to fight for their rights according to these very principles and these lofty ideals. . . . The Egyptian revolution lead by Nasser made Egypt the base for the African revolution much the same way Egypt had been the base for the Arab revolution. . . . The Egyptian revolution radiated to Africa the spirit of a united struggle and the spirit of a united goal. . . . Indeed Nasser is worthy of his definition as the pioneer and herald of the African revolution. (Pp. 7–8)

Most of Fa'iq's book is a survey of Nasser's aid to various anticolonial movements in Africa, and the reference to the French Revolution is made primarily in this context. However, the author also emphasized the antifeudal, antimonarchical nature of the French Revolution. In this context he made no secret of what he (and Nasser?) thought of Haile Selassie and his regime. They were feudal and oppressive, just like the foreign imperialists with whom they collaborated.

Significantly, the section on Ethiopia was not included in the chapters describing the anticolonial struggles or in those on the Pan-African process leading to the establishment of the OAU. Instead, Ethiopia was discussed in a chapter titled "Egypt's Support to Africa's Muslims and Its Impact on Her African Policy" (pp. 87–91). In no ambivalent terms Fa'iq portrayed Haile Selassie as an enemy of Islam. He was a systematic oppressor of Muslims and Islam in Eritrea, and it was for this reason that Egypt opened its gates, mainly those of Al-Azhar, to Eritrean Muslims. Moreover, Fa'iq disclosed, Egypt provided aid to the ELF, not only until 1963, but also after the establishment of the OAU. Fa'iq added:

> The Muslims of Eritrea were oppressed mainly because they were Muslims. Muslims were equally oppressed elsewhere in Ethiopia.

Though Muslims constituted a good half of Ethiopia's population, we cannot find any trace of them in high governmental offices. They were left in poverty and backwardness. Haile Selassie was in the habit of describing Ethiopia as a Christian island besieged by Islam from all directions. This was even written in official tourist books that every visitor received upon landing in Addis Ababa. This is how the Ethiopian government ignored half of her citizens—the Muslims. (P. 89)

According to Fa'iq, Haile Selassie's hatred of Islam was part of his hatred of everything progressive. In Eritrea, because it had an Islamic majority, he abolished all the human, cultural, and political rights that had been achieved by Eritreans and were endorsed by the UN. In so doing, the emperor oppressed Christians just as he had Muslims. Ethiopia also fought against the Somali Muslims and incited the southern Sudanese Christians against Sudanese unity. Among Ethiopia's many other sins, Fa'iq also mentioned its efforts in 1957–1959 to talk the Sudanese out of negotiating a new bilateral water agreement with Egypt. Failing to mention that Egypt at that time bluntly ignored Ethiopia as a Nile country, Fa'iq blamed Ethiopia for working to prevent an all-Nile understanding "which was so needed to enable Egypt to fulfill the idea of the High Dam." "Haile Selassie's hatred of the Egyptian revolution was so deep," he wrote, making a more valid point, "that he went as far as separating the Ethiopian Church from that of Alexandria." Last but not least, "Ethiopia was an American influence zone. Haile Selassie allowed the Americans to build an air and communication base in Asmara. He also enabled Israel to build factories and trading stations in Eritrea, aiming to make Eritrea a springboard for [Ethiopia's] economic and commercial plans in the whole of East Africa. Ethiopia also allowed Israel to make Asmara a center for its intelligence gathering in the entire region" (p. 89).

Summarizing Nasser's African perspective of Ethiopia, Fa'iq concluded:

Even though Egypt's African policy abstained from interfering with the internal matters of other independent states, and even though Egypt rendered assistance to liberation movements that fought against foreign imperialism, the story of Ethiopia was totally different. First, Haile Selassie was the first to initiate a hostile policy against Egypt by allying himself with Israel. Second, the struggle of the Eritrean people was different than other separatist movements. They were fighting for their rights as endorsed by the United Nations, while Haile Selassie was the aggressor against them. When the OAU [Organization of African Unity] was established in 1963, Haile Selassie tried to improve his image . . . but he was and he remained an integral part of all the reactionary forces in Africa. His African policy was never really different

from his internal Ethiopian policy, a policy of oppression, backwardness, reaction, and religious discrimination. (Pp. 90–91)

We can afford only a very brief survey of the anti-Ethiopian literature produced in Egypt during Nasser's time. Most of it repeated the
same arguments. Rashid al-Barawi, for example, published his book
Ethiopia Between Feudalism and Modern Times in 1961.[7] He portrayed
medieval Ethiopia as committed to fighting Islam in alliance with a crusading Europe (p. 53) and discussed modern Ethiopia (judging by the
1955 Constitution) as still anti-Islamic (p. 39). Egypt, he argued, had always stood for the welfare of local Muslims. When fighting Ethiopia at
Gura in 1876, Egypt's goal was the liberation of the Somalis and the Eritreans. Egypt's defeat in that battle perpetuated Ethiopian Christian oppression of Islam (pp. 59–60). Ethiopia, according to Barawi, was hardly
a better place for its Christians. Under Haile Selassie the country remained backward, lacking essential infrastructure; in many ways it was
still run by a system of medieval feudalism (pp. 111–115).

'Abduh Badawi, another prolific writer on Ethiopia, published many
articles in which he provided a similar picture of an anti-Islamic medieval Ethiopia. In his 1970 book *With the Islamic Movement in Africa,*
Badawi made the same argument about Haile Selassie's government (pp.
4–5, 119–121).[8] In this book he also blamed Ethiopia for joining European imperialism by occupying Somali territories during the "scramble
for Africa" (pp. 187–189). In two other articles Badawi emphasized the
historic ethnic connection between Ethiopia's Muslims and the ancient
Arabs of the nearby Arabian Peninsula.[9] Though he did not say so
specifically, he clearly implied that their salvation would be by way of
Arab reunification.

One more author worth mentioning as a promoter of Arab-Islamic
revolutionaries in the Horn of Africa is Jalal Yahya. In his various articles, as well as in his two books, *The Red Sea and Imperialism* (1962)
and *African Egypt* (1967), he discussed "The Arabs in the Horn of
Africa," the Somali-Arab struggle against imperialism, and Ethiopia as a
colonial collaborator.[10]

Nasser's Own Words: An Admiring Brother

Compared to the radically anti-Ethiopian literature published in the interwar period, these expressions were quite mild. During Nasser's time
militant Islam was restrained in Egypt, and Islam, politically speaking,
was primarily promoted as a dimension of Arabism (or Africanism). No
books were published in the old spirit of *"Islam al-najashi,"* depicting

Ethiopia as essentially illegitimate. The writings of the 1930s in the vein
of Yusuf Ahmad or Shakib Arslan and the portrayal of Ethiopia as the ultimate enemy of Islam were not to be recycled in Egypt prior to the
1980s. The regime, though flexibly allowing publications not entirely
compatible with its party line, was definitely not interested in further ex-
acerbating relations with Haile Selassie. What Nasser did in practice—
ignoring Ethiopia's water rights, supporting both the Eritrean separatists
and the Somali claims—was alienating enough. Nasser's first priorities
were in the Middle East and could hardly afford an actively hostile Haile
Selassie in Africa. Diplomatically and verbally, he worked instead to appease the Ethiopians. By 1963 he had compromised on a rather conservative OAU based in Addis Ababa. Indeed, throughout this period
Nasser did his best, quite successfully, to befriend Haile Selassie in person. One can only assume that his real thoughts were closer to Muhammad Fa'iq's. One may speculate that Nasser would have tried to undermine imperial Ethiopia had he been more successful in his Middle
Eastern "Arab circle." Concretely, however, we are left with the fact that
the main bulk of literature on Ethiopia produced during Nasser's period
was positive.

Nasser himself led the praise of Ethiopia and its emperor. In 1954
the regime offered a new book in its very popular series "We Chose It
for You." It was one of the first (number 6) in a long list of inexpensive
and immensely popular books selected to shape public opinion. *Lights
on Ethiopia* was ostensibly prepared by Amin Shakir, Sa'id al-'Iryan,
and Mustafa Amin, but it was actually a collection of hastily translated
chapters from A. H. M. Jones and Elizabeth Monroe's 1935 classic, *A
History of Ethiopia*.[11] In 1957 (or 1958) a new edition was printed, apparently to enable Nasser himself to add an introduction. His five-page
"The Kingdom of Ethiopia: A Sister State" was to appear later in additional publications in Egypt and other Arab countries.[12] Nasser wrote:

> Between ourselves and Ethiopia there are eternal relations of love in-
> comparable to anything else between two close brothers. We and
> Ethiopia are two neighborly states on a continent in which imperialism
> attacked in order to feed itself and not its children. . . . In addition to
> this the two of us share this eternal river that brings good and blessings
> to its banks from the heights of Ethiopia to Sudan and down to the
> Mediterranean Sea. Every drop of these waters . . . reflects the shared
> beliefs that tie the feelings of the Egyptians, the Sudanese, and the
> Ethiopians together. For all of us first and foremost believe in God as
> if we shared the same religion. The Muslims of Ethiopia, in all of their
> thoughts, bring forward the memory of that distant day in which the
> first Muslim *muhajirun* of Muhammad's *sahaba* stepped on the *na-
> jashi*'s carpet seeking asylum from the pagans of Mecca. He gave them

shelter and security and all his pure justice, and he blessed them and
their prophet. And the Christians among us, like the Christians of
Ethiopia, are of the same religious sect, worshiping God and asking his
help in the same way. . . . They receive the blessings of the bishop appointed by the patriarch of Alexandria.

Nasser, as discussed earlier, was about to give up the church connection and, in practice, ignore Ethiopia as a Nile country. Despite these
major decisions, he nevertheless sought friendship. He provided the ultimate expression of Islamic acceptance of Ethiopia by endorsing the
positive aspect of the *najashi*-Muhammad story (literature distributed in
Cairo also spread the idea of Haile Selassie as the spiritual successor of
the benevolent *najashi*).[13] But Nasser's diplomatic message was to play
Haile Selassie's game and rebuild Egyptian-Ethiopian relations on the
new African premise. Here his line was praising Ethiopia's historic and
symbolic Pan-African role as the pioneer of the anti-imperialist struggle.
It was Western aggression, Nasser argued, that had tried to separate
Ethiopia and Egypt throughout. Refraining from even a hint at any of the
many Egyptian-Ethiopian, Islamic-Christian confrontations, Nasser
placed all the blame on Westerners: first the European crusaders, who, in
the twelfth to thirteenth century, incited Ethiopia against Egypt; later the
fanatic Portuguese, who tried to make Ethiopia a base against Islam;
then, in the late nineteenth century, the British, French, and Italians,
who, in the name of Christianity, tried to penetrate Ethiopia but were re-
pulsed. Now it is the United States, Nasser wrote, that is trying to build
a wall between Ethiopia and Egypt.

Imperialism, Nasser argued (again ignoring the historical role of
Islam), was successful in Ethiopia in one sense only. It instilled a sense
of siege in the Ethiopians' minds and made them suspicious of everything originating beyond the sea, thus closing themselves to Egypt as
well. But one modern imperialist chapter shattered this wall. Mussolini's
invasion of Ethiopia and his 1935–1941 conquest ended the mental self-
isolation of the Ethiopians and reconnected them to Egypt. "As for
today," Nasser concluded, "we are free to act as we understand. We must
look around us and shed light on Ethiopia to let the Arab and African
readers know what they are missing in this sisterly country, so that they
will come to know her and help to strengthen the relations of fraternity
with a nation that has been so strongly connected to us from the very
early days of history."

This line, praising Ethiopia as the symbol of Africa's stand against
imperialism, was Nasser's main theme to the end. If other Egyptian
army officers could hardly forgive Ethiopia for defeating Egypt in 1876
or for fighting for its independence while they could not do so, Nasser

was apparently ready to admire it. The Ethiopian-Italian war of 1935–1936 was a formative event in his youth.[14] (On one occasion, in a public speech, Nasser reminded the emperor that they had met personally in Khartoum in 1940, when Haile Selassie was preparing to reenter Ethiopia and Nasser was a young officer stationed in the Sudan.) When Haile Selassie arrived in Cairo in June 1959 to sever the "oriental" church relations, Nasser plied him with African anticolonial brotherhood, making several speeches that practically crowned Haile Selassie as the elder statesman, if not the leader of the emerging continent.[15] On the one hand, he let Muhammad Fa'iq prepare his revolutionary option in Africa and the Horn; on the other, he instructed Mahmud Fawzi to work with Aklilu Habta-Wold in establishing the OAU.

In terms of overt verbal and diplomatic relations, Ethiopia was embraced by Nasser as the heart of Africa. When Haile Selassie visited Cairo in October 1966, the *Egyptian Gazette* ran a lengthy article titled "Africa's Silent Servant." The paper praised Ethiopia for its historic stand in defending Africa's honor and Haile Selassie's role in uniting the continent around the OAU. In sharp contrast to the writings of Fa'iq, Barawi, Badawi, and others, it went on to depict Ethiopia as the guardian of human and national rights. Without mentioning the *najashi*'s hosting of the *sahaba,* the article recycled and modernized the concept of Ethiopia as "the land of righteousness":

> Ethiopia's assistance to Africans has taken many forms throughout several decades. Africans, no matter from what territory they came, have received Ethiopian patronage. None who have ever appealed to Ethiopia have gone away empty handed or unnoticed. Thus Ethiopia's policy of nonintervention in the affairs of other independent African states cannot be construed to mean that it advocates the principle that any government can violate the fundamental human rights of its citizens; . . . neither should it be interpreted to refer to governments that have not been voluntarily established by the people of their own free will and accord. For Ethiopia is historically committed to the philosophy that all peoples have an inherent right to live in freedom and independence.[16]

Mainstream Public Opinion Shapers

The Nasserist regime helped enhance the positive image of Ethiopia among Egypt's general public, intellectuals, and academicians. The emphasis on the historic role of European aggression against Africa shed new light on their common history. Thus literature now being produced on the Mamluks' relations with medieval Ethiopia attributed much of the mutual misunderstanding to European involvement.[17] Revolutionary

Egypt also had a new perspective on the ousted Muhammad 'Ali dynasty and especially on Khedive Isma'il. The latter was now seen as more a collaborator with Western interests and his war with Emperor Yohannes IV as part of an Egyptian imperialistic dream. Of the many examples available, I will mention only one book, Fathi Ghith's *Islam and Ethiopia over History,* published in Cairo in 1967.[18]

Fathi Ghith was an engineer and an intellectual who, on his own evidence, had devoted twenty years to the study of Ethiopia. He had worked in Ethiopia and had met several times with Haile Selassie (p. 299). His book was an attempt at a serious, well-balanced history based on the study of both Western and Islamic (but no Ethiopian) sources. Throughout the book one can sense very little emotional bias, and the discussion, even of the most delicate issues, is objective and sober. The fourth chapter, "History of Ethiopia During Early Islam," delved into the heart of the initial *najashi-sahaba* legacy. The author presented the various Islamic sources and their differences, and he quoted European scholars. He finally concluded that the noble Ethiopian *najashi* rendered vital aid to Islam, and it was for this that a grateful Muhammad ordered the Muslims to "leave the Abyssinians alone." The *najashi,* wrote Ghith, making his main point, never converted to Islam but only respected it (pp. 46–59). In so stating, Ghith set the tone for the rest of his book.

Ethiopia in his eyes was a legitimate, very important, good neighbor of Islam and Egypt. His presentation of medieval history, especially the Mamluk-Solomonian dialogue (chapter 7) and Ahmad Gragn's conquest of Ethiopia (chapter 9), was written in this same spirit (he also blamed the Europeans for inciting these medieval conflicts; see chapter 6). He devoted chapters to Tewodros and Yohannes, in which he analyzed their anti-Islamic policies in very factual language and aimed his criticism against Khedive Isma'il. In the long chapter 14, titled "Egyptian Attacks on Ethiopia" (pp. 209–239), he blamed the Egyptian ruler for recklessly waging war on Ethiopia. Isma'il, he wrote, collaborated with European interests, provoked Yohannes, and brought about a great disaster upon Egypt.

Fathi Ghith's last chapters, devoted to the historical role of Haile Selassie, were written in the same spirit of intellectual independence. He admired Haile Selassie for his courageous effort to thwart Mussolini and revive Ethiopia's independence. He also praised him for introducing modern education and becoming a symbol of African pride. But he was critical of the emperor on two major issues. The first was his failure to introduce political modernization to Ethiopia. Beyond the facade of the 1955 Constitution and the Ethiopian Parliament, the system remained a feudal autocracy. The abortive 1960 coup, he stated, was just the first warning sign for Haile Selassie (p. 308). The second issue was Haile

Selassie's policy vis-à-vis Islam. In his early period of rule, before the Italian conquest (chapter 17), the emperor tried moderately to amend previous injustices by allowing Muslims to own land. When the Italians occupied Ethiopia during 1936–1941 (chapter 18), the Muslims were granted all their rights and prospered. But their situation during Haile Selassie's second period of rule (pp. 298–314) deteriorated again. The emperor, like the rest of the Christian elite, feared that once the Muslims made progress, they would do away with Christian dominance. He therefore began to oppress them again. Here, in blaming Haile Selassie for depriving Muslims of good education and governmental jobs, Ghith allowed himself some isolated emotional expressions. He was careful, however, to balance his judgment by concluding that though Haile Selassie was far from being a benevolent *najashi,* he was nevertheless a great historic figure.

It is obvious that the Egyptian regime did not dictate one homogenous concept of Ethiopia and was willing to tolerate a debate within limits. Representative of the academic, intellectual discourse on Ethiopia and its inner dichotomies was a new monthly magazine that began publication in 1957. Titled *Nahdat Ifriqya,* Africa's Awakening, it aimed at "promoting the African national awareness, advancing inter-African acquaintance, and publishing various studies of interest to any African" (vol. 1, no. 2 [1957]). It became an important forum for Egypt's Africanists, and a good part of every issue was devoted to Ethiopia and the Horn of Africa. Among the many contributors was 'Abduh Badawi, who led a fairly anti-Ethiopian faction. In his various articles and book reviews, Badawi helped spread the idea that Muslims in Ethiopia and the Horn were Arabs, or at least strongly connected to the Arabs.[19] This theme was repeated in many other articles analyzing and supporting the Somali liberation struggle as part of an Arab revolution and referring to Ethiopian control of the Ogaden as subjugation of Islam.

Eritrean leaders also published their strong anti-Ethiopian views in *Nahdat Ifriqya* (for example, the April 1959 issue). Ethiopian history, with an emphasis on the abuse of Islam (especially by Tewodros and Yohannes but also by Haile Selassie), was a major theme. However, this kind of anti-Ethiopian literature published in the magazine was far from being blunt or aggressive. Badawi wrote persistently that all problems in the Horn should be solved through a peaceful, friendly dialogue with Ethiopia (June 1959, February 1964). Moreover, anti-Ethiopian radical Islamic literature was not published, though one article, "Chapters in the History of Islam in Ethiopia and Eritrea" by Dr. Jamal al-Din al-Ramadi (February 1963), came quite close. It began with a long section describing the *najashi*-Muhammad dialogue, concluding that the *najashi* had converted to Islam. But this premise served the author in describing how widespread Islam was in Ethiopia, and he made no mention of *"Islam al-najashi"* as the main argument of Ethiopia's illegitimacy.

Nahdat Ifriqya also contained many scholarly, objective pieces (such as one on Emperor Menelik II in January 1961) and well-balanced book reviews (the Egyptian army's chief of staff, 'Abd al-Fattah Ibrahim, wrote a two-part impartial review of Spencer Trimingham's *Islam in Ethiopia*, June and July 1959). There was, however, a similarly active pro-Ethiopian faction among the contributors to *Nahdat Ifriqya* (notably Dr. Zahir Riyad, to whom I shall soon return), led primarily by Coptic intellectuals.

Coptic Intellectuals: Through Ethiopia Back to Egypt

As we have seen, the Coptic Church establishment under Nasser was deprived of its tremendously important patronage over the Ethiopian Church, and the regime abolished much of its judicial-religious autonomy. The new patriarch, Cyril VI, however, managed to stand up to Nasser, and in October 1959 they reached an understanding. The church, under Cyril VI's revitalized leadership, came to terms with the Nasserist state.[20] But it was a severely weakened institution (a fact that would be exposed during the 1970s with the return of radical Islam to Egypt). The church proved incapable of repairing its relations with the Ethiopians and thus, perhaps, improving its position at home. Coptic intellectuals nevertheless remained appreciative of the historic bond between their own community and the source land of the Nile. Though many of them, like Makram 'Ubayd in the 1930s, embraced secular Arabism, they did their best to retain their special Egyptian Nile identity. They were happy to serve the new Nasserist cause of establishing Egypt's position in the "African circle," and the regime, on its part, enabled them to work.

In 1954 the Institute of Coptic Studies was opened, including ten departments, among them one African and one Ethiopian.[21] But leading Coptic intellectuals, in helping promote the concept of continental Africa, made a special point of reemphasizing Ethiopia's centrality. They responded to the call to relate to Africa but focused mainly on the Nile Valley and its Christian-Islamic history. It was through Africa, so it seems, that they wanted to direct Egypt back to its Nile identity.

Two members of the old guard, Mirrit Boutros-Ghali and Murad Kamil, were still very active. Mirrit remained closely attached to church affairs, writing an article in 1966 on the historic relations between the churches,[22] and he continued to visit Ethiopia even during the 1980s. Murad Kamil also tried to save whatever was possible of church relations.

In 1957, still before the final break, he published an important article on the church connection up to 1952.[23] Its message was quite clear: modern Egyptian nationalism and modern Ethiopia needed their mutual Christian bond, and people of goodwill on both sides had managed to modernize these relations in the late 1940s. In 1967 Murad wrote another article on the same subject, updating it and lamenting the 1959 separation. Earlier in 1958 he had published an edition of the seventeenth-century *Sirat al-habasha* by the Yemenite traveler and envoy al-Haymi al-Hasan ibn Ahmad. The latter visited the Ethiopian capital of Gondar and described its Muslim quarter. Murad, in his long introduction and annotations, made an effort to depict Christian-Islamic relations in Ethiopia of that time as characterized by great tolerance.[24]

The most prolific Coptic intellectual, when it came to African-Ethiopian affairs, was Zahir Riyad. In 1934 he had been sent by the Egyptian Ministry of Education to teach history for three years in the new secondary school opened by Haile Selassie in Addis Ababa. Mastering Amharic, he later returned to Ethiopia in 1943 for two more years to help Murad Kamil rebuild the education system the Fascists had destroyed. He also helped Murad Kamil, still under the parliamentarian regime, spread the concept of benevolent Ethiopia.[25] In 1954 Riyad joined the African Department of the Institute of Coptic Studies and became its living spirit. He also published extensively in *Nahdat Ifriqya* (e.g., his memories of the antifascist Ethiopian stand; the Fascists' "divide and rule" policy undermining good Christian-Islamic relations in Ethiopia; and a piece on the Egyptian Church helping the Ethiopians fight Western aggression in medieval and modern times).[26] In 1957 Riyad published an extensive book review on Trimingham's classic *Islam in Ethiopia*, blaming it for grossly overemphasizing Christian-Islamic dichotomies. He himself published a book in 1964 entitled *Islam in Ethiopia in Medieval Times* portraying a much more positive picture of interreligious tolerance. Earlier in 1962 he published a book on *The Alexandrian Church in Africa*, largely focusing on the church's very important mutual relations with Ethiopia.[27] Riyad also published numerous studies on internal Ethiopian politics and society and a more comprehensive *History of Ethiopia*, which appeared in 1966. Riyad's writings have been discussed elsewhere,[28] and his ideas shall also be referred to when discussing Sadat's period. His message, however, was unambiguous: Ethiopian society, culture, and history, though flawed, should be respected. Ethiopia was a natural ally and a natural friend of Egypt.

The most important Coptic intellectual relevant to this study was Boutros Boutros-Ghali. Educated in Egypt and France, he received his doctorate in international law and by the early 1960s had become renowned as a roving lecturer, an editor of *Al-Ahram*'s economic supplement, and a professor at Cairo University. He has already been mentioned as the man behind the Egyptian-Ethiopian rapprochement of the mid-1980s; indeed, he would become a major architect of Egypt's foreign policy under Sadat and Mubarak. In time he would become a global figure, the Secretary-General of the United Nations from 1992 to 1997. While still serving Nasser, however, Boutros Boutros-Ghali made his principles clear: Egypt's "African circle" was no less significant than its "Arab circle." In fact, he maintained, it was first in importance, for the Nile flowed through Africa, and the Nile was Egypt's life and identity.

In 1963 Boutros Boutros-Ghali summarized his ideas in the article "The Foreign Policy of Egypt."[29] It opened with a section titled "The Challenge of the Nile": "From Cheops to Muhammed Ali, from Muhammed Ali to Gamal Abdel Nasser, Egyptian foreign policy has been dominated by two challenges: the first has been the physical task of mastering the waters of the Nile; the second has been the moral task of deciding how the Egyptian rulers should use the wealth resulting from the cultivation of the Nile Valley. . . . [W]ithout the struggle to make the most lasting and economic use of the Nile's waters, Egypt would be still a narrower land, and famine would be her fate." He then began a geographical and cultural analysis: "Egypt is not simply one country but four: an African country, a Mediterranean country, an Islamic country and an Arab country." Putting Africa first, Boutros-Ghali explained Egypt's psychological and emotional links with the continent. He did so by referring to the famous "Afrocentrist" W. E. B. DuBois, a proponent of the idea that ancient Egypt, and therefore human civilization, had begun in the African heartland, in the Upper Nile, "African Ethiopia." The "up the river–down the river" relations between ancient Egypt and ancient Africa, wrote Boutros-Ghali, had been summarized by DuBois. He quoted:

> In Ethiopia the sunrise of human culture took place, spreading down into the Nile Valley. Beyond Ethiopia, in central Africa, lay the gold of Ophir and the rich trade of Punt on which the prosperity of Egypt largely depended. Egypt brought slaves from black Africa as she did from Europe and Asia. But she also brought citizens and leaders from Africa. When Egypt conquered Asia, she used black soldiers to a wide extent. When Asia overwhelmed Egypt, Egypt sought refuge in Ethiopia as a child returns to his mother, and Ethiopia then for centuries dominated Egypt and successfully invaded Asia.[30]

By reemphasizing the pre-Islamic, pre-Arab roots of Egypt's identity, Boutros-Ghali remained loyal to the Pharaonicism of the liberal interwar period. Contrary to the regime's ideology, he implied that the African Nile countries were closer to Egypt than the Arabs of Asia. Yet, as the OAU was inaugurated and Nasser worked to enhance Egypt's status on the continent, Boutros-Ghali went from strength to strength. In 1965 the semiofficial *Al-Ahram* began publishing a new quarterly, *Al-Siyasa al-Duwaliyya* (International Politics). It soon became the most important platform of discussion on Egypt's foreign policy, and under Boutros-Ghali's editorship it pursued a pro-African, pro-Ethiopian line. Dozens of articles written by the Coptic intellectuals mentioned above, by Boutros-Ghali himself, and by many others diverted public attention back to the Upper Nile.[31] They gradually paved the way for what would be labeled in the late 1970s "the Boutros-Ghali thesis": namely, that rather than promoting revolutions in the Nile countries, Egypt should work for stability and cooperation with the governments of Sudan and Ethiopia. After Nasser's death, while Muhammad Fa'iq was in jail, Boutros Boutros-Ghali became Sadat's chief adviser on African affairs.

The Nasserist regime undertook to revolutionize Egypt, its infrastructure, society, and identity. Our Ethiopian dimension gave us a few glimpses at some deep-rooted changes. It also gave us an opportunity to go deeper and observe the more subtle discussion beyond such concrete issues. Here we found that rather than divorcing the old Egyptian past, the period mostly recycled old concepts. The discussion of the Ethiopian "other," delving through the Nile and the cross into the very heart of the Egyptian "self," was not essentially different from similar discussions that had been held in the formative days of Islam and of early Egyptian nationalism, as well as in the mid-1930s, the years of early Pan-Arabism in Egypt. Indeed, all discussions of Ethiopia throughout all the periods that have been mentioned were polarized, reflective of the essential strategic dilemmas and the complexity of self-determination. The Nasserist period, emphasizing its own premises and terminology, deriving from its own reservoir of revolutionary Arabism, was also just another chapter in the Nile's continuum.

SADAT AND MUBARAK:
THE RETURN TO EGYPT AND THE NILE

The death of Nasser in late September 1970 marked the end of an era in Egypt and in its relations with the surrounding regions. The Nasserist emphasis on the Arab dimension no longer dominated the struggle over Egypt's self-definition. In many ways the rise of Sadat signaled the revival of the Egyptian territorial element and its growing influence at the expense of Arabism. Though Egyptian nationalism and Arabism were greatly compatible, the change in emphasis reflected a major multifaceted shift. From the perspective of our discussion this change was accompanied by the abandonment of both Arab and African revolutionary terminology, as well as a strategic reorientation on the United States rather than the Soviet Union. Egyptian society and domestic politics now became more open to various forces, old and new, which stretched from liberalism on one end to Islamic radicalism on the other. The regime itself, less concerned about external "circles," focused more on the land of the Nile itself, its integrity and welfare. It was ready to make peace with Israel in order to retrieve the Egyptian Sinai. Naturally, it attached growing importance to Egypt's traditional spheres of interest, the Red Sea and the Nile basin.

"The Boutros-Ghali Thesis"

The renewed emphasis on values that had been formed in the first half of the twentieth century did not mean a return to the "Unity of the Nile Valley" concept. Egypt would no longer strive for political unification with Sudan nor for actual control over parts of the Upper Nile basin. However, Egypt's interest in the Red Sea, the Horn, and Sudan intensified.[32] The centrality of the Nile in Egypt's revitalized territorial identity rendered developments in its upper basin more relevant. Although Africa and its continental diplomacy remained important to Egypt, real concern was focused on Sudan, Ethiopia, and Somalia.

As of 1977 Boutros Boutros-Ghali was made responsible for promoting Egypt's policy. He wrote in his memoirs:

> I tried repeatedly to convince Sadat of my views and maintained that Egypt's national interest required us to establish relations with Ethiopia, where 85 percent of the Nile waters originate. To guarantee the flow of the Nile, there is no alternative to cooperation with Ethiopia, particularly in view of the Ethiopian irrigation project at Lake Tana, which could reduce the Nile waters reaching Egypt. As long as relations between Cairo and Addis Ababa were strained or hostile, we risked serious problems. Preserving Nile waters for Egypt was not only an economic and hydrological issue but a question of national survival. . . . Our security depended on the south more than on the east, in spite of Israel's military power. . . . I told him about my plan to associate all the states bordering the Nile in a common supranational authority. It would create a highway from Alexandria to the heart of the continent, an electricity grid taking advantage of all the new dams on the river. We could even export electricity to the European Common Community. . . . Lake Nasser, with Abu Simbel and its temple, restored by UNESCO [United Nations Educational, Scientific, and Cultural

Organization], as the capital of this new region, would become a population center with new fields, towns, and tourist projects on its banks.
Now it was a barrier between Egypt and the Sudan, but it could become a magnet drawing the region together beyond the megalopolis of
Cairo. We could conquer the desert.[33]

In the reality of the Sadat-Mangistu deep animosity, the so-called
Boutros-Ghali thesis became rather a down-to-earth policy of contain-
ment. Seeking to minimize the risks to Egypt stemming from Soviet involvement (in Somalia and Ethiopia) on the one hand and from radical
Islam (in the Sudan) on the other, the main thrust of this policy was to
promote stability in the entire region. The new strategy proved successful first in Sudan, where Egypt supported a stable and friendly government under Ja'far al-Numayri that lasted until the mid-1980s. (The Sudanese policy was then about to culminate successfully with the
inauguration of the Jonglei Canal in the Sudd marshes of southern
Sudan, a project that, if completed, would have substantially increased
the waters of Lake Nasser. But in 1983 Numayri began losing his control, and the renewed war with southern Sudanese Christian rebels halted
the work on the canal until the project was finally abandoned.)[34] If Haile
Selassie's imperial regime had survived or been replaced by some moderate system, Egypt and Ethiopia might have rebuilt their mutual understanding of the pre-Nasserist period. However, with Ethiopia under
Mangistu looking to the Soviet Union as a model and ally, Ethiopian-
Egyptian relations deteriorated, reaching a historic low in the aftermath
of the Ogaden War.

Sadat worked during 1975–1977 to build an "Arab" (in fact an
Egyptian-Sudanese-Saudi) alliance in the Red Sea aimed at curbing the
Soviets, then entrenched primarily in Somalia. After the Soviet-equipped
Somalis invaded the Ethiopian Ogaden, the Soviets, in an apparent attempt to control the entire Horn, came to Mangistu's aid. In February
1978, when Sadat tried to prevent an Ethiopian Soviet-backed retaliatory
invasion of Somalia, Mangistu threatened to interfere with the Nile. Mutual threats and unrealistic rhetoric of suspicion prevailed to the end of
Sadat's rule, but minimal confidence was not restored prior to 1985. It
was only then, as discussed previously, that Boutros-Ghali's relentless
efforts at appeasement drew Mangistu and Mubarak closer. In 1987
Mangistu, for reasons of his own, began seeking Egyptian sympathy.
Mubarak was ready to reciprocate because in that same year the Egyptians realized that the Aswan High Dam, Nasser's legacy, could no
longer serve as their ultimate guardian.

Until the great drought in Ethiopia of the mid-1980s, Egyptians
were not really concerned with the Nile. The idea that the High Dam had

created Lake Nasser as their controlled source of life was effectively instilled during Nasser's period. In fact, according to the literature surveyed above on Egyptian concepts of Ethiopia in the 1960s, the cen-
turies-old fear of Ethiopian interference with the Nile was now a matter
of history. In many ways this assumption was to be preserved until 1987.

Reflective of Egyptian attitudes toward the Nile waters issue is the
case of Egyptian journalist and researcher 'Abd al-Tawwab 'Abd al-
Hayy. In March 1973 he was invited by the Ethiopian government to
visit and meet the emperor. Haile Selassie, already sensing the new spirit
emanating from Cairo, was anxious to cement his relations with Sadat.
Indeed, he was soon to pay the highest price for this desire by breaking
relations with Israel in the middle of the Yom Kippur War (6–24 October
1973) initiated by Sadat. The emperor wanted to revive the Nile issue
and insert it into the middle of the dialogue, and he approached it in the
old Ethiopian way. The journalist was shown maps and was briefed
about Ethiopian designs for the Blue Nile and Lake Tana. He was then
flown to the Blue Nile area to see the actual sites. The barely disguised
threat proved partially effective. 'Abd al-Hayy returned to Egypt and
met with Sadat.

A few weeks later, in May 1973, Sadat and Haile Selassie met at an
OAU summit, where Haile Selassie quickly promised Sadat that Ethiopia would never interfere with the Nile before consulting with the other
riparian countries. This was only the beginning of the story for the
Egyptian journalist. Despite the High Dam, he made it his business to
worry about the future of the Nile. During the next few years he studied
the relevant data and history of hydropolitics and toured extensively
along the river and its sources. He came to the conclusion that without
all-Nile plans and without a coordinated regional effort to increase the
water quantities reaching Lake Nasser, a catastrophe would eventually
occur. In fact, he finally published a book titled *The Nile and the Future*.[35] However, he did so only in 1988, after his fears were proven valid.

Again, we cannot afford a full, balanced discussion here of the
Egyptian literature on Ethiopia produced in the 1970s and 1980s. Inescapably, we shall have to skip much of what was written by mainstream
researchers and academicians. But Ethiopian and African studies in Egypt
continued to develop and yielded a goodly amount of scholarly works on
Ethiopia. I can only repeat the observation that the Nile dimension in
Ethiopian-Egyptian relations was marginalized in mainstream writings of
that time. In the vast literature produced on the Nile, the general tendency
was to minimize the relevance of Ethiopia and reemphasize the complete,
nearly exclusive identification between Egypt and the river.

Representative of this approach, for example, was a book published in 1985, *The Nile River: The Past, the Present, and the Future.*[36] The authors, Dr. 'Abd al-'Azim Abu al-'Ata, Dr. Mufid Shihab, and Professor Daf'allah Rida, in discussing the river's history, made only brief mention of other riparian civilizations and primarily analyzed the history of the river as the shaper of Egypt (pp. 32–33). The main issue concerning the present, they wrote, was a Zionist plot to control the Nile and divert its waters to Israel (pp. 5–15, 85–115). Faced with this external threat, they argued, Egypt was the guardian of the Nile and the Aswan High Dam the main security precaution. References to Ethiopia as a Nile country are sparse and minimizing. Even when the sources of the Nile are discussed, the reader is led to understand that Ethiopia is just one of the contributing countries (pp. 28–29, 43, 52–54). They are also led to believe that Ethiopia is a potential ally of Israel and might collaborate with the Zionist plot (p. 113). All in all, the book pays ten times more attention to a presumed Israeli plot than to the reality of Ethiopia as a Nile country. In dealing with the future of the river, Ethiopia is again referred to as just one of the upstream countries with which Egypt should cultivate good relations. The future, the authors stated, can be better assured by promoting understanding among all riparian countries. However, the cornerstone of future all-Nile cooperation is the 1959 Nile Waters Agreement (pp. 66–71). The 1959 agreement, remember, divided historical rights over the Nile waters between Egypt and Sudan only.

Voices for Friendship with Ethiopia

The following paragraphs are devoted to those whose writings reflected the conceptual polarization regarding Ethiopia. During the period under discussion this polarization continued to widen and, in fact, reached its outer limit. As in the past it was the Coptic intellectuals who led one of the factions that worked to spread the concept of Ethiopia as a very important, friendly neighbor.

I shall mention only one book by Zahir Riyad. *Egypt and Africa*[37] was published in 1976, the year Sadat's slogan of "Arabization of the Red Sea" ignited the crisis with Mangistu. Riyad, however, had a very different message than rivalry. Recycling some of his earlier studies, he analyzed the centrality of Africa in Egypt's identity. Egypt was the Nile, he asserted, and the Nile stemmed from Africa. He made his main point in the opening lines of the very first page, which contained barely concealed criticism of the Nasserist illusion that the Aswan High Dam separated Egypt from the African sources of the river:

Egyptian-African relations did not begin in our time nor are they the product of a certain leader or the work of his generation. It is the work of nature that Egypt is a part of Africa. For it is the Nile River that connects them. The Nile has flowed to Egypt from the heart of Africa ever since God created them both. It is therefore natural that Egypt is connected to Africa more than to any other part of the world. It is a human, historical, and territorial connection that no one can escape, even though people have tried to do so at certain times.

Riyad's message was that Africa was primarily Ethiopia, and indeed, much of the book was devoted to Egyptian-Ethiopian relations. These relations were not without their problems, he admitted, but essentially they were those of close brotherhood. An entire chapter is devoted to "The Period of the Mamluks: The Height of Ethiopian-Egyptian Relations" (pp. 81–104). While for Europe, he wrote, "Prester John's" Ethiopia was a myth, for the Mamluks it was very real—it was the Nile. The Ethiopians, on their part, desired to maintain their church relations and "saw the people of Egypt and the Church of Egypt as their brothers who never aimed for their conquest and were never interested in controlling them. The Ethiopians [of that time] never saw an Egyptian army advancing towards their country" (p. 90). Riyad described Ethiopian threats toward the Nile, the Mamluks' counterattack, and the delay in sending an *abun,* but the whole mood of the chapter is one of internal family affairs (pp. 95–96). In analyzing Egyptian-Ethiopian relations during early modern times (pp. 151–160), Riyad emphasized the role of Khedive Isma'il. Though Isma'il first tried to mediate between the British and Emperor Tewodros, he later became a full collaborator with the Western imperialists. He made it his ambition to build an Egyptian-African empire, really endeavoring to establish a name for himself in Europe. He thus became the agent of the British in the Sudan. When he collided with Ethiopia, "he did not hesitate to exchange the old policy of friendship and mutual understanding for a new policy of invasion, aggression, and hostility. . . . Egyptian expansion in the Red Sea further deteriorated Ethiopian-Egyptian relations, moving from friendship to enmity" (p. 154–155). Riyad made no mention of Yohannes's anti-Islamic policy and put all the blame for the 1876 fateful collision solely on Isma'il.

Riyad devoted an extensive chapter to Egyptian-African relations between 1885 and 1952 (pp. 165–232), its main portions again focusing on Ethiopia. After Isma'il the Ethiopian-Egyptian dialogue returned to its friendly track. Riyad described Egypt's significant aid in introducing modern education during the reign of Menelik II (p. 167) and later Ras Tafari's rivalry with Abuna Matewos (pp. 169–170). The victory of the modernizing Tafari, Riyad wrote, and his coronation in 1930 as Haile

Selassie paved the way for ever-improving relations in various fields. They culminated during the "Abyssinian crisis," when the entire Egyptian people and its government supported Ethiopia against Mussolini (Riyad made no mention of anti-Ethiopian expressions of that time). When Haile Selassie returned in 1941, he not only restored church relations but also called for more Egyptian aid in economy, medicine, and education. Riyad himself, as mentioned earlier, took part in one such education mission to Ethiopia, which had been headed by Murad Kamil. Ethiopian-Egyptian friendship, he wrote, grew out of more than the Coptic-Ethiopian connection, and he discussed the educational aid rendered at that time by the Islamic Al-Azhar (pp. 171–173).

Riyad's chapter dealing with the Nasserist period (pp. 233–265) was too short to contain much detail on Ethiopia, but whatever was discussed (pp. 241–245) was less positive. Riyad placed part of the blame on Ethiopia's response to Israeli politics and the establishment of relations between these two countries. It was the Coptic community, he said, that ensured the maintenance of good relations, but church relations themselves were now marred by the internal crisis in the Coptic Church during the era of Patriarch Yusab. This crisis resulted in the 1959 separation between the churches and the intensification of their old conflict over Deir al-Sultan. Riyad's last chapter, "How Did Egypt Find the African Revolution," again reemphasized his initial premise—namely, that of the three "circles" of Egypt (he used Nasser's terms), the African circle was by far the most meaningful. Though he did not implicitly blame Nasser and his Arab revolution for trying to challenge this order of priorities, his message was quite clear: Egypt is African before anything else, and in Africa it is Ethiopia that, despite all the problems, had always been Egypt's sister and natural partner.

The political importance of Riyad (and his colleagues) lay in the fact that his ideas were fully consonant with those of Boutros Boutros-Ghali (who himself continued to write in the same spirit), and Boutros-Ghali, as we have seen, was a major force behind Mubarak's policy. The Coptic intellectuals continued to remind the Egyptian policymakers and public opinion shapers that the Nile, despite the Aswan Dam, was also Ethiopia. Though none of them ever mentioned Ethiopian water rights (at least not in the 1980s), their concepts of Ethiopia were all geared toward the reconstruction of mutual understanding.

Radical Muslims and Ethiopia's Illegitimacy

Sadat's declared policy of "openness" not only strengthened the liberals and the Coptic intellectuals; beginning in the early 1970s the voice of radical Islam had become no less effective in competing for the reshaping of post-Nasserist Egypt. The tension between what Sadat called "[an Egyptian] state of [modern] institutions" and the radical Muslim vision of a religious state was an issue around which revolved much of Egypt's history during this period. The differences of opinion were also reflected in our particular area of interest. Islamic radicals, even fundamentalists, as soon as they resurfaced following Nasser's death, were also active in spreading their perceptions of Ethiopia. Again, Ethiopia was a very significant "other," meaningful enough to make the discussion a matter of principle, a discussion of the Islamic "self." Advocates of political Islam in Egypt could naturally resort to their old reservoir of Ethiopia's negative images in order to promote their cause of Islamic militancy. Fortunately for them, the new Ethiopia under Mangistu Haile Mariam could easily serve as a model of evil and peril.

Of the vast literature available on this topic, this section will address only three books. In 1974 an Arabic edition of the sixteenth-century Islamic description of Ahmad Gragn's conquest of Ethiopia appeared in Cairo.[38] *Tuhfat al-zaman* or *Futuh al-habasha* was written by one of Gragn's Islamic scholars, Shihab al-Din Ahmad ibn 'Abd al-Qadir, known also as 'Arab Faqih. The text itself, along with a French translation and notes, was published by R. Basset in Paris in 1897.[39] *The Conquest of Ethiopia* was the most detailed description of that important period, and the fall of Ethiopia under Islam was described in the most anti-Ethiopian spirit and terminology. According to *The Conquest,* Ethiopia's downfall was ordered by the Prophet himself, for the Christian state was persecuting Muslims and conquering its Islamic neighbors.

The text of *Futuh al-habasha* (perhaps because it was so radical?) was not preserved by mainstream Muslims. When Shakib Arslan, Mussolini's anti-Ethiopian supporter, published an annotated portion of the text in Cairo in 1933,[40] he had to borrow it from Basset. Fahim Muhammad Shaltut's 1974 edition of the text added notes as well as a new subtitle: "The Somali-Ethiopian Struggle in the Sixteenth Century." It is doubtful Gragn spoke Somali, and in any case his unifying revolution was Pan-Islamic and Arab. Adding such a subtitle in 1974 was a sure means of rendering the text concretely relevant. The new introduction explained that "this is a rare book on the jihad of the Somali people and of the Islamic warriors in this region of the Islamic homeland. . . . [I]t would be a calamity for Islamic history not to publish it and spread it once more." The text, the editor went on, had been neglected by Islam, and the entire story of Ahmad Gragn had been twisted by hostile historians and Western "orientalists." They depicted Gragn as an aggressor, whereas the essence of his war was defensive. It was a jihad of Muslims defying their enemies, those who conquered and subjugated them. They had no choice but "to launch a jihad to save their religion and their liberty, to ensure their lives and ensure freedom for the followers of Islam in the land of the Somalis." The Ahmad Gragn story, needless to reiterate, was arguably the most significant chapter in the history of Islamic-Ethiopian relations. The publication of *Futuh al-habasha* in itself was to declare Ethiopia a historic, illegitimate enemy of Islam. To relate the story to the contemporary Somali-Ethiopian conflict over one-third of Ethiopia's territory was much more. It was tantamount to a call for the destruction of Ethiopia.

If the "Ahmad Gragn trauma" was the most formative historical chapter from the Ethiopian perspective, the Prophet-*najashi* dialogue, as I have argued from the beginning, was the most important chapter from the Islamic point of view. It has been obvious, throughout this study, what the rescue by the Christian Ethiopian king of Muhammad's first followers has meant to mainstream Muslims. I have also noted that radical Muslims chose to emphasize the end of that episode as it was narrated by Islamic sources: namely, that twelve years after the first Muslims found asylum with the *najashi,* he himself answered the call of Muhammad and converted to Islam. It followed, according to Islamic radicals, that Ethiopia was already Muslim and that its Christian essence, the result of its clergy defying their king, should not be tolerated.

'Abd al-Fattah 'Aliyyan's book *The Hegira to Ethiopia and the Argument About the Issue of Islam al-Najashi,* published in Cairo in 1987[41] (with a new edition in 1993), is a detailed summary of this major anti-Ethiopia point. In 122 pages the author failed to mention the positive Islamic traditions about Ethiopia and the famous saying attributed to Muhammad to "leave the Abyssinians alone." Rather, he made only one point, proving that the *najashi* converted to Islam. Quoting nearly all relevant early sources and using quotations from the Muhammad-*najashi* correspondence (pp. 78–81), his argument finally rests on the assumption that early Islamic sources could not be wrong. The *najashi,* a righteous person of great vision, 'Aliyyan asserted, saw the light and converted to Islam (p. 48). However, this was a manifestation of his own personal greatness, not Ethiopia's, and when he died, deserted by his own people, they deserved no gratitude for his action. Christian Ethiopia was spared Islamic conquest for various practical, and therefore temporary, reasons (p. 103).

Much of 'Aliyyan's book (pp. 69–122) is devoted to an exposé of Muslim writers who denied "*Islam al-najashi,*" calling them worse than "foreign" writers, who did the same for their religion (pp. 118–119). 'Aliyyan attacked various modern Muslim authors, including the above-mentioned Fathi Ghith (pp. 106–107). He was more selective in referring to medieval classical Islamic literature. For example, he avoided any

reference to al-Suyuti's *Raising of the Status of the Abyssinians,* but he
used another, irrelevant book by him. As a professor of Islamic history
on the faculty of humanistic studies at Al-Azhar University, 'Aliyyan
must surely have been familiar with the voluminous work of his predecessor, Ahmad al-Hifni al-Qina'i, mentioned in Chapter 5. The latter
had exhausted the Al-Azhar library in producing his 1902–1903 work on
Ethiopia. His presentation of the Muhammad-*najashi* story, we recall,
did include the argument that the Ethiopian king embraced Islam, but
this was not the essence of the episode as far as he was concerned. In
line with most moderate Muslims, al-Qina'i had focused on Ethiopia's
rescue of early Islam, and he recycled the friendly legacy of this formative story. 'Aliyyan failed to mention al-Qina'i at all, for his entire purpose was to recycle the message of radical Islam, that of Christian
Ethiopia's inherent illegitimacy.

Radicalization of Islam in Al-Azhar was perhaps less surprising than
in the core of Egypt's academia. One of the harshest attacks on historical Ethiopia and on its legitimacy was produced by Dr. Muhammad
Rajab 'Abd al-Halim of the Institute of African Research and Study at
Cairo University. His book *The Political Relations Between the Muslims
of Zeila and the Christians of Ethiopia in Medieval Times*[42] discussed
history from the *najashi* to Ahmad Gragn and was published in 1985.
Though it resorted to an academic apparatus and used a rich variety of
sources, it portrayed Ethiopia in the vein of Yusuf Ahmad's *Islam in
Ethiopia* of Mussolini's days in 1935, and it worked equally to foment
anti-Ethiopian racist attitudes. In exposing Ethiopia as the ultimate embodiment of enmity to Islam, it was perhaps even more categorical.

One premise of the book is reflected in its title, specifically that
none of the Muslims of the Horn of Africa should be divided by language or region. 'Abd al-Halim refrained from referring to local medieval Muslims as "Adalites," "Hararis," "Somalis," and the like, or to
modern ones as "Eritreans," "Afars," "Oromos," "Jabarties," or "Ethiopians." Instead, he called them all "Zayla'un," after the Red Sea port of
Zeila, which connected them to the Middle Eastern core of Islam. The
main argument of the book is that the Zayla'un, unfortunately, failed to
implement Islamic unity as they faced one of Islam's sworn enemies.

Indeed, the first of the book's four parts is devoted to "The Attitudes
of the Ethiopians Toward Islam and Zeila." The Ethiopians, 'Abd al-
Halim argued, were first and foremost crusaders. Even before the rise of
Islam they wanted to destroy the Kaaba and Christianize all Arabs. The
prophet Muhammad knew this very well, and the *najashi* with whom he
was in contact was not the king of Ethiopia, but rather a local ruler of the
coastal zone. As for the Ethiopians themselves, the Prophet ordered the

Muslims to beware of them, for he said, "the lean-legged Ethiopians, they will destroy the Kaaba." When the Prophet ordered Islam to "leave the Abyssinians alone," it was another warning against their evil nature (see pp. 31–38, mainly p. 36). Early Muslims, 'Abd al-Halim wrote, rushed to control the Red Sea and occupied the Dahlak Islands (A.D. 702) to prevent the Ethiopians from destroying Mecca and the Kaaba: "Indeed, the Ethiopians revealed their enmity to Islam from the very beginning. It was mostly out of their fear of Islam, for the new religion proved so powerful in uniting the Arabs on the other shore of the Red Sea. They were hostile from the very start . . . and the *najashi* affair made no difference, for when he died it ended in any case, and their fanatic priests took over in fighting Islam" (p. 37).

The second part of the book is devoted to the medieval struggle between the Solomonian emperors and the Zayla'un (namely, those of the Islamic sultanates of Ifat and Adal). According to 'Abd al-Halim, the entire story was motivated by the Ethiopians' inherent crusading zeal and their envy of the Muslims' prosperity, which stemmed from their own backwardness. The third part of the book describes the Ethiopian subjugation of Islam, their destruction of mosques, coerced Christianization, and the overtaxation of conquered Islamic communities. Finally, the fourth and final part attempts to explain the failure of the Zayla'un, including the final collapse of Ahmad Gragn's jihad. This failure, 'Abd al-Halim explains, was due to the Ethiopian alliance with European crusaders and the Muslims' failure to help one another. Islamic weakness resulted in the survival of Christian Ethiopia and the perpetuation of its enmity and hostility. In his conclusion 'Abd al-Halim put it all in a contemporary perspective: Ethiopia, the enemy of Islam, is still here oppressing Muslims because the Muslims have failed to unite.

1987–1988: A Turning Point?

In 1985, while Dr. 'Abd al-Halim published his radical anti-Ethiopian work and Dr. Abu al-'Ata and his coauthors analyzed the future of the Nile as they ignored Ethiopia, the water level in Lake Nasser had already begun to drop. By November, as the drought in Ethiopia culminated, the lake had fallen 3 meters. Recognition of the approaching crisis slowly began to dawn. During the next two years the Egyptian government took some measures toward water conservation, but the scope of the problem was exposed only two years later. When rain in Ethiopia failed to arrive in 1986 and then in the summer of 1987, the water level in Lake Nasser dropped to 12 meters below its normal level. As the lake continued to shrink it became clear that cutbacks in electricity and irrigation would be of no use. The magnitude of the potential disaster was unprecedented. The possibility that the eternal Nile would virtually dry up should rains in Ethiopia continue to fail seemed only a very few years away, perhaps only two. Desperate plans, such as quickly erecting a barrage at the mouth of the river, were aired.[43] The thirty-year-old illusion that Egypt would control the Nile by building the Aswan High Dam was shattered.[44] Ethiopia was to be readdressed as the actual source of the river. In March 1987, as Mubarak invited Mangistu to Egypt for the first time, a Cairo symposium on the Nile ended with the conclusion that all-Nile cooperation was vitally needed.[45]

From this study's perspective a new book published in 1988 ushered in a new era. *The Crisis of the Nile Waters: Where To?*[46] was published by the Center for Arab Studies in Cairo and is a collection of eleven short articles. "Its publication is most timely," the center's researchers stated on the cover and in their introduction, "for the Nile, between drought and flood . . . is calling for new inquiries and studies. . . . It is not only the longest river in the world, it is also the home of nine countries, Arab and African, each with its various interests and concerns, each experiencing different issues of unity and disunity, and each with its different ways of development and progress. . . . It was inevitable that our research center would recognize the fact that the Nile is not just an Egyptian river, but is also connected to eight other peoples, and especially those two who are mostly relevant—the Sudanese and the Ethiopians." In order to reflect the diversity of the Nile, stated the Egyptian editors, they also included in their volume articles by a British, a Sudanese, and an Ethiopian author.

The first article was the most significant, written by Professor Rushdi Sa'id, one of Egypt's leading geologists, an expert of global reputation, and an authority on the Nile's geography. Professor Sa'id had studied and written on the Nile ever since 1962, and in 1992 he would publish his authoritative *The River Nile: Its Development and the Usage of Its Waters in the Past and in the Future,* in which he would directly attack the Aswan High Dam.[47] The pretentious attempt to exclusively Egyptianize the Nile, he wrote, had led to geological and ecological disasters that would be exposed in the long run (pp. 245, 260–262). No less disastrous was the blow to all-Nile planning. This point was made clear in Sa'id's opening article in the 1988 collection: "The Future of Nile Waters Exploitation." It begins with his statement that in 1979 he delivered a lecture in Cairo stating that Egypt's source of life was external and, painful as it was, would continue to remain so in the future. This notion, however, was hardly acceptable in a country where dependence on water was so absolute and faith in the High Dam so entrenched

(p. 11). The article went on to explain the essential water data, some of it derived from John Waterbury's *Hydropolitics of the Nile Valley*, also published in 1979. (The two scholars saw eye to eye on most issues and published their observations even though 1978 witnessed the highest water level ever recorded at Lake Nasser.) Egypt's reliance on a one-sided solution, Sa'id continued, is illusory. Then, in a section on Ethiopia (pp. 20–22), Professor Sa'id asserted that Ethiopia was the main source of water for Egypt and Sudan. He also added that Ethiopia had its own concerns and interests, as well as its own demographic growth and economic needs, all of which should be addressed.

However, he went on, Ethiopia, for its part, should neither work unilaterally nor air "ugly threats." Ethiopia was not in a position to interfere with the river without external financial help, and this help must be conditional on interregional coordination. Such coordination, Sa'id asserted, should be based on full consideration of the acute needs of Egypt and Sudan, as well as Ethiopia's wealth of rain and other water sources. The spirit and principle of the 1902 agreement between the British and the Ethiopians, he argued, should be maintained. Ethiopia should benefit from general development and electric power without harming the downstream nations.

Sa'id's emphasis was on multilateral cooperation. It is only through regional understanding and agreements, he concluded, that the vitally important all-Nile plan can be formulated and implemented. Only a shared integrative approach, common institutions of mutual consultation, planning, and enterprise can save the Nile. Only if each party adopts a comprehensive vision that simultaneously satisfies its own needs can the future be assured.

The Crisis of the Nile Waters presented other approaches as well. A short article by a famous thinker Dr. 'Abd al-'Azim Anis, "Waters and Politics" (pp. 114–117), argued that the ideas raised by the international community for all-Nile cooperation were merely "a new version of the old imperialistic designs regarding the river." Hilmi Sha'rawi, a researcher at the Center for Arab Studies, also opposed his colleagues. In his article, "With the Drought Crisis: How Israel and the USA Think on the Nile's Waters" (pp. 118–121), he argued that the primary need was to pay attention to the designs of these imperialists.

Perhaps most reflective of the new spirit was the fact that the editors chose to include the Ethiopian point of view. They chose no less the anti-Egyptian work by Wondimneh Tilahun discussed previously, *Egypt's Imperial Aspirations over Lake Tana and the Blue Nile*, translating it into Arabic and publishing a summary (pp. 71–89). As we will recall, Wondimneh's book, published in 1979, was a radical attack on Egypt, portraying it as an inherently Nilo-imperialist country. It depicted Sadat as the aggressive successor of Isma'il and equated the latter with Hitler. It also clearly conveyed Ethiopian anger and its threat to punish Egypt by interfering with the Nile. The summary of Wondimneh's book was accompanied by an introduction and counterremarks, but the very willingness to include such an Ethiopian viewpoint was innovative. Though the controversy demonstrated by *The Crisis of the Nile Waters* left little hope for outright solutions, its very publication symbolized a new readiness to listen. Ironically, the same week the book hit the shelves, beginning 10 August 1988, heavy rainfall began in Ethiopia. It would continue at least to the end of the twentieth century.

NOTES

1. See Meital, "The Aswan High Dam."
2. See Warburg, "The Nile in Egyptian-Sudanese Relations."
3. See *Al-Ahram*, 27 June 1959.
4. For a comprehensive analysis of Nasser's relevant policy, see Ismael, *The U.A.R. in Africa.*
5. Fa'iq, *'Abd al-Nasir wal-thawra al-ifriqiyya.*
6. For an episode reflecting Fa'iq's identification with the Nasserist regime, see Vatikiotis, *Nasser and His Generation*, p. 364, n. 15.
7. Barawi, *Al-Habasha bayna al-iqta'.* In the same year he published a pro-Somali, anti-Ethiopian book: *Al-Sumal al-kabir.*
8. Badawi, *Ma'a harakat al-Islam fi ifriqya.*
9. Badawi, "Adwa' 'ala ithyubya al-mu'asira," *Nahdat Ifriqya* (January 1959): 16–18; "Naqd al-kitab," *Nahdat Ifriqya* (June 1963): 61–64.
10. Yahya, "Al-'Arab fi sharq ifriqya" (September 1959), "Kifah al-sumal" (January 1960), and "Misr wal-sumal" (March 1960), all in *Nahdat Ifriqya*. The original-language titles of his books mentioned in the text are *Al-Bahr al-ahmar wal-isti'mar* and *Misr al-ifriqiyya*. In 1968 Yahya also issued a biography of the Moroccan Islamic-Arab anticolonial revolutionary 'Abd al-Karim al-Khattabi. Based in Cairo, al-Khattabi helped inspire various Arab liberation fronts in North Africa in the 1950s. He also helped the Eritrean students form the ELF.
11. Shakir, al-'Iryan, and Amin, *Adwa' 'ala al-habasha*. Nasser's introduction was added to a second edition in 1957 or 1958.
12. The essay is included as a chapter in a book by Lebanese author and journalist Mahmud al-Huss, *Ithyubya fi 'ahd Hayla Silasi al-awwal*, pp. 20–24 (see more below).
13. Sadiq al-Habashi, an Ethiopian Muslim studying at Al-Azhar (who later returned to Ethiopia to become a member of the Ethiopian Parliament), published a book in 1954 in Cairo titled *Ithyubya fi 'asriha al-dhahabi, fi 'asr Hayla Silasi al-awwal* (Ethiopia in Her Golden Age: The Age of Haile Selassie I). True to its title, it praised Haile Selassie's promotion of Islam in Ethiopia as well as his amicable relations with Egypt. The journalist 'Aziz Abaza added a foreword on Ethiopia, the land of justice under a benevolent Christian king. In 1960 the

Lebanese Nasserist journalist Mahmud al-Huss published *Ethiopia in the Period of Haile Selassie* in Beirut (see previous note), to which Nasser added the same "The Kingdom of Ethiopia" introduction discussed above. Al-Huss's book contains extensive quotations on the benevolence of the medieval *najashi* and praises Haile Selassie in similar terms. The main theme of the book is the historical bond between Nasser and Haile Selassie.

14. See Stephens, *Nasser,* pp. 35–37; Vatikiotis, *Nasser and His Generation,* chap. 1.

15. See texts and pictures reflecting Nasser's cordiality in the *Ethiopian Herald* and in *Al-Ahram,* 29 and 30 June 1959. Nasser's speech was also published in al-Huss, *Ithyubya fi 'ahd Hayla Silasi al-awwal,* pp. 129–130.

16. *Ethiopian Herald,* 18 October 1966, quoting *Egyptian Gazette* "of last Sunday."

17. See 'Ashur, "Ba'd adwa' jadida."

18. Ghith, *Al-Islam wal-habasha 'ibra al-ta'rikh.*

19. Badawi's articles in *Nahdat Ifriqya* included "Adwa' 'ala Ithyubya al-mu'asira" (January 1959). See also his book review in June 1960 on Murad Kamil's *Bayna al-habasha wal-'Arab* in the below-mentioned edition of *Sirat al-habasha.*

20. See Fawzi, *Al-Baba Qirilus wa'Abd al-Nasir,* esp. pp. 57–63.

21. See Riyad, *Misr wa-Ifriqya,* p. 242.

22. See Mirrit's article in *Al-Siyasa al-Duwaliyya,* no. 3 (1966).

23. Kamil, "La Dernier phase des relations historiques."

24. Kamil, ed., *Sirat al-habasha,* by al-Haymi al-Hasan ibn Ahmad.

25. See his article on relations between Christians and Muslims in medieval Ethiopia: "Al-'Alaqat bayna al-muslimin wal-masihiyyin fi al-habasha fi al-'usur al-wusta," *Al-Muqtataf* (December 1950).

26. See Riyad's articles in *Nahdat Ifriqya* in December 1957, May 1958, and June 1959.

27. Riyad, *Kanisat al-iskandiriyya fi ifriqya.*

28. See an analysis of Riyad's writings on Ethiopia in Erlich, *Ethiopia and the Middle East,* pp. 143–145.

29. Boutros-Ghali, "The Foreign Policy of Egypt"; he made the very same points in a somewhat shorter article: "Siyasatuna al-kharijiyya tujaha ifriqya," *Al-Ahram al-Iqtisadi,* no. 204 (1964).

30. The quotation Boutros-Ghali cites here is from DuBois's *The World and Africa,* p. 117. For a discussion of Afrocentrism and the Nile, see Shavit, "Up the River or Down the River?"

31. See more in the section "Boutros-Ghali and Egypt's Strategic Continuity," in Erlich, *Ethiopia and the Middle East,* pp. 147–149.

32. For Egyptian relations with Sudan and for general background on Egypt's regional strategy, see Warburg, *Egypt and the Sudan,* mainly pt. 2: "Regional and Political Considerations."

33. Boutros-Ghali, *Egypt's Road to Jerusalem,* pp. 321–323.

34. See Collins, *Waters of the Nile.*

35. 'Abd al-Hayy, *Al-Nil wal-mustaqbal,* see mainly pp. 120–125, 141–143. See also Warburg's discussion of the book in "The Nile in Egyptian-Sudanese Relations," p. 228.

36. Abu al-'Ata, Shihab, and Rida, *Nahr al-Nil.*

37. Riyad, *Misr wa-Ifriqya.*

38. Shaltut, *Tuhfat al-zaman aw futuh al-habasha*.

39. The original text appeared as: Chihab ed-Din Ahmed Ben Abd el-Qader ('Arab Faqih), *Futuh al-habasha: Histoire de la conquête de l'Abyssinie,* ed. and trans. R. Basset, Paris, 1897.

40. Shakib Arslan published extensive portions of *Futuh al-habasha* in his book *Hadir al-'alam al-Islami*.

41. 'Aliyyan, *Al-Hijra ila al-habasha*.

42. 'Abd al-Halim, *Al-'Alaqat al-siyasiyya bayna muslimi*.

43. See *Al-Akhbar,* 8 March 1988; *Jerusalem Post,* 29 June 1988.

44. See Sofer, *Rivers of Fire,* chap. 2.

45. *Al-Musawwar,* 20 March 1987.

46. Sa'id et al., *Azmat miyah al-nil*.

47. Sa'id, *Nahr al-nil*.

10

Conclusion: The 1990s and the Legacies of History

RENEWED DIALOGUE, RESURFACING SUSPICIONS

This book concludes with its practical-strategic dimension unfinished. The issue of the Nile waters in the first years of the twenty-first century is still an Egyptian-Ethiopian bone of contention. The realization forced upon Egypt and Ethiopia by the chaotic 1987–1988 period—that they must listen to each other—has borne some fruit. Indeed, the 1990s witnessed the establishment and institutionalization of a dialogue between the parties. On 1 July 1993 the heads of the two states, Hosni Mubarak and Meles Zenawi, signed a framework of cooperation and committed themselves to reaching an agreement. Egypt agreed in principle that Ethiopia deserved a share in the waters, and the two parties agreed not to engage in activities regarding the use of the Nile that might damage the interests of other riparian countries.[1] The Nile 2002 Conference, which had started in 1992, continued to convene every year, enabling Egyptian and Ethiopian officials, as well as international water experts, to air their views. At these meetings (the seventh of which was held in Addis Ababa in June 2000), issues of interest involving historical, diplomatic, legal, and technical matters were discussed from an academic outlook.[2]

In February 1999 the Nile Basin Initiative, a new all-riparian body, was launched in Dar es Salaam. The ministers of water affairs of nine countries (Egypt, Ethiopia, Burundi, Rwanda, Sudan, Tanzania, Congo, Kenya, and Uganda, with Eritrea as an observer) stated jointly that "for the first time in history, all Nile basin countries have expressed a serious concern about the need for serious discourse," and they declared that their "shared vision" was to "achieve sustainable socioeconomic development through the equitable utilization of, and benefit from, the common Nile basin water resources."[3] The rains that followed in the summer

213

of 1999—as though Mother Nature were pleased with this international understanding—were the heaviest in thirty years, and the Nile swelled to record levels.

Beyond achieving a better atmosphere and carrying on a continuous dialogue within such new frameworks, Ethiopian-Egyptian relations do not yet contain an element of complete trust. In June 1996 Ethiopia announced that it was planning to construct two small dams on tributaries of the Blue Nile and that the government would "undertake the construction of required projects, with or without foreign assistance, once its master plan for the highlands has been completed."[4] In January 1997 the Egyptian government launched an ambitious desert irrigation plan, the Toshka Canal, which, upon completion, would increase Egyptian dependency on the Nile and intensify Egypt's commitment to exploit its "historic rights" to the fullest. The idea underlying the canal, known also as the Southern Valley Project, was first raised in the 1950s and then recycled by Anwar al-Sadat. Water pumped from Lake Nasser and brought to the Western Desert, to the oases of Farafra and Al Kharj, would irrigate vast areas and provide the infrastructure for eighteen new towns and hundreds of villages. A huge pumping station, the largest in the world, at Lake Nasser would be completed by 2002. By the year 2017 these waters, representing some 10 percent of the quantity collected each year in Lake Nasser, will give life to a new region inhabited by up to seven million people, providing wheat, cotton, and fruit, and will become a new tourist center. The Egyptians say that these waters will be a part of their 55.5-billion-cubic-meter annual share allotted them by the 1959 Nile Waters Agreement.[5] While the first phase of the Southern Valley Project, the canal, will cost about $2 billion, further phases focused on agriculture, industry, and tourism will bring the total estimated cost to $88 billion.[6] By the year 2000 some 60 of the canal's 168 kilometers had already been dug.

Reacting to the launching of the Toshka project, Ethiopian Prime Minister Meles Zenawi accused Egypt of striking a "proprietorial attitude" over the waters of the Nile River. In May 1998 the Ethiopian government announced a plan for constructing dams on the Blue Nile that included 175 small irrigation projects. Meles Zenawi implicitly warned Egypt that these projects on the upper reaches of the Nile would eventually reduce the amount of water flowing downstream to Sudan and Egypt. Expressing disbelief that the Egyptians would irrigate the southern valley with waters they saved elsewhere, he charged that Egypt was trying to maximize its use of Nile water in order to make it impossible for an equitable quota system to be negotiated. "The Egyptians treated the waters of the Nile," he asserted about both Toshka and the 1959 agreement, "as though they were a purely Egyptian affair rather than one concerning all the states in the basin."[7] The chances of reaching a vital, comprehensive, all-river understanding and plan, in light of such unilateral moves, have hardly improved.[8]

WHERE ARE THE SCHOLARS?

Against this background of a promising renewed dialogue combined with the old threatening messages, the 1990s produced another cycle of relevant Ethiopian and Egyptian literature. It continued to reflect the same old dichotomies between the will to cooperate with the most meaningful "other" and the inclination to demonize this other. Egyptians and Ethiopians wavered between the various options, concepts, and images analyzed above. Militants on both sides persisted in spreading their versions. Some Ethiopian writers suggested that Egypt was not trustworthy, that Cairo had always needed to undermine Ethiopia to prevent Addis Ababa from developing the Nile.[9] They called for unilateral action, implementation of the 1964 U.S. report on the Blue Nile that recommended some twenty-six projects, and a disregard for international law, which, in any case, worked only for the strong.[10] Islamic radicals in Egypt continued to produce anti-Ethiopian literature.[11] A new argument was put forward in 1993 that the righteous *najashi* was not an Ethiopian but a Sudanese.[12] The Coptic Church helped the Eritrean Church secede from its Ethiopian mother institution,[13] further deteriorating already strained church relations.[14]

More sober were the professional water experts on both sides. They published studies presenting the comprehensive reality of the Nile that reflected great anxiety. The Egyptian Rushdi Sa'id[15] and the Ethiopian Zewdie Abate,[16] for example, did not see everything eye to eye. The Egyptian reiterated, albeit indirectly, the "historic rights" concept, while the Ethiopian insisted on the principle of "equitable shares." But their analyses of the factual data and their calls for comprehensive cooperation were very similar in terms. Historians and authors in both countries readdressed chapters of common history.[17]

No less meaningful, from the point of view of this book, was the resumption of active cultural ties. The medieval enterprise of translating works from Arabic into Ethiopian languages was now resumed. For example, in 1990 and 1992 two books by Egyptian Nobel Prize winner Nagib Mahfuz were published in Addis Ababa in Amharic. In analyzing one of these, *The Search* (written in 1964), Ethiopian intellectual Mulugeta Gudeta described both Egypt and Ethiopia as societies constantly in search of their identity. He stated that such translations would "bring the two cultures and two peoples closer. The striking similarity of the two societies, Egyptian and Ethiopian, has become apparent in *The Search,* whose characters, their aspirations and tragedies are emotionally appealing to the local [Ethiopian] audience."[18]

However, the academic communities of the two countries, as well as communities of international scholars studying them, hardly helped to enhance understanding. Historians of Egypt continued to pay little attention to the country's Ethiopian aspects. After the demise in the 1950s of the "Unity of the Nile Valley" idea, the old tendency to "leave the Abyssinians alone" strengthened further. The rediscovery of Ethiopia's crucial relevance in the late 1980s did not reignite professional academic interest among Egyptianists. The international and national communities of Ethiopianists also contributed only little to mutual awareness. Most of them, loyal to their training as Africanists, continued to focus their Ethiopian studies on issues and analogies connecting Ethiopian studies to the black continent. Though they were justified in this, the result was to marginalize Ethiopia's oriental dimensions. Ethiopian historiography of the last generation has practically isolated the country from its integral Middle Eastern contexts.[19] Where diplomats and water experts have resumed contact, at conferences like Nile 2002 and in bodies such as the Nile Basin Initiative, academic circles have failed. At the Fourteenth International Conference of Ethiopian Studies held in Addis Ababa in November 2000, like at all previous scholarly gatherings of this sort since the 1960s, not one Egyptian scholar attended.

BACK TO A FATAL COLLISION?

In the 1990s the two regimes became generally similar in terms of their systems and global orientations. Both were now a mixture of authoritarian leadership, some political openness, and a free market economy in pursuit of foreign investments. Each also proved similarly sensitive to the need to address the issue of water limitations and population growth. President Mubarak of Egypt approached this issue accordingly. The Toshka Canal project is indeed a major undertaking, in line with the ambitious visions of Egypt's great rulers. As of the mid-1980s Mubarak resisted all opposition and personally pushed for airing the idea, initiating surveys, and raising funds. He gave his full backing to overcoming political circles (headed by the Wafd Party) and water experts (headed by Professor Rushdi Sa'id and many others) who strongly opposed Toshka, arguing that for climatic, geological, and financial reasons, the idea would prove a disastrous waste. (Most opponents of Toshka had also been critical of the Aswan High Dam.) Identifying with the project, Mubarak nevertheless conceived Toshka as the ushering in of a "new civilization" in the deserts of Egypt. In so doing, however, Mubarak was definitely not following in the footsteps of Nasser, who built the Aswan High Dam in defiance of world experts and Western strategists. In contrast, the Toshka project had been endorsed by foreign investors, most significantly, investors from Saudi Arabia and the United Arab Emirates (the main canal is to be named Shaykh Zayd Canal after the shaikh of Abu Dhabi). Toshka may, rather, prove to be a project as valid as the Suez Canal, built with Western money and foreign consent. But here again, the historical analogy to that enterprise raises worries. What will be the consequence of growing Egyptian dependence on foreign investments? Of the dramatically different scope of Egyptian dependence on Nile waters? Can Egypt live up to its promise not to use more water than the amounts allocated by the 1959 agreement? Can Egypt save such enormous quantities elsewhere? Can it persuade the other riparian countries that it is entitled, by "historic rights," to those quantities and more? Or is Mubarak heading in the direction of Khedive Isma'il—that is, through a costly canal project and an ambitious vision of the Nile to an Ethiopian war?

The times of Khedive Isma'il and the Tigrean Ethiopian emperor Yohannes IV, the years of their fatal collision in the 1870s, come to mind on the Ethiopian side as well. The new regime in Addis Ababa, as of 1991, has been led by the former fighters of the Tigrean People's Liberation Front and is in many ways molded after the Tigreans' concepts of Ethiopia. Meles Zenawi, unlike all of his predecessors, does not aspire to be a centralizing ruler of Ethiopia. Like Mubarak, he combines authoritative leadership with some political openness, which in this case also stems from the Tigreans' traditional ideas of Ethiopian decentralization and ethnic pluralism. The new regime is much more attentive to Ethiopia's own diversity and, consequently, much more open to the world and its free economy. Ethiopia of the 1990s indeed saw the beginnings of a revolution that may change its very identity—and perhaps also the nature of our Ethio-Egyptian story.

Here again, nothing is one-dimensional. On the one hand, the ethnic-regional restructuring and the new emphasis on a free market economy combine to enable the resurgence of Ethiopian Islam. As trade and commerce begin to flourish and as money trickles in from Arabia, Ethiopian Muslims are entering the very core of the country's new elite. The growing business community of Addis Ababa already reflects a new Ethiopian inner Islamic-Christian dialogue based on renewed concepts of pluralist Ethiopianism. A new urban, open market and Middle Eastern–oriented economic formulas may well facilitate a grand solution to regional water problems. Ethiopia can be compensated, through commercial and financial arrangements, by the global community and the Arab world, for not depriving Egypt of its lifeblood.

On the other hand, however, this is only one aspect of the developing Ethiopian reality. The new regime is equally committed to the welfare of Ethiopia's peasants, perhaps more so than all of its predecessors. The TPLF leaders, most of them sons of poor families, grew up on the ethos of the peasantry-soldiery bond, a core element of Christian Ethiopian culture. They made it their main cause in fighting to liberate the country from Mangistu's dictatorship. Moreover, they are also integrally committed to the welfare of northern Ethiopia, consisting of regions that had been neglected—as we have seen—by the previous regimes, where peasants were exposed to famine and drought. For these reasons the new leadership of Ethiopia views the development of rural areas as its top priority. The ultimate concern is "food security" for the peasants. In this the government seems to enjoy the support of the capital's intellectual elite and the academic community.[20] There seems to be a near consensus that irrigation projects for northern Ethiopia are the key not only to the physical survival of most Ethiopians, but also to the survival of Ethiopia's culture and its Christian character.

No wonder the Ethiopian-Egyptian dialogue is difficult. Beyond its very existence—a major positive new development—the actual positions are essentially contradictory. Egypt, concerned with its strategy of "water security," is full of goodwill regarding general cooperation and regional development. The Egyptians realize that without ecological conservation in the whole basin, reforestation of the Ethiopian highlands, and other cooperative enterprises aimed at securing more waters, the Aswan High Dam will not save their country forever. They offer the other Nile riparian countries their hydrological expertise and ecological know-how, and they also call for diplomatic and cultural all-Nile cooperation. At the Fifth Nile 2002 Conference, held in Addis Ababa in February 1997, the Egyptian government's official "Country Paper" urged the riparian countries to promote studies of local water problems and share this information in order to implement needed all-Nile projects. The main point of the paper was to point to the successful construction of the Aswan High Dam in the 1960s as an Egyptian-Sudanese model for needed regional cooperation.[21]

The position of the Ethiopians is to accept the principle of regional cooperation in the same spirit but to focus mainly on what they think Egypt wants to ignore: the redistribution of water. They consider the Toshka Canal project in much the same terms that Haile Selassie in his time viewed the construction of the Aswan High Dam—namely, a one-sided step that ignored Ethiopia, a humiliating provocation by a patronizing Egypt. The Ethiopian "Country Paper" presented at the Fifth Nile 2002 Conference in 1997 asserted that

> attempts by downstream co-basin countries to maintain the status-quo and/or expand water resources projects were seen to negate the principle of equitable utilization and cooperation principles accepted under International Law. . . . There is a felt need [in Ethiopia] to develop the country's water resources by building hydraulic structures (dams and reservoirs) . . . so that the standard of living of the Ethiopian people will be raised. . . . [We] need to engage in continuous dialogue with the objective of coming up with an equitable allocation of water resources of the basin through the application of internationally acceptable legal principles.[22]

THE MESSAGE OF THIS BOOK

For those who are attempting to deal with the Nile's unfolding reality and for those working to promote mutual Ethiopian-Egyptian understanding, I have offered this historical-cultural perspective. It may prove no less useful than examining current affairs. Both Egypt and Ethiopia are history-oriented cultures, and their interrelations have been a meaningful part of their histories. The future of the Nile issue, in whatever direction it may lead, will rest solidly on the long, multifaceted saga that has been related here. What remains to be seen is which of the various legacies of this rich history the present leaders will opt to pursue.

One major lesson of the history reconstructed in this volume is its versatility. On the one hand, we have seen strong elements of continuity: the eternal flow of the Nile, the enduring myths, the persisting anxieties, the entrenched suspicions, the ever-recycled game of mutual dependency and relevance. On the other hand, however, we have seen that the complexity of this long history has produced almost endless nuances and options. A reexamination of this story will reveal no single leading, determining aspect. In fact, the Ethiopian-Egyptian narrative has been polarized between cordial neighborliness and demonizing enmity, but it has, for the most part, developed around a varied, middle-of-the-road blend. None of the many factors, the constant interplay of which has created these relations, has, in itself, been one-dimensional.

On both sides the conceptualization of the significant "other" has stemmed from the multidimensional "self" and its own internal, ever-developing dynamism. In discussing Egyptian attitudes and policies regarding Ethiopia, we followed the interplay among Islam, Egyptian-ism, and Arabism. Each of these dimensions of Egyptian identity is, on its own, rich in nuances. Islam inherited its Ethiopian dichotomy from its very beginnings, and its transformation continued. The earlier mes-sage of Muhammad's gratitude and Ethiopia's special status was spread in Egypt from the time of the medieval Jalal al-Din al-Suyuti to that of the early modern Ahmad al-Hifni al-Qina'i, then to that of the great Is-lamic modernizer Rashid Rida and his followers in 1935. Concurrently, we have followed Islam's negative concepts. We have seen how the ini-tial *"Islam al-najashi"* message of Christian Ethiopia's inherent illegiti-macy was interpreted and spread in Egypt by Yusuf Ahmad in the 1930s and by Rajab 'Abd al-Halim and 'Abd al-Fattah 'Aliyyan in the 1980s. In examining Egypt's Arab nationalism during the formative, stormy 1930s, as well as during the Nasserite 1950s–1960s, a similar dichotomy was apparent. It was reflected, for example, in Nasser's praise of Ethio-pia as a symbol of African anticolonialism coupled with Muhammad Fa'iq's simultaneous condemnation of Ethiopia as the embodiment of re-action, oppression, and collaboration with imperialism.

Modern Egyptian nationalism similarly wavered between such po-larized images. In the early stages of this nationalism, Colonel Muham-mad Rif'at and others spread the notion of Ethiopia as the destroyer of the "Unity of the Nile Valley" dream, and in the 1980s authors such as 'Abd al-'Azim Abu al-'Ata openly ignored Ethiopia as a Nile country. This negative image of Ethiopia competed, however, with a positive, unique concept of a neighborly Ethiopia promoted by better-known pro-ponents of Egyptian nationalism, from Ahmad 'Urabi to Muhammad Lutfi Jum'a and Muhammad 'Abdallah 'Inan. The latter were forcefully joined by modern Copts, from Ramzi Tadrus to Mirrit Boutros-Ghali, Murad Kamil, Zahir Riyad, and Boutros Boutros-Ghali.

The substantial input of the Coptic intellectuals reflects the organic connection between external relations and domestic affairs. In premod-ern times the special Ethiopian-Coptic religious ties helped the Copts in their domestic relations with the Islamic state. Modern Copts worked to rebuild and modify these ties in order to fortify their place in a new Egyptian society. Their intellectual effort to spread the concept of his-toric Ethiopian-Egyptian relations was indeed a part of their struggle for internal Egyptian pluralism. No wonder the Islamic radicals, whose in-terpretation of the "self" is rigidly monolithic, stood at the forefront in declaring Ethiopia an illegitimate, evil "other."

The Islamic radicals, by excluding the political rights of all non-Muslims, also provided the most radical argument for Egypt's claim to "historic rights" over the Nile. Their concept of Ethiopia's illegitimacy, transmitted to and modified by modern militant Egyptianists and Arab revolutionaries, was much in the background of modern history. The construction of the Aswan High Dam, while declaring Ethiopia irrelevant to the waters of the Nile, was a somewhat more mellow, modern version of the initial Islamic radical delegitimization of Ethiopia.

But what about those—indeed, the majority—who have sustained and recycled Ethiopia's positive image from the start? When we relate their ideas to the modern issue of the Nile waters, we again find a world of double messages. The initial Islamic premise of acceptance, "Leave the Abyssinians alone as long as they leave you alone," was in itself subject to interpretation. On the one hand, it meant benevolent recognition of Ethiopia's existence despite its Christianity. This flexible interpretation of Islam itself, as we have seen, was transmitted to and modified by Arab and Egyptian liberals and served their visions of a pluralist "self" as well as a neighborly "other." But the message to "leave the Abyssinians alone" also meant marginalization of Ethiopia. Moreover, it was tantamount to an expectation that Ethiopia "leave us alone"—that is, become distant, abstract, and irrelevant. Thus the same message of medieval grace also helped to legitimize the exclusion of Ethiopia's rights to Nile waters. Indeed, even the most liberal, modern, pro-Ethiopian Egyptians, including Coptic intellectuals, continued to defend the concept of Egypt's "historic rights." Will they now be able to update this message, accepting the fact that Ethiopia cannot live up to this old idea, that this is a vital need, that Ethiopia cannot "leave" any of them "alone," not Egypt, not the Middle East, and not the Nile?

Ethiopian concepts of Egypt and the Nile also stemmed from the very depths of its identity. The Ethiopian self was no less dynamic a concept than the Egyptian self. It had a similarly strong sense of uniqueness, closely related to external "circles" of affiliation. Ethiopia's self-image has always had an ever-evolving "African" dimension. However, because of the limitations of this study, I can barely do justice to Ethiopia's Africanism, having discussed it only in the phase when Egyptian-Ethiopian relations were transferred to the African sphere. Beginning in the late 1950s, renewed emphasis on the "African-ness" of Ethiopia has had a tremendous impact on its history, enhancing its international standing and conferring seniority to it on the continent. At home it has helped many ethnic groups, especially in southern and central Ethiopia, to reassert their own particular identities, confronted as they are by a centralized state and culture. Having said this, Africanism has also helped those who have preferred to ignore Middle Eastern–related issues, especially the Eritrean problem. Insofar as the Africanization of the last generations caused Ethiopia to turn its back on the Middle East, it proved self-defeating.

This study has focused on the Middle Eastern dimension of historic Ethiopia and its development vis-à-vis the centrality of Egypt. Here again, to summarize our findings, we dealt with an ever-evolving dichotomy. On the one hand, Egypt was the center of everything that Christian Ethiopians dreaded in the Middle East. Egypt was the capital of both state and political Islam. It was the Nile-centered state that aspired to control the greater Nile basin. It also became the capital of the modern Arab revolution that threatened to unite the Muslims of the Horn of Africa. From the period of Ethiopia's medieval wars with Ifat and Adal, and Khedive Isma'il's early modern effort to build an African empire, to the modern Arab-inspired Eritrean "fronts" and the Somali Ogaden War, Egypt was always there. In Ethiopian eyes Egypt embodied the threat of the Middle East, from the time of King Lalibela and Emperor Zar'a Ya'qob to that of Prime Minister Aklilu Habta-Wold, Ambassador Emmanuel Abraham, and Professor Wondimneh Tilahun. "The Ahmad Gragn trauma"—the Ethiopian fear that Islam or Arabism would reunite to destroy the Ethiopian state—was fixed primarily on Cairo.

On the other hand, however, the Middle East was a world to which Ethiopia had always belonged, and Egypt was the main source of its richness and promise. Egypt was a center of Eastern Christian culture, which contributed to the very foundations of Ethiopian identity. The sixteen-centuries-old institution of the *abun*—the fact that the head of the Ethiopian Church was an Egyptian bishop—was the utmost expression of Ethiopia's need to belong to the East. The Christian Ethiopian-Egyptian bond was, throughout history, a main channel to the outside world, ever essential for Ethiopia's development. The church's canonical writings, the state's legislative code, the national royal ethos, the Ethiopian monastic system, state administration, military technology, modern education—indeed, almost all avenues of medieval and modern progress—were derived from this connection.

For sixteen centuries Ethiopia has persisted in being a part of the Middle East. Though this connection has eroded since 1959, Ethiopia is more than ever in dire need of being reinstated in the Middle East. The historical importance of the Eastern-oriental connection has been stressed by nearly all Ethiopian politicians and scholars, and returning to the Middle East has become a declared policy of the new regime that came to power in 1991. The new role of Muslims in Ethiopia, their leadership in the transformation toward a free market, urban economy, seems already to be influencing the very nature of the Ethiopian self, further connecting it to the Middle East. Can the new Ethiopian leadership work for a constructive dialogue with Egypt? Can it give wider meaning to the concept of "equitable shares," which suggests placing less emphasis on the redistribution of water and focusing more on Ethiopia's greater share in the other resources that Egypt and the Middle East can offer?

The nature of Ethiopia's relations with Egypt and the Middle East has had much to do with the nature of its domestic affairs. Rulers and leaders who interpreted the Ethiopian self in one-dimensional terms tended to activate the so-called Ahmad Gragn trauma and failed to open the country to the East. Those who viewed Ethiopia in more pluralist terms, who were more concerned with its regional, religious, and ethnic identities, compromised on central absolutism. They were also better prepared, in most cases, to relate confidently to the Middle East, cope with its challenges, and benefit from its resources. The rivalry between Asrate Kassa and Aklilu Habta-Wold and that between Aman Andom and Mangistu Haile Mariam, as described above, revolved around these different options.

The leadership of Ethiopia that emerged in 1991 claims to aspire to pluralism. The new Tigrean-led regime has reshaped Ethiopia as a federal republic comprised of different states, each expressing a different ethnic identity. Will it be successful in pluralizing Ethiopia? Will the revived Muslim community serve as a bridge to the Arab East? Will Egypt proceed on the road of its own liberalization? Will the modern Coptic community regain confidence and resume its efforts at enhancing good relations with Ethiopia? Will Egypt continue to influence the entire Middle East in this pluralist direction?

In 1897 the leader of Islamic modernism in Egypt, Rashid Rida, predicted that in some fifty years Ethiopia would develop to a point at which it would reach the level of modernity of Japan. In 1924 Ras Tafari regarded Cairo as a corridor to the marvels of Europe, a modern entity comparable to London, Paris, and Rome. Both visions proved to be illusory. Are these two countries, which share so much history, now ready to build mutual trust and finally work together? Will they give the twenty-first century a better chance? We certainly hope so, for the alternative is frightening.

NOTES

1. See "Egypt Recognizes Ethiopia's Rights to Nile Waters," *Ethiopian Herald*, 3 July 1993.
2. Gabre-Selassie, "The Nile River Question."

3. See "Policy Guidelines for the Nile River Basin Strategic Action Program," posted on the Nile Basin Initiative's Web site at: www.nilebasin.org (accessed 22 February 1999).

4. Swain, "The Nile River Dispute."

5. See Goldman, "Massive Nile River Diversion Planned."

6. See: http://american.edu/projects/mandala/ted/ice/bluenile.htm.

7. Quoted in *Mideast Mirror* (May 1998), available online at: www. ethiopians.com/abay/news.html. See also *Arabic News* at: www.arabicnews.com/ansub/daily/day 980523/1998052309.html.

8. See Mark Huband, "Egypt: A Step Nearer to Taming the Nile," *Financial Times,* 20 February 1998; *Al-Hayat,* 28 February, 2 March, and 22 May 1998.

9. See "Egypt and the Horn: A Case of Misplaced Hostility," *Ethioscope* (January 1985): 32–35.

10. Mettaferia, "The Nile River"; see the introduction to this five-article series. The author assisted the American researchers in their 1957–1962 surveys.

11. In 1991 Dr. 'Abd al-Wahhab Fadl of Al-Azhar University published an annotated text of al-Suyuti's *Raf' sha'n al-hubshan.* Though al-Suyuti's medieval book was pro-Ethiopian (see Chapter 3 above), Fadl's introduction and notes were extremely anti-Ethiopian, for example: "After the death of the *najashi,* the period of understanding between the Muslims and the Ethiopians ended, and a new *najashi* took over. He did not follow Ashama in preserving the good relations with the Muslims . . . and thus the Ethiopians revealed their spirit of enmity to Islam and to Muslims from the very beginning" (pp. 21–22).

12. See Dr. Muhammad 'Abd al-Mun'im Khifaji, "Al-Sudan dar al-hijratayn," *Al-Azhar* (May 1999): 18–21; this article also reviews the literature on this idea.

13. In September 1993, after Eritrea was proclaimed independent, the Ethiopian government, in a step perhaps reminiscent of Nasser's 1959 relinquishing of the Coptic-Ethiopian connection, agreed to the separation of the churches. (The Eritrean Church had not been separated from the Ethiopian Church even under the 1890–1941 Italian colonial regime.) A year later, in September 1994, much to the anger of many Ethiopian clergy, the Coptic patriarch ordained five Eritrean monks as bishops. In May 1998 he consecrated the first Eritrean patriarch, Abuna Filepos. Meanwhile, Ethiopian-Eritrean relations deteriorated and war broke out between the two countries. Coptic support for the Eritrean Church was viewed with anger in Addis Ababa. See *New African* (October 1994): 36–37 and (July 1998): 29.

14. See Antuni 'Abd al-Sayyid Suriyal's comprehensive study of the relations between the Ethiopian and the Egyptian Churches, *Al-Istiqlal al-dhati likanisat ithyubya,* which contains well-documented research but also very strong anti-Ethiopian biases. The Copt author puts much of the blame for the contemporary crisis of the Copts in Egypt on what he describes as Ethiopian undermining of the ancient interchurch relations.

15. See Sa'id, *Nahr al-nil,* mainly pp. 279–280, 288–309. In the same vein see also Nawfal, "Al-Itar al-ta'rikhi wal-mustaqbali."

16. Abate, *Water Resources Development,* chap. 8. See also Tadesse, "The Nile River Basin."

17. Muhammad, *Thiyudur al-thani imbiratur ithyubia;* Wudnah, *Atse Yohannes.* The first is quite an objective assessment of the Ethiopian emperor's

relations with the British. The second is a most favorable discussion of the Ethiopian Tigrean emperor and a strong condemnation of the Egyptian Khedive Isma'il and his anti-Ethiopian campaign (see esp. pp. 200–225).

18. See Mulugeta Gudeta, "Mahfouz's *The Search* Comes to the Ethiopian Audience," *Ethiopian Herald,* 9 February 1992.

19. In a special issue dedicated to the Fourteenth International Conference of Ethiopian Studies, the *Journal of Ethiopian Studies* (vol. 33, no. 2 [November 2000]) published articles discussing the state of the art in relevant fields. Professor Bahru Zewde, a leading historian and former head of the Institute of Ethiopian Studies, presented a general overview titled "A Century of Ethiopian Historiography" (pp. 1–26). He mainly analyzed the works of his colleagues in the Department of History of Addis Ababa University and did so against the background of global historiography and the "African continental setting." Having identified African historical studies as revolving around schools and methods developed mainly in Nigeria and Tanzania (and also in Ghana, Kenya, and Uganda), he concluded that "the integration of Ethiopian historiography into the African mainstream, a perennial concern, is still far from being achieved to a satisfactory degree." However, throughout this detailed and thorough survey of Ethiopian historiography of the last generation, there is no mention of Ethiopia's Middle Eastern contexts, nor is there a single reference to the relevance of Egypt in either historical or historiographical terms.

20. At the Fourteenth International Conference of Ethiopian Studies held in Addis Ababa in November 2000, most papers presented in the section "Development and Environment" focused on the peasantry. This was also the subject of a plenary session that hosted three leading professors, Desalegn Rahmato, Berhanu Nega, and Mesfin Wolde-Mariam.

21. See "Country Papers: The Arab Republic of Egypt," in Ethiopian Ministry of Water Resources, *Fifth Nile 2002 Conference: Proceedings,* pp. 27–36.

22. See "Country Papers: Federal Democratic Republic of Ethiopia," in ibid., pp. 37–44.

Bibliography

ARCHIVAL MATERIAL

Institute of Ethiopian Studies (IES), Addis Ababa University
Israel State Archives (Ginzach haMedinah, IGM), Jerusalem
Ministero degli Affari Esteri, Archivio Storico (ASMAE), Rome
Public Record Office (PRO), London

NEWSPAPERS AND MAGAZINES

Addis Zaman, Addis Ababa
Al-Ahram, Cairo
Al-Akhbar, Cairo
Akhir Sa'a, Cairo
Al-Azhar, Cairo
Al-Balagh, Cairo
Berhannena Salam, Addis Ababa
Egyptian Gazette, Cairo
Ethiopian Herald, Addis Ababa
Ethioscope (journal of the Ethiopian Foreign Ministry), Addis Ababa
Financial Times, London
Ha'aretz, Tel Aviv
Al-Hayat, London
Al-Hilal, Cairo
Jerusalem Post, Jerusalem
Jihad, Cairo
Al-Kashkul, Cairo
Lamerhav, Tel Aviv
Ma'ariv, Tel Aviv
Al-Majalla al-Jadida, Cairo
Majallati, Cairo
Al-Manar, Cairo

Al-Misri, Cairo
Al-Muqattam, Cairo
Al-Muqtataf, Cairo
Al-Musawwar, Cairo
Nahdat Ifriqya, Cairo
New African, London
New York Times
La Reforme, Alexandria
Al-Risala, Cairo
Ruz al-Yusuf, Cairo
Al-Siyasa al-Duwaliyya, Cairo
Times, London
Al-Watan al-Arabi, Algeria

BOOKS AND ARTICLES

Abate, Zewdie. *Water Resources Development in Ethiopia*. Ithaca, 1994.
'Abd al-Halim, Muhammad Rajab. *Al-'Alaqat al-siyasiyya bayna muslimi al-zayla' wa-nusara al-habasha fi al-'usur al-wusta* (The Political Relations Between the Muslims of Zeila and the Christians of Ethiopia in Medieval Times). Cairo, 1985.
'Abd al-Hayy, 'Abd al-Tawwab. *Al-Nil wal-mustaqbal* (The Nile and the Future). Cairo, 1988.
Abir, Mordechai. "The Origins of the Ethiopian-Egyptian Border Problem in the Nineteenth Century." *Journal of African History*, vol. 8 (1967): 443–461.
———. *Ethiopia: The Era of the Princes. The Challenge of Islam, and the Reunification of the Christian Empire, 1769–1855*. New York, 1968.
———. *Ethiopia and the Red Sea*. London, 1980.
Abou El Fadl, Khaled. "Islamic Law and Muslim Minorities." *Islamic Law and Society*, vol. 1 (1994): 141–187.
Abraham, Emmanuel. *Reminiscences of My Life*. Oslo, 1995.
Abraham, Kinfe. "The Nile Issue: Psycho-Political Hurdles to an Agreement and the Way Forward Toward a Rapprochement." In Ethiopian Ministry of Water Resources, ed., *Fifth Nile 2002 Conference: Proceedings: Comprehensive Water Resources Development of the Nile Basin: Basis for Cooperation*, pp. 597–610. Addis Ababa, 1998.
Abu al-'Ata, 'Abd al-'Azim, Mufid Shihab, and Daf'allah Rida. *Nahr al-Nil, al-madi wal-hadir wal-mustaqbal* (The Nile River: The Past, the Present, and the Future). Cairo, 1985.
Abu Bakr, 'Ali al-Shaykh. *Ma'alim al-hijratayn ila ard al-habasha* (Aspects of the Two Hegiras to the Land of the Ethiopians). Riyad, 1993.
Ahmad, Abdussamad. "Gojjam: Trade, Early Merchant Capital, and World Economy, 1901–1935." Ph.D. diss., University of Illinois, 1986.
———. "Lake Tana in Italian Expansionist Thinking of the Mid-1930s." Paper presented at the conference "The Nile: History, Civilizations, and Myths," Tel Aviv University, May 1997.
Ahmad, Yusuf. *Al-Islam fi al-habasha* (Islam in Ethiopia). Cairo, 1935.

Ahmed, Hussein. "The Historiography of Islam in Ethiopia." *Journal of Islamic Studies*, vol. 3, no. 1 (1992): 15–46.

'Aliyyan, 'Abd al-Fattah. *Al-Hijra ila al-habasha wamunaqashat qadiyyat islam al-najashi* (The Hegira to Ethiopia and the Argument About the Issue of the King of Ethiopia to Islam). Cairo, 1987.

Amanu, Adunga. "The Ethiopian Orthodox Church Becomes Autocephalous." B.A. paper, Haile Selassie University, 1969. Available at IES, Addis Ababa University.

Arbel, Benjamin. "Renaissance Geographical Literature and the Nile." In Haggai Erlich and Israel Gershoni, eds., *The Nile: Histories, Cultures, Myths*, pp. 105–120. Boulder, 1999.

Arslan, Shakib. *Hadir al-'alam al-Islami* (The Present of the Arab World). Cairo, 1933.

'Ashur, Sa'id 'Abd al-Fattah. "Ba'd adwa' jadida 'ala al-'alaqat bayna misr wal-habasha fi al-'usur al-wusta" (Some New Lights on the Relations Between Egypt and Ethiopia in the Middle Ages). *Al-Majalla al-Ta'rikhiyya al-Misriyya* (Egyptian Historical Journal) vol. 14 (1968): 1–43.

Ayalon, David. "The Spread of Islam and the Nubian Dam." In Haggai Erlich and Israel Gershoni, eds., *The Nile: Histories, Cultures, Myths*, pp. 17–24. Boulder, 1999.

Ayele, Negussay. "The Blue Nile and Hydropolitics Among Egypt, Ethiopia, Sudan." In A. Gromyko, ed., *Proceedings of the Ninth International Congress of Ethiopian Studies*, vol. 2, pp. 38–50. Moscow, 1988.

'Azm, Sadiq al-Mua'ayyad al-. *Rihlat al-habasha* (The Voyage to Ethiopia). Cairo, 1908.

Badawi, 'Abduh. *Ma'a harakat al-Islam fi ifriqya* (With the Islamic Movement in Africa). Cairo, 1970.

Bakr, Muhammad Num. *Italia wa-musta'amaratuha* (Italy and Her Colonies). Cairo, 1936.

Barawi, Rashid al-. *Al-Habasha bayna al-iqta' wal-'asr al-hadith* (Ethiopia Between Feudalism and Modern Times). Cairo, 1961.

———. *Al-Sumal al-kabir: Haqiqa wa-hadaf* (Greater Somalia: Truth and Aim). Cairo, 1961.

Bayumi, 'Abdallah. *Mawsu'at al-ta'rikh al-'askari al-misri fi al-'ahd al-hadith, al-kitab al-thalith: Al-jaysh al-misri fi 'asr khulafa Muhammad 'Ali* (Military History of Egypt in Modern Times, Vol. 3: The Egyptian Army in the Period of Muhammad 'Ali's Successors). Cairo, n.d.

Begashaw, Kassaye. "A Note on the Ethiopian Der es-Sultan." Ministry of Culture, Addis Ababa, August 1993.

Bekele, Shiferaw. "Kassa and Kassa: The State of Their Historiography." In Shiferaw Bekele, ed., *Kassa and Kassa: Papers on the Lives, Times, and Images of Tewodros II and Yohannes IV (1855–1889)*, pp. 289–404. Addis Ababa, 1990.

Ben-Gurion, David. *Rosh hamemshala harishon, mivhar te'udut, 1947–1963* (The First Prime Minister of Israel, Selection of Documents, 1947–1963). IGM, Jerusalem, 1997.

Boutros-Ghali, Boutros. "The Foreign Policy of Egypt." In Joseph Black and Kenneth Thompson, eds., *Foreign Policies in a World of Change*, pp. 319–331. New York, 1963.

———. *Egypt's Road to Jerusalem*. New York, 1997.

Bruce, James. *Travels to Discover the Source of the Nile (1768–1773)*. Edinburgh, 1813.

Budge, E. A. W. *A History of Ethiopia*. London, 1928.

Butler, Alfred J. *The Arab Conquest of Egypt*. 2nd ed. Oxford, 1978.

Buxton, David. *Travels in Abyssinia*. New York, 1967.

Carter, B. L. *The Copts in Egyptian Politics*. London, 1986.

Caulk, Richard. "Religion and State in Nineteenth-Century Ethiopia." *Journal of Ethiopian Studies*, vol. 10 (1972): 23–41.

Cerulli, Enrico. *Il libro etiopico dei miracoli di Maria*. Rome, 1943.

———. *Etiopi in Palestina, I and II*. Rome, 1943 and 1947.

Church of Ethiopia. *The Church of Ethiopia: A Panorama of History and Spiritual Life*. Addis Ababa, 1997.

Collins, Robert. *The Waters of the Nile, Hydropolitics, and the Jonglei Canal, 1900–1988*. Oxford, 1990.

———. "A Nile Policy Conservancy and Development Strategy." Paper prepared for the meeting of the International Advisory Group for the Nile Basin of the World Bank, November 1997.

———. "In Search of the Nile Waters." In Haggai Erlich and Israel Gershoni, eds., *The Nile: Histories, Cultures, Myths*, pp. 245–267. Boulder, 1999.

Conti Rossini, Carlo. *Storia d'Etiopia*. Bergamo, 1928.

Crummey, Donald. *Priests and Politicians: Protestant and Catholic Missions in Orthodox Ethiopia, 1830–1868*. Oxford, 1972.

Cuoq, Joseph. *L'Islam en Ethiopie, des origines au XVIe siecle*. Paris, 1981.

Dirar, Uoldelul Chelati. "The Nile as a Gateway for the Missionary Activity in Abyssinia." In Haggai Erlich and Israel Gershoni, eds., *The Nile: Histories, Cultures, Myths*, pp. 139–149. Boulder, 1999.

Dombrowski, F. *Ethiopia's Access to the Red Sea*. Leiden, 1985.

DuBois, W. E. B. *The World and Africa*. New York, 1947.

Dunn, Ross. *The Adventures of Ibn Battuta, a Muslim Traveler of the Fourteenth Century*. London, 1986.

Erlich, Haggai. *The Struggle over Eritrea, 1962–1978*. Stanford, 1983.

———. *Ethiopia and the Challenge of Independence*. Boulder, 1986.

———. *Ethiopia and the Middle East*. Boulder, 1994.

———. *Ras Alula and the Scramble for Africa*. East Lansing, 1982 (2nd ed., 1996).

Erlich, Haggai, and Israel Gershoni, eds. *The Nile: Histories, Cultures, Myths*. Boulder, 1999.

Eshete, Alame. "Une Ambassade du Ras Ali en Egypte, 1852." *Journal of Ethiopian Studies*, vol. 9 (1971): 1–8.

———. "Egypt and the Conflict in the Horn of Africa, 1941–1974." Paper presented at the Conference on the Horn of Africa, January 1985, Cairo. Available at IES, Addis Ababa University.

Ethiopian Ministry of Water Resources, ed. *Fifth Nile 2002 Conference: Proceedings: Comprehensive Water Resources Development of the Nile Basin: Basis for Cooperation*. Addis Ababa, 1998.

Ethiopian Orthodox Church. *The Church of Ethiopia: A Panorama of History and Spiritual Life*. Addis Ababa, 1970 (2nd printing, 1997).

Fadab, Tahir Ibrahim. *Harakat tahrir iritriya wa-masiratuha al-ta'rikhiyya* (The Egyptian Liberation Front and Its Historical Destiny). Cairo, 1994.

Fadl, Muhammad 'Abd al-Wahhab, ed. *Raf' sha'n al-hubshan* (Raising the Status of the Abyssinians), by Jalal al-Din al-Suyuti. Cairo, 1991.

Fa'iq, Muhammad Muhammad. *'Abd al-Nasir wal-thawra al-ifriqiyya* (Nasser and the African Revolution). Beirut, 1980.

Fawzi, Mahmud. *Al-Baba Qirilus wa'Abd al-Nasir* (Pope Cyril and Abdel Nasser). Cairo, 1993.

Gabre-Selassie, Zewde. *Yohannes IV of Ethiopia.* Oxford, 1975.

———. "The Nile River Question in a New Era of Cooperation Among Riparian States." Paper presented to the Nile 2002 Conference, Addis Ababa, June 2000.

Gaudefroy-Demombynes, M., ed. *Masalik el Absar fi Mamalik el Amsar,* by Ibn Fadl Allah al-'Omari. Paris, 1927.

Gershoni, Israel. "Geographers and Nationalism in Egypt: Huzayyin and the Unity of the Nile Valley, 1945–1948." In Haggai Erlich and Israel Gershoni, eds., *The Nile: Histories, Cultures, Myths,* pp. 199–213. Boulder, 1999.

———. *Light in the Shade: Egypt and Fascism, 1922–1937.* (In Hebrew.) Tel Aviv, 1999.

Gershoni, Israel, and J. Jankowski. *Redefining the Egyptian Nation, 1930–1945.* Cambridge, 1995.

Gervers, Michael. "The Mediterranean Context of the Rock-Cut Churches of Ethiopia." In Taddese Beyene, ed., *Proceedings of the Eighth International Conference of Ethiopian Studies,* vol. 1, pp. 171–184. Addis Ababa, 1988.

Ghith, Fathi. *Al-Islam wal-habasha 'ibra al-ta'rikh* (Islam and Ethiopia over History). Cairo, 1967.

Goldman, Aaron. "Massive Nile River Diversion Planned." *World Rivers Review,* vol. 12, no. 3 (1997). Available online at: www.irn.org/pubs/wrr/9706/nile.html.

Guidi, Ignazio. "Due nuovi manoscritti della Cronaca Abbreviata di Abissinia." *Rendiconti della Reale Accademia dei Lincei,* vol. 2 (1926).

Guillaume, A. *The Life of Muhammad.* Oxford, 1955.

Habashi, Sadiq al-. *Ithyubya fi 'asriha al-dhahabi, fi 'asr Hayla Silasi al-awwal* (Ethiopia in Its Golden Era, the Era of Haile Selassie I). Cairo, 1954.

Hable Selassie, Sergew. *Ancient and Medieval Ethiopian History to 1270.* Addis Ababa, 1972.

Habte Selassie, Bereket. *Conflict and Intervention in the Horn of Africa.* New York, 1980.

Habtewold, Aklilu. *Aklilu Remembers: Historical Recollections from a Prison Cell,* trans. Getachew Tedla. Uppsala, 1994.

Haddad, Y. "The Challenge of Muslim Minorities: The American Experience." In W. A. R. Shadid and P. S. van-Koningsveld, eds., *Integration of Islam and Hinduism in Western Europe,* pp. 134–151. Kampen, 1991.

Haile Selassie. *Autobiography of Emperor Haile Selassie: My Life and Ethiopia's Progress,* trans. Edward Ullendorff. Oxford, 1976.

Harraz, Muhammad Rajab. *Iritriya al-haditha, 1557–1952.* Cairo, 1974.

———. *Al-'Umam al-muttahida wa-qadiyyat Iritriya, 1945–1952* (Modern Eritrea, 1945–1952). Cairo, 1974.

Harun, 'Abd al-Sallam, ed. *Rasa'il al-Jahiz* (The Messages of Jahiz). Beirut, 1991.

Hecht, D. "Ethiopia Threatens to Block the Nile." *Azania,* vol. 23 (1988): 1–11.

Heikal, Mohamad. *The Road to Ramadan*. London, 1975.

Henze, Paul. "The Strategic Long View: The Nile Valley and the Horn of Africa." In A. Bennigsen, P. Henze, G. Tahnam, S. Wimbush, eds., *Soviet Strategy and Islam*, pp. 120–142. London, 1989.

———. *The Horn of Africa: From War to Peace*. New York, 1991.

———. "Consolidation of Christianity Around the Source of the Blue Nile." In Haggai Erlich and Israel Gershoni, eds., *The Nile: Histories, Cultures, Myths*, pp. 39–56. Boulder, 1999.

———. *Layers of Time: A History of Ethiopia*. London, 2000.

Hess, Robert. *Ethiopia: The Modernization of Autocracy*. Ithaca, 1970.

Husayn, 'Abdalla. *Al-Mas'ala al-habashiyya* (The Ethiopian Question). Cairo, 1935.

Huss, 'Abd al-Rahman al-. *Ithyubya fi 'ahd Hayla Silasi al-awwal* (Ethiopia in the Period of Haile Selassie I). Beirut, 1960.

Ismael, Tareq. *The U.A.R. in Africa: Egypt's Policy Under Nasser*. Evanston, 1971.

Jalata, Asafa. *Oromia and Ethiopia: State Formation and Ethnonational Conflict, 1868–1992*. Boulder, 1993.

Jones, A. H. M., and Elizabeth Monroe. *A History of Ethiopia*. Oxford, 1968 (1st ed., 1935).

Jum'a, Muhammad Lutfi. *Al-Asad al-ifriqi wal-nimr al-itali* (The African Lion and the Italian Tiger). Cairo, 1935.

Kamil, Murad. "Translations from Arabic in Ethiopian Literature." *Bulletin de la Societe d'Archeologie Copte*, vol. 2 (1941): 61–71.

———. *'Amani fi al-habasha* (Two Years in Ethiopia). Cairo, 1945.

———. "Al-Rahbaniyya fi al-habasha" (Monastism in Ethiopia). *Majallat risalat marmina*, vol. 3 (1948): 30.

———. *Fi bilad al-najashi* (In the Land of the *Najashi*). Cairo, 1949.

———. "The Ethiopian Calendar." *Bulletin of the Faculty of Arts* (1950). Fouad University, Cairo.

———. "La Dernier phase des relations historiques entre l'Eglise Copte d'Egypte et Celle d'Ethiopie (Jusque'en 1952)." *Bulletin de la Societe d'Archeologie Copte*, vol. 14 (1950–1951): 1–22.

———, ed. *Sirat al-habasha*, by Al-Haymi al-Hasan bin Ahmad. Cairo, 1958 (2nd ed., 1972).

Kaplan, Steven. "Can the Ethiopian Change His Skin? The Beta Israel and Racial Discourse." *African Affairs*, vol. 98 (1999): 535–550.

Kendie, Daniel. "The Internal and External Dimensions of the Eritrean Conflict." Ph.D. diss., Department of History, Michigan State University, 1994.

Khaddouri, Majid. *War and Peace in the Law of Islam*. Baltimore, 1955.

Khattab, Mahmud Shit. *Islam al-najashi*. Riyad, n.d.

Kirlus, Al-Sayyid. *Muhadara 'an al-habasha* (A Lecture on Ethiopia). Cairo, 1896.

Lamlam, Alaqa. *Ya'atse Takla-Giyorgisna ya'atse Yohannes tarik* (History of Emperor Takla-Giyorgis and Emperor Yohannes). Ms. Ethiopiens no. 259, Bibliotheque Nationale, Paris.

Levtzion, Nehemia. "Arab Geographers, the Nile, and the History of Bilad al-Sudan." In Haggai Erlich and Israel Gershoni, eds., *The Nile: Histories, Cultures, Myths*, pp. 71–76. Boulder, 1999.

Lewis, Bernard. *Race and Slavery in the Middle East: A Historical Inquiry*. New York, 1990.

Makuriya, Takla-Tsadiq. *Ya'ityopia tarik, ka'atse Lebna Dengel eska atse Tewodros* (History of Ethiopia from Emperor Lebna Dengel to Emperor Tewodros). Addis Ababa, 1961.

———. *YaGragn Ahmad Warara* (Ahmad Gragn's Invasion). Addis Ababa, 1974.

Mansur, Lutfi. *Al-Hijra ila al-habasha wal-'alaqat al-islamiyya al-masihiyya fi bidayat al-islam* (The Emigration to Ethiopia and Islamic Christian Relations at the Beginning of Islam). Kafr Qara', 1998.

Maqrizi, Ahmad bin 'Ali al-. *Kitab al-Ilmam bi-akhbar man bi-ard al-habasha min muluk al-Islam* (The Book of the True Knowledge of the History of the Muslim Kings in Abyssinia). Issued by Matba'at al-ta'lif, Cairo, 1895.

Marcus, Harold. *Haile Selassie I: The Formative Years, 1892–1936.* Berkeley, 1987.

Markaz al-Buhuth al-Arabiyya. *Azmat miyah al-nil: Ila ayna?* (The Water Crisis of the Nile: Where To?). Cairo, 1988.

Mas'ad, Bulus. *Ithyubia, aw al-habasha fi munqalab min ta'rikhiha* (Ethiopia, or Abyssinia in a Turning Point in Its History). Cairo, 1935.

Massaia, G. *I miei trentacinque anni di missione nell'alta Etiopia.* Rome, 1921.

McCann, James. "Ethiopia, Britain, and Negotiations for the Lake Tana Dam, 1922–1935." *International Journal of African Historical Studies,* vol. 14 (1981): 667–699.

Meinardus, Otto. *Christian Egypt: Faith and Life.* Cairo, 1970.

Meital, Yoram. "The Aswan High Dam and Revolutionary Symbolism in Egypt." In Haggai Erlich and Israel Gershoni, eds., *The Nile: Histories, Cultures, Myths,* pp. 219–226. Boulder, 1999.

Mettaferia, Dammaka. "The Nile River: Need for Equitable Use of Its Waters." Series of five articles in *Ethiopian Register* (July–December 1994).

Morell, Virginia, and Nevada Wier. "The Blue Nile: Ethiopia's Sacred Waters." *National Geographic* (December 2000): 2–29.

Muhammad, Ibrahim 'Abd al-Majid. *Thiyudur al-thani imbiratur ithyubia wal-'alaqat al-ithyubiya al-baritaniyya fi 'ahdihi* (Tewodros II, Emperor of Ethiopia, and Ethiopian-British Relations in His Time). Cairo, 1989.

Muir, W. *The Life of Mohammed.* London, 1923.

Munro-Hay, Stuart. *Aksum: An African Civilization of Late Antiquity.* Edinburgh, 1991.

———. *Ethiopia and Alexandria: The Metropolitan Episcopacy of Ethiopia.* Warsaw, 1997.

Nasr, Yusuf. *Juhud misr al-kashfiyya fi ifriqya fi al-qarn al-tasi' 'ashr* (Egypt's Discovery Enterprise in Nineteenth-Century Africa). Cairo, 1979.

Nawfal, Muhammad Na'man. "Al-Itar al-ta'rikhi wal-mustaqbali li'darat miyah al-nil bayna misr wa-duwal hawd al-nil" (The Historical and Future Framework for the Administration of the Nile Waters Between Egypt and the Countries of the Upper Nile). In Samir Sarhan and 'Abd al-'Azim Ramadan, eds., *Ta'rikh al-misriyyin* (History of the Egyptians), no. 95: *Misr wa'ifriqya* (Egypt and Africa), pp. 385–408. Cairo, 1996.

Negash, Tekeste. "The Blue Nile as Bait: Ethiopian Policy Versus Egypt in the Twelfth Century." Paper presented at the conference "The Nile: History, Civilizations, and Myths," Tel Aviv University, May 1997.

Pankhurst, Richard. *The Ethiopians.* Oxford, 1998.

———. "Ethiopia's Alleged Control of the Nile." In Haggai Erlich and Israel Gershoni, eds., *The Nile: Histories, Cultures, Myths,* pp. 25–37. Boulder, 1999.

Pankhurst, Rita. "An Unpublished Letter of King of Kings Tewodros II to the Egyptian Governor of the Sudan." In A. Gromyko, ed., *Proceedings of the Ninth International Congress of Ethiopian Studies,* vol. 4, pp. 167–176. Moscow, 1988.

———. "The First International Conference of Ethiopian Studies." *Institute of Ethiopian Studies Bulletin,* vols. 23–24 (September–December 2000): 1–8.

Pedersen, Kirsten. *The History of the Holy Community in the Holy Land from the Time of Emperor Tewodros II Until 1974.* Jerusalem, 1983.

———. *The Ethiopian Church and Its Community in Jerusalem.* Jerusalem, 1994.

———. "The Ethiopian Community in Jerusalem, 1200–1530." Paper presented to the Fourteenth International Conference of Ethiopian Studies, Addis Ababa, November 2000.

Perruchon, J. *La Vie de Lalibala.* Paris, 1892.

Philipp, Thomas. "Copts and Other Minorities in the Development of the Egyptian Nation State." In S. Shamir, ed., *Egypt from Monarchy to Republic,* pp. 131–150. Boulder, 1995.

Plante, J. "The Ethiopian Embassy to Cairo of 1443." *Journal of Ethiopian Studies,* vol. 13, no. 2 (1975): 133–140.

Qasim, 'Abduh Qasim. "'Alaqat misr bil-habasha fi 'asr salatin al-mamalik" (Egyptian-Ethiopian Relations During the Mamluk Period). In Ra'uf 'Abd al-Hamid, ed., *Al-Arab fi Ifriqya* (The Arabs in Africa), pp. 57–84. Cairo, 1987.

Qina'i, Ahmad al-Hifni al-. *Al-Jawahir al-hisan fi ta'rikh al-hubshan* (The Beautiful Diamonds in the History of the Ethiopians). Cairo, 1902–1903.

Rafi'i, 'Abd al-Rahman al-. *'Asr Isma'il* (Isma'il's Period). Vol. 1. Cairo, 1948.

Renaudot, E. *Historia Patriarcharum Alexandrinorum Jacobitarum.* Paris, 1713.

Rif'at, Muhammad. *Kitab jabr al-kasr fi al-khilas min al-asr* (Overcoming the Calamity in Release from Captivity). Cairo, 1896–1897.

Riyad, Zahir. *Kanisat al-iskandiriyya fi ifriqya* (The Alexandrian Church in Africa). Cairo, 1962.

———. *Misr wa-Ifriqya* (Egypt and Africa). Cairo, 1976.

Rohlfs, G. *Meine Mission nach Abessinien.* Leipzig, 1883.

Rubenson, Sven. *The Survival of Ethiopian Independence.* London, 1976.

———. "Shaikh Kassa Hailu." In Sven Rubenson, ed., *Proceedings of the Seventh International Conference of Ethiopian Studies* (in Addis Ababa), pp. 279–285. Uppsala, 1984.

———, ed. *Acta Aethiopica, Vol. 1: Correspondence and Treaties, 1800–1854.* Evanston, 1987.

Sabri, Muhammad. *Misr fi Ifriqya al-sharqiyya* (Egypt in East Africa). Cairo, 1939.

Sa'id, Rushdi. *Nahr al-nil, nash'atuhu wa-istikhdam miyahihi fi al-madi wal-mustaqbal* (The River Nile: Its Development and the Usage of Its Waters in the Past and in the Future). Cairo, 1992.

Sa'id, Rushdi, et al. *Azmat miyah al-nil: Ila ayna?* (The Crisis of the Nile Waters: Where To?). Center for Arab Studies, Cairo, 1988.

Salim, Rija'. *Al-Tabadul al-tulabi bayna misr wal-duwal al-ifriqiyya, 1952–1985* (Students Exchange Between Egypt and African Countries, 1952–1985). Cairo, 1989.

Sarhank, Isma'il. *Haqa'iq al-akhbar fi duwal al-bihar* (The Truthful News About the Countries of the Sea). Cairo, 1896–1897.

Sbacchi, Alberto. *Legacy of Bitterness: Ethiopia and Fascist Italy, 1935–1941.* New Jersey, 1997.

Schwab, Peter. *Decision-Making in Ethiopia.* London, 1972.

Shafiq, Suliman. *Al-Aqbat bayna al-harman al-kanisi wal-watani* (The Copts Between the Church and the National Hierarchies). Cairo, 1996.

Shakir, Amin, Sa'id al-'Iryan, and Mustafa Amin. *Adwa' 'ala al-habasha* (Lights on Ethiopia). Cairo, 1954 (2nd ed., 1957 or 1958).

Shaltut, Fahim Muhammad, ed. *Tuhfat al-zaman aw futuh al-habasha* (The Conquest of Ethiopia), by Shihab al-Din Ahmad ibn 'Abd al-Qadir. Cairo, 1974. (Originally published as: Chihab ed-Din Ahmed Ben Abd el-Qader ['Arab Faqih]. *Futuh al-habasha: Histoire de la conquete de l'Abyssinie,* ed. and trans. R. Basset. Paris, 1897.)

Shanuda, Zakki. *Ta'rikh al-aqbat* (History of the Copts). Cairo, 1962.

Shavit, Yaacov. "Up the River or Down the River? An Afrocentrist Dilemma." In Haggai Erlich and Israel Gershoni, eds., *The Nile: Histories, Cultures, Myths,* pp. 79–104. Boulder, 1999.

Six, Veronika. "Water, the Nile, and the *Ta'amra Maryam:* Miracles of Virgin Mary in the Ethiopian Version." *Aethiopica,* vol. 2 (1999): 53–68.

Sofer, Arnon. *Rivers of Fire: The Conflict over Water in the Middle East.* Lanham, 1999.

Stephens, Robert. *Nasser: A Political Biography.* London, 1971.

Sultan, 'Abdallah 'Abd al-Muhsin al-. *Al-Bahr al-ahmar wal-sira' al-'arabi al-israili* (The Red Sea and the Arab-Israeli Conflict). Beirut, 1984.

Suriyal, Antuni 'Abd al-Sayyid. *Mushkilat dir al-sultan bil-quds* (The Issue of Deir al-Sultan in Jerusalem). Cairo, 1991.

———. *Al-Istiqlal al-dhati likanisat Ithyubya, 1941–1959* (The Self-Determination of the Ethiopian Church, 1941–1959). Cairo, 1994.

Swain, Ashok. "The Nile River Dispute: Ethiopia, the Sudan, and Egypt." *Journal of Modern African Studies,* vol. 35, no. 4 (1997).

Tadesse, Hillawi. "The Nile River Basin: Its Use and Development." *Ethioscope,* no. 1 (1998): 13–23.

Tadrus, Ramzi. *Hadir al-habasha wa-mustaqbaluha* (Ethiopia's Present and Future). Cairo, 1906.

Tafla, Bairu. "The Father of Rivers: The Nile in Ethiopian Literature." In Haggai Erlich and Israel Gershoni, eds., *The Nile: Histories, Cultures, Myths,* pp. 153–170. Boulder, 1999.

Tamrat, Taddesse. *Church and State in Ethiopia.* Oxford, 1972.

———. *The Ethiopian Church and Its Doctrine.* Addis Ababa, 1982.

Teklahaymanot, Abba Ayele. "The Egyptian Metropolitans of the Ethiopian Church." *Orientalia Cristiana Peridica,* vol. 54 (1988): 175–222.

Tilahun, Wondimneh. *Egypt's Imperial Aspirations over Lake Tana and the Blue Nile.* Addis Ababa, 1979.

Trimingham, J. Spencer. *Islam in Ethiopia.* Oxford, 1952 (London, 1965).

Troutt Powell, Eve. "Brothers Along the Nile: Egyptian Concepts of Race and Ethnicity, 1895–1910." In Haggai Erlich and Israel Gershoni, eds. *The Nile: Histories, Cultures, Myths,* pp. 171–181. Boulder, 1999.

'Umari, Fadlallah al-. *Ta'rif.* Cairo, 1312.

'Urabi, Ahmad. *Kashf al-sitar 'an sirr al-asrar* (Raising the Curtain of the Secret of Secrets). Cairo, 1929.

van Donzel, Emeri. *Enbaqom: Anqasa Amin* (The Gate of Faith). Leiden, 1969.

————. "Al-Nadjashi." *Encyclopedia of Islam.* Emeri van Donzel, ed. Leiden, 1993.

————. "Ethiopia's Lalibela and the Fall of Jerusalem, 1187." *Aethiopica,* vol. 1 (1998): 27–49.

————. "The Legend of the Blue Nile in Europe." In Haggai Erlich and Israel Gershoni, eds., *The Nile: Histories, Cultures, Myths,* pp. 121–130. Boulder, 1999.

————. "Badr al-Jamali: The Copts in Egypt and the Muslims in Ethiopia." In Carol Hillenbrand, ed., *Studies in Honor of Clifford Edmond Bosworth,* pp. 297–309. Leiden, 2000.

Vatikiotis, P. J. *Nasser and His Generation.* London, 1978.

Wakin, Edward. *A Lonely Minority.* New York, 1963.

Waldagiorgis, Aklilaberhan. *Kagibts baityopya yatashamut papasat* (Egyptian Bishops Appointed to the Ethiopian Church). Addis Ababa, 1953.

Walda-Selassie, Heruy. *Wazema* (Vigil). Addis Ababa, 1921.

————. *Yale'lat wayzaro Manan mangad ba'irusalemna bamisr* (The Trip of Princess Manan in Jerusalem and Egypt). Addis Ababa, 1923.

————. *Dastana kibir* (Happiness and Honor). Addis Ababa, 1924.

————. *Ba'adame masinbat hulun lamayet* (Witnessing It All by Myself). Addis Ababa, 1934.

Warburg, Gabriel. *Egypt and the Sudan: Studies in History and Politics.* London, 1985.

————. "The Nile in Egyptian-Sudanese Relations, 1956–1995." In Haggai Erlich and Israel Gershoni, eds., *The Nile: Histories, Cultures, Myths,* pp. 227–234. Boulder, 1999.

Waterbury, John. *Hydropolitics of the Nile Valley.* Syracuse, 1979.

————. "Is the Status Quo in the Nile Basin Viable?" Draft article. Princeton, June 1996.

————. "Policy and Strategic Considerations Affecting Cooperative Use of Nile Basin Water Resources." In Ethiopian Ministry of Water Resources, ed., *Fifth Nile 2002 Conference: Proceedings: Comprehensive Water Resources Development of the Nile Basin,* pp. 613–624. Addis Ababa, 1998.

Webman, Esther. "Havnayat zehut islamit bebritanya" (Maintaining Islamic Identity in Britain.) M.A. thesis, School of History, Tel Aviv University, 1997.

Wiet, G. "Les Relations Egypto-Abyssines sous les sultans mamlouks." *Bulletin de la Société d'Archéologie Copte,* vol. 4 (1938): 115–140.

World Bank. "The World Bank, Ethiopia, and the Nile: A Strategy for Support to Ethiopia." In Country Department for Ethiopia, "Eastern Nile Development Program: A Draft." Washington, D.C., June 1998.

Wudnah, Mamo. *Atse Yohannes* (Emperor Yohannes). Addis Ababa, 1993.

Yahya, Jalal. *Al-'Alaqat al-Misriyya al-Sumaliyya* (Egyptian-Somali Relations). Cairo, 1960.

————. *Al-Bahr al-ahmar wal-isti'mar* (The Red Sea and Imperialism). Cairo, 1962.

————. *Misr al-ifriqiyya* (African Egypt). Cairo, 1967.

Zabiyan, Muhammad. *Al-habasha al-muslima* (Islamic Ethiopia). Damascus, 1937.

Zakkar, Suhayl, ed. *Kitab al-futan* (The Book of Heresies), by 'Abdallah Nu'aym ibn Hammad. Beirut, 1993.

Zewde, Bahru. *A History of Modern Ethiopia.* London, 1991.

————. "A Century of Ethiopian Historiography." *Journal of Ethiopian Studies,* vol. 2 (2000): 1–26.

Index

About the Book

The ongoing Egyptian-Ethiopian dispute over the Nile waters is potentially one of the most difficult issues on the current international agenda, central to the very life of the two countries. Analyzing the context of the dispute across a span of more than a thousand years, *The Cross and the River* delves into the heart of both countries' identities and cultures.

Erlich deftly weaves together three themes: the political relationship between successive Ethiopian and Egyptian regimes; the complex connection between the Christian churches in the two countries; and the influence of the Nile river system on Ethiopian and Egyptian definitions of national identity and mutual perceptions of "the Other." Drawing on a vast range of sources, his study is key to an understanding of a bond built on both interdependence and conflict.

Haggai Erlich is professor emeritus of Middle East and African history at Tel Aviv University. His many publications include *Ethiopia and the Middle East* and *The Nile: Histories, Cultures, Myths*.